Jewish Biblical Legends

Jewish Biblical Legends

Rabbinic Wisdom for Christian Readers

JOEL S. ALLEN

CASCADE *Books* • Eugene, Oregon

JEWISH BIBLICAL LEGENDS
Rabbinic Wisdom for Christian Readers

Copyright © 2013 Joel S. Allen. All rights reserved. Except for brief quotations in critical publications or reviews, no part of this book may be reproduced in any manner without prior written permission from the publisher. Write: Permissions, Wipf and Stock Publishers, 199 W. 8th Ave., Suite 3, Eugene, OR 97401.

Cascade Books
An Imprint of Wipf and Stock Publishers
199 W. 8th Ave., Suite 3
Eugene, OR 97401

www.wipfandstock.com

ISBN 13: 978-1-62032-840-8

Cataloguing-in-Publication data:

Allen, Joel Stevens.

    Jewish biblical legends : rabbinic wisdom for Christian readers / Joel S. Allen.

    xii + 162 pp. ; 23 cm. Includes bibliographical references.

    ISBN 13: 978-1-62032-840-8

    1. Legends, Jewish. 2. Jewish legends. 3. Talmud—Legends. 4. Rabbis—Legends. 5. Haggadot—Commentaries. I. Title.

BM530 A44 2013

Manufactured in the U.S.A.

Dedicated to my wife, Kitty
אשת־חיל מי ימצא

Content

	Foreword by Edward Goldman	ix
	Acknowledgments	xi
	Introduction	1
1	The Work of Creation	14
2	The Serpent and Sin	40
3	The World after Sin	47
4	Abraham, Our Father	60
5	Jacob and Esau	80
6	Israel in Egypt	90
7	The Plundering of Egypt	112
8	At the Sea and Beyond	137
9	Moses, Torah, and Sinai	142
10	The Ethics of the Fathers	151
	Glossary	161
	Bibliography	165

Foreword

AN IMPORTANT BY-PRODUCT OF increased interest on the part of Christian scholars and lay people in their Jewish roots is an attraction to early Rabbinic Literature. After all, Jesus and Paul were Jews who were clearly familiar with and greatly influenced by rabbinic thinking. Relationships, as well as disputations, can be discerned between early Rabbinic and early Christian Literature. The student of Christianity who wishes to fully understand his or her heritage needs to read it in the context and against the backdrop of early Rabbinic thought and interpretation. To fill that niche, Dr. Joel S. Allen has written this engaging work: *Jewish Biblical Legends: Rabbinic Wisdom for Christian Readers*.

As Dr. Allen states in his introduction, the book represents his own personal syntheses of Rabbinic Literature courses he took as a doctoral student at the Hebrew Union College in Cincinnati with his prior training for the United Methodist ministry. In utilizing the Rabbinic Literature he was learning in class for preaching and teaching in his Methodist congregation, he recognized the need for and value of a volume of this type and vowed to write it. Sixteen years later he has admirably fulfilled his vow. The book is eminently usable for the very purposes he envisioned it. His target audience—pastors, teachers, interested lay people—can all benefit from this careful and thoughtful presentation.

The introduction contains an excellent primer on the methodology and function of Early Rabbinic Aggadic Literature. Dr. Allen presents the beginner in the academic discipline of Midrash with an overview of the field that contains the positions and thinking of numerous important scholars. For those readers who wish to engage more deeply in the technical aspects of the field, helpful footnotes, an extensive bibliography, and a glossary are included.

Foreword

The body of the volume contains nine chapters, each focusing on the rabbinic presentation and interpretation of one biblical theme. The first is "The Work of Creation." The next eight chapters present additional themes that follow the biblical chronology. The ninth, the latest biblical theme included in this work, is "Moses, Torah, and Sinai." However, there is a non-biblical final chapter, the tenth, which deals with "The Ethics of the Fathers," an inspiring ethical guidebook from the *Mishnah*. For each chapter, Dr. Allen has judiciously selected rabbinic passages that would be of interest to his target audience. He has translated and interpreted the material, and most importantly he has laid out the implications of these passages for the Christian reader. Whether for personal study or for the college or seminary classroom, this book is highly suited. It opens the world of rabbinic thought to those Christians who may not have had prior exposure.

Edward Goldman,
Hebrew Union College—Jewish Institute of Religion, Cincinnati

Acknowledgments

I ACKNOWLEDGE MY INDEBTEDNESS to all of my teachers at both Asbury Theological Seminary and Hebrew Union College—Jewish Institute of Religion. Their commitment to faith, knowledge, and wisdom has shaped me beyond description. For them, the dictum *fides quaerens intellectum* was more than a saying; it was a way of life. In particular, I acknowledge my debt to Edward Goldman. He introduced me to these stories and sayings and taught me how to understand them.

In one course, for some reason, I was the only student who registered. He did not cancel the course but spent the whole semester with me one-on-one. While this thought initially intimidated me, it turned out to be one of the best educational experiences of my life. He patiently corrected my pronunciation and translation; mainly he taught me how to think like a rabbi. To this day I call this my "Rabbi and I" class. I hope I can communicate something of that great experience here so that other Christians can come to appreciate this body of wisdom and insight. As one rabbi said of the Bible, "Turn it and turn it; for everything is in it."

Introduction

LET ME IMAGINE—SO FAR as I am able—the kind of person who is likely to pick up a book with the title *Jewish Biblical Legends: Rabbinic Wisdom for Christian Readers*. Yes. I'm going to try to describe you since you just picked up this book or opened it in an e-reader. You must be interested in the Bible or you wouldn't have any interest in the topic. That part was easy. I'm going to guess that you've grown up hearing the Bible read in church and you've read quite of bit of it yourself. You may be a pastor, a teacher, or just the kind of person who really listens to sermons and thinks about the Bible when you hear it being read. You are committed, so far as you are able, to living in accordance with the light of Scripture. But you didn't get started on this Christian journey yesterday. In fact, you started out quite a while ago and it is all starting to feel just a little tedious.

These stories have come at you a thousand ways. You sang Bible songs in camp, you learned Bible stories at VBS maybe like many of us on flannel graph. You've read, heard, and maybe taught countless Sunday School lessons. You have seen movies about the Bible, and of course you have heard a million and ten sermons from the Bible. If you have attended church over ten years and were given academic credit for every sermon, you would likely have a PhD! Reading the Bible can be something like going to work; you can appreciate the value of what you do even if it gets a little tiresome to walk into the same office year after year.

If you identify, this book is for you. This is an entree into unusual and sometimes bizarre ways of divining the meaning of divine revelation. You will discover how the rabbis of ancient times and synagogues sought to keep their congregations engaged by telling tales and parables that do not appear in the texts of Scripture but shed light on it. They were gifted story-tellers and sometimes—almost like "Doc" in *Back to the Future*—crazy but brilliant

Jewish Biblical Legends

inventors. And like Marty McFly, we can climb into this literary DeLorean and speed back to a time when sages saw things in Scripture we could never see. We don't know Hebrew like them—either at all or not as well—and we are separated from the culture of the biblical world more than they. Their interpretive insights were based upon immense knowledge of what we call the Old Testament—of course, they were reading it in Hebrew, the original language—which they employed to keep the congregations engaged and informed. They may end up doing the same for us if I do my job well.

The vastness of this *haggadic* literature makes any definitive summary a treacherous task indeed. We embark on an ocean that is deep and sweet; our little vessel can only hold a few buckets. There are legends and wisdom sayings by rabbis on every topic and theme imaginable. We focus here mainly on rabbinic wisdom sayings and legends (called *haggadah* or plural *haggadoth*) related to the first five books we call the Pentateuch (for rabbis, "Torah"). Particularly, we will examine *haggadoth* from the creation of the world to the giving of the law on Mt. Sinai. In the final chapter we will survey a few very famous wisdom sayings from *Pirke Avot*—an important collection of *haggadic* sayings in the Mishnah. These stories and sayings were sprinkled throughout the *midrashic* and Talmudic literature and have been collected together in various publications following different methods. I'll say more about these collections below (see "*Haggadic* Literature: What is it?").

I have done this work in three steps. First, I read through these collections and selected what seemed intelligible and applicable in a Christian setting.[1] As a Methodist preacher who has had extensive experience in other denominations, I have some idea of what would be of interest. Second, I sought to make the text itself accessible in English. Some translations use out-of-date language. I translated most texts from Mishnaic Hebrew but also consulted translations. Third, I imaginatively explored implications the text has or might have for us.

I have allowed myself to be repetitious in a way that may be tedious to a person reading this from front to back. However, I realize that many if not most readers will not read this book completely or from start to finish. Some may well read from the back to the front and read this introduction

---

1. Another similar work on this topic is Silverman, *Rabbinic Stories*. Rabbi Silverman's excellent work is topical in nature while mine follows biblical order (that is, the biblical events in the Pentateuch). James Kugel's excellent *The Bible as It Was* is somewhat similar to my presentation, although he does not restrict himself to the *haggadic* traditions and covers more of the biblical materials with less theological commentary. I chose to cover less territory but plow a little deeper.

Introduction

last. That is what I might have done. If you are a linear reader, you have my permission to skip around at will. If you are not a linear reader, you probably will not read the Introduction at all or have already skipped around quite a bit. Plunder at will. I'll try to help a bit with an index but the book follows the biblical order from creation to Mt. Sinai.

This kind of rabbinic literature is sometimes dead serious, sometimes light-hearted. Many times we should imagine rabbis almost playing games with Scripture with an eye to getting a chuckle from the pews. I have become increasingly aware of the whimsical spirit with which much of this literature is written. I try to write in something of the same whimsical spirit. This is not a book of weighty theology but a joyous journey into a strange—sometimes downright eccentric—new world of biblical meanings. I do try to find a serious "point" that might have some relevance today. I also explain the biblical "hook" from which the saying hangs. But feel free to cast what I say aside and discover a new meanings in the text. As you will read below (chapter 10), one rabbi famously said of Scripture, "Turn it, turn it; for everything is in it." If you are a preacher, you can use that one on Sunday morning.

So my point here is to pursue new insights through the confluence of ancient Jewish wisdom and contemporary Christian culture. Perhaps this will provide a tonic if what ails us is the boredom that comes from listening to the same voices in the same echo chamber. Here we travel back to a radically new-for-us world of absolutely wild *midrash* and we can hardly help but be stunned by what we discover. I certainly was surprised when I first encountered this literature and have made exploration of it my life's work.[2]

This book flows directly from my personal story. In the fall of 1997 I began to study Rabbinic Literature at Hebrew Union College in Cincinnati, Ohio with several eminent scholars: Richard Sarason, Edward Goldman, David Aaron, and Adam Kamesar.[3] I am also a United Methodist minis-

---

2. To describe *midrash* as "wild" isn't completely fair. The rabbis had specified rules called *middoth* that guided their thinking. Some of these we see exemplified in Jesus' teaching. Jesus was, after all, the first person in human history known to be called "rabbi"! However, from a modern vantage point, especially for those trained in the historical critical methods of interpretation, rabbinic interpretation seems positively unrestricted and free-wheeling.

3. Adam Kamesar is a specialist in the Judaism of the Greco-Roman world and not a rabbinics scholar per se. However, as I read Josephus, Philo, Septuagint, Stoic literature, and Christian Fathers under his wise guidance, I learned how rabbinic methods of biblical interpretation and *haggadic* legends came to be understood and employed by those outside their immediate circles. He has written an excellent introduction to

ter and was at the time serving my first United Methodist congregation in Kentucky. During the week I was translating and interpreting rabbinic literature and on Sundays preaching to my small Kentucky congregation. The words of the rabbis simply exploded from one world into another; I could not keep them hermetically sealed in the classroom. I found myself without fail making reference to rabbinic sayings, parables, and biblical conjecture in the course of my preaching. At the time I determined that as soon as I had completed my dissertation—which also dealt with one specific *haggadic* tradition—I would indeed write my first post-doctorate book on this topic. I had no idea at that time that I would end up taking all of nine years to complete my Ph.D. and another year to prepare the dissertation for publication.[4] But now I dive back into the world of *haggadah* to explore how it can be helpful to Christian biblical knowledge.

Reading these legends can sometimes be quite unsettling to a Christian interpreter. Rabbis have a very different reading agenda and methodology than Christians, and their interpretations can sometimes be inspirational, sometimes confusing, sometimes irritating and off-putting. The main impression Christians have when they first encounter these texts is that they are cavalier in nature. They seem to be masters at forcing Scripture to their wishes and will. As one of my teachers said, "The rabbis just don't care about what the Bible meant in its original context. They only want to know what it means for them in their own day." For anyone trained in the historical method of biblical interpretation—one that seeks to interpret in accordance to original contextual meaning—this will seem quite random and haphazard.

Two things are important to remember. First, Rabbis usually do have a feature of the biblical text that is the focus of their attention. They are not simply ignoring the text and the meaning it had in its historical context. We know that rabbis were fastidious to preserve the text in perfection; the care their scribes took with sacred writ is legendary. Second, as we said above, rabbis are sometimes serious and sometimes having fun with Scripture. Often, after hours of exhausting work studying and debating legal texts, rabbis turned to this non-legal work for comedic relief. Over and over we will

---

the way in which church fathers understood and employed the traditions of narrative *haggadah* ("The Church Fathers and Rabbinic Midrash," 20–40). It has truly been one of the great privileges of my life to have been able to read such wonderful literature with these brilliant men. I took courses with other wonderful instructors, but these four—and especially Drs. Goldman and Sarason—helped me learn and love the *haggadic* literature.

4. Allen, *The Despoliation of Egypt*.

find the rabbis almost playing with Scripture—often by tweaking a feature of the Hebrew text.

For instance, in Genesis where Rebekah is coming to meet her future husband, we read in English that when she saw Isaac, she quickly slipped off her camel to run to him (Gen 24:64). The Hebrew actually uses a verb that usually means "to fall" (*naphal*)! Why did Rebekah "fall" off her camel when she saw Isaac? The rabbis answer, "Because in a revelation, God showed her that the wicked Esau would be her son and she fell off the camel in dismay." Rabbis know that the verb *naphal* here means "to dismount quickly." But they are having some fun and saying something about their persecutors at the same time (who they understood as descendants of Esau). You need to hear the rabbi chuckle with that interpretation. Associated with this playfulness in Scripture interpretation is a playful competition among the interpreters. Sometimes Rabbis and their disciples would spin out interpretations in a competitive way; as in, "Top that!"

The Broadway musical *Wicked*—if you haven't seen it, you must!—illustrates something strikingly similar to rabbinic interpretive methodology. *Wicked* transforms *The Wizard of Oz* by providing a new backstory that alters the story and its meaning. New perspectives on the moral quality of key figures come to light; the Wizard wasn't so wonderful after all and the witch was tragically heroic. Glinda was not good but she was popular, which was "everything that really counts" for her. Similarly, rabbis also love to spin out new background stories to illuminate a well-known biblical story with new coloration and signification. Usually their new perspective responds to a feature of the biblical text. It was all a way of being playful and yet inquisitive about differing shades of meaning in the sacred Scriptures.

In the remaining portion of this introductory chapter, several related topics will be briefly explored. First, we must learn what *haggadic* literature is and how it works. Second, we will learn what early Christian theologians thought about these stories. What we will find is that many Christians considered these stories to be critical biblical background that helped to explain the Bible itself. Finally, we'll take a quick overview of rabbinic biblical interpretation (*midrash*) and some of the issues involved. If you aren't interested in these topics, just skip to the first chapter. You have my permission. It isn't a sin.

Jewish Biblical Legends

HAGGADIC LITERATURE: WHAT IS IT?

The rabbinic texts we will explore are called in Hebrew, as mentioned above, *Haggadah*, meaning, "what is told." *Haggadic* literature includes anything the rabbis said that fell outside the bounds of *halakah* (that is, legal literature). *Halakah* means "the walk"—as in "the walk of life"—and comes from the verb "to walk" (*halak*). All the legal texts of the rabbinic world (namely the *Mishnah, Tosefta,* and the *Talmuds*) concerned the daily living of a typical Jew. The great majority of what they debated and wrote about was legal in nature. *Haggadah* refers to everything else: simple sayings of wisdom, anecdotes about the lives of the rabbis, parables about kings and palaces, stories about characters in the Bible, and even fully-developed sermons. In rabbinic literature, this is the fun stuff. Legal literature is dense, highly cryptic, extraordinarily complicated, and often quite burdensome, even to the pious. But everyone enjoys the *haggadic* literature.

Rabbis themselves sometimes wrote about *haggadah* as if it contained an almost seductive power. "The delights of the sons of men" (Eccl 2:8) is said to refer to the *haggadah*, which gives delight to the study of Scripture. *Haggadah* is described to be fragrant with aroma redolent of the lilies mentioned in the Song of Solomon. Whole episodes in the life of Abraham, Isaac, Jacob, Moses, which are completely unmentioned in the Bible, seem to be spun out of thin air. They felt that where the Bible left things unmentioned one could, by carefully reading of contextual clues, fill in the gaps. So they made up stories to plug the gaps in the scriptural story. In so doing, they shed light on the meaning of the biblical stories. From the *haggadah* we learn virtually everything the rabbis believed about God, creation, various reasons for commandments, and much on topics such as beliefs about angels and demons, magic, superstition, various folktales, folk medicine, charms, and so on.[5]

More importantly, for the rabbis, the study of *haggadah* qualifies as a distinct and direct pathway to the worship and knowledge of God. "If you wish to know Him by whose word the world came into being, study *Aggadah;* you will thereby come to know the Holy One, blessed be He, and hold fast to His ways."[6] For the rabbis, the Bible was not only a source of Torah—divine instruction for the patterning of life—the words of Torah

---

5. Stern, "Introduction," xvii. Much of the description of *haggadic* literature comes from this source.

6. Ibid., xxi. *Aggadah* is an alternative spelling for *haggadah*.

Introduction

became a lens through which the rabbis viewed every element of life. The Torah gave them the vocabulary by which they interpreted the tragedies and triumphs of life. The study of Torah became the sacred temple of divine presence that replaced the Jerusalem Temple after its destruction. As they searched the meaning of particular verses, "they would search after it, first, in themselves, in their own experiences and in what they knew to be true. If Scripture could not lie, neither could it be false or contradictory to the rabbis' own selves and to their knowledge, their sense of the world and of their place in it."[7]

These traditions are not recorded in special books of *haggadic* wisdom (except for *Pirke Avot* and *Midrash Rabbah*). They are sprinkled throughout the whole breadth of rabbinic legal literature like the marbling of fat on the flesh in a good steak. A word is necessary at this point about collections of *haggadic* literature that will serve as our primary source. The Israeli poet and scholar Hayim Bialik and editor Yehoshua Ravnitzky produced a marvelous and beloved collection called *Sefer Ha-Aggadah*. They thought of this collection as something like restoring a ruined palace to its original glory. The re-construction project required three years just to comb through the literature and select the texts they wished to include.

Interestingly, they carried out this work in the early part of the twentieth century in Palestine and saw it as something of a metaphor for the need for Jews, dispersed into many lands, to be drawn back to their homeland again. "The Jews, too, were scattered, dispersed among the nations; they, too, could recapture their special glory, their singular worldview and perspective on life, only by being reassembled and reconstituted in their homeland, their 'palace.'"[8] Bialik saw this work as a support and encouragement for those dispersed Jews who were being physically reconstituted into their homeland; it was an encouragement to become not only geographically but culturally and spiritually reconstituted in their homeland.

Sefer Ha-Aggadah is available in vocalized Hebrew (with a volume of English translation by William G. Braude) and includes materials not specifically related to Bible stories. For this and other reasons, I relied on it more than the more famous *Legends of the Jews* by Louis Ginzerg who essentially re-wrote the story of the Bible by weaving the legends together into a new fuller story. It was this "creating a new story out of countless individual traditions" that made Ginzberg less useful for me. Bialik and

---

7. Ibid., xx.
8. Ibid., xix.

Jewish Biblical Legends

Ravnitzky preserved the voices of the rabbis in a way that Ginzberg did not. This is not to discredit in any way Ginzberg's remarkable achievement. The footnotes alone are stunning in their encyclopedic completeness. Typically I used Ginzberg when I wanted to summarize the trajectory of the *haggadah* and Bialik when I wanted to grapple with a specific text. I also often consulted the English translation of ancient collections of *haggadah* called *Midrash Rabbah*.

EARLY CHRISTIAN APPRECIATION FOR *HAGGADIC* LITERATURE

What outlook did early Christian biblical scholars have toward these Jewish biblical legends? Throughout the history of the church many of our best biblical expositors believed that in order to understand parts of the Old Testament, especially on the literal level, the *haggadic* traditions of the rabbis played a major role. These traditions were sometimes understood as historical background helpful for Christian Bible interpretation. Some conceived of the Jewish traditions as legitimate speculation that was helpful in filling in gaps in the biblical text. They appreciated the legendary knowledge the rabbis brought to bear and knew that rabbis understood better the context and background of the Hebrew Bible. Who better to speculate so as to fill in the gaps left in the biblical narrative?

To illustrate, I will briefly survey the Christian teacher whose biblical erudition was broadly known in the ancient world: Origen (ca. 185–254). While Origen was a theologian and spiritual writer *par excellence*, his influence as a biblical critic and exegete constitutes what is essentially the beginning of the golden era of scientific Christian biblical exegesis. N. de Lange in *Origen and the Jews* has set the stage for much of the recent discussion on the topic. De Lange sought to demonstrate Origen's knowledge of rabbinic traditions and the sweeping influence of these rabbinic traditions on Origen's exegesis. Origen's reliance upon the exegetical traditions learned directly from the rabbis he knew in Caesarea is one of the distinctive features of his exegesis. Hardly any aspect of his exegesis has not been affected by these rabbis and their exegeses.[9]

R. Kimmelman had already effectively argued that Rabbi Yohanan and Origen's lengthy disputations concerning the interpretation of the Song

---

9. De Lange, *Origen and the Jews*, 134.

of Songs produced substantive cross-fertilization.[10] I took a class at Hebrew Union College in which we read in Aramaic the Targum on Song of Songs, and read this article by Kimmelman at the same time. Since we were reading the very rabbinic text to which Kimmelman refers, it was easy for us to evaluate his argument and to see how cross-pollination of interpretation was indeed on display. In other words, the rabbis in the Targum were responding to what they knew Origen was saying about the Song of Songs, and Origen was responding to and learning from the rabbis he knew in Caesarea. D. Halperin discovers in Origen's sermons on Ezekiel imagery taken from the sermons of Galilean rabbis.[11] There is reason to say that Origen had an open and intellectually stimulating relationship with the Jews of Caesarea of his time.[12]

A. Kamesar draws attention to Origen's scientific interest in rabbinic exegesis, especially as a tool in the explanation of the literal sense of the text. This is indicated by his usage of rabbinical exegesis in the prologues to his commentaries.[13] According to Greek and Latin procedure, the prologue of a commentary is where the scientific questions of title, authenticity, number of books, occasion, and utility were addressed. For instance, in his prologue to the *Commentary on the Psalms*, Origen notes that "the Hebrews" divide the psalter into five books. He includes what he has learned from Jewish oral tradition concerning the authorship of individual psalms and tells of his consultation with a Jewish scholar on this subject. "The Alexandrian and Palestinian Fathers sometimes viewed narrative aggadic traditions as historical data to be employed in the interpretation of the biblical text. This means that they viewed such aggadot as relevant to . . . the explanation of 'matters of fact.'"[14]

These narrative traditions were often seen as "legitimate attempts, based on conjecture, to explain the narrative gaps in the biblical text."[15] It was already well recognized in the world of Greek scholarship that often

---

10. Kimmelman, "Rabbi Yohanan and Origen," 567–95. Perhaps "disputations" is too strong a term for what Kimmelman argues. What he claims is that these interpreters seem to know and to be responding to what the other is saying.

11. Halperin, "Origen," 261–75.

12. Crouzel, *Origen*, 78, and Bietenhard, *Caesarea, Origenes und die Juden*.

13. Kamesar, "The Church Fathers and Rabbinic Midrash," 29. This article is an excellent overview of the depth of interest in Jewish biblical interpretation among many early Christian leaders.

14. Ibid., 31.

15. Ibid., 32.

authors intentionally left gaps in their writings that they expected wise readers to be able to fill in for themselves based upon intelligent guesswork and foreshadowing. Therefore, good readers will feel free to listen carefully to the minutia of the story and when there are narrative gaps that seem to beg for an explanation such readers will recreate and imagine what would fit the general tone and implication of what is extant in the narration.

Therefore, it may well be that the church fathers didn't look to *haggadah* as a source of historical information retained in Jewish oral tradition but as the legitimate contemplation and speculation of the rabbis. As such, the Fathers may well have had an understanding of *haggadah*, which was roughly equivalent to what was actually going on in the *beth midrash* (schools of rabbinic Torah-study). The rabbis certainly knew that the *haggadot* were not secret oral traditions of the hoary past but playful and theological conjecture based on and filling out the biblical story.

MIDRASH: RABBINIC BIBLICAL INTERPRETATION[16]

There has been a long-running debate over the question of whether traditional Jewish biblical interpreters sought to *interpret* the holy text or to *manipulate* it to advance their own theological perspective or ideological agenda. Traditionally collections of Jewish biblical interpretation were seen to be essentially collections of interpretations from the *beth midrash* or synagogue, which could be read in isolation from one another and which individually tended to divine the deeper meanings of Scripture. Even though the sage may be seeking at times to buttress *halakhic* traditions with scriptural authority or to develop a particular line of argument, according to this view, the *darshan* (or *midrashic* exegete) was truly struggling with the meaning of Scripture and Scripture itself played a significant role in shaping the theology and ideology of the rabbinic community. In this view, *midrash* collections have no sustained argument or theological agenda *qua* collection; their focus, not wholly but substantively and primarily, is the explication of Scripture.

James Kugel is of the view that the primary concept of *midrash* is exegetical (as opposed to eisegetical). He identifies four basic assumptions

---

16. *Midrash* refers to rabbinic biblical interpretation. *Haggadah* is a broader term that includes all the non-legal rabbinic sayings and wisdom. We are dealing here with *haggadic* interpretation of Scripture, which is a type of *midrash*. The two words are closely related.

that, in spite of the wide variety of styles and genres and even interpretive methods, underlie all traditional biblical interpretation. The first assumption was that the Bible is fundamentally a cryptic document. Second, the Scriptures are fundamentally relevant to contemporary life and its challenges. Third, the Scriptures are perfect and perfectly harmonious. While there might appear to be discrepancies in the Bible, these apparent variances are fraught with deeper meaning and are not mistakes but opportunities for the interpreter to search for the deeper substance of the text. Because there is perfect harmony within all parts of the Bible, any biblical text can be used to illustrate another. In its extreme form, the doctrine of "omnisignificance" claims that nothing is said in vain or even for rhetorical flourish. Every detail of Scripture is an opportunity to interpret; that is, to search for a deeper meaning. Fourth, all Scripture is of divine provenance, or divinely inspired.[17]

Interpreters of the Scriptures are sometimes thought of as being completely cavalier in their attitude, altering meanings willy-nilly to fit their whims and fancies, or more commonly, their theological/political agendas. This, according to Kugel, is not correct. While all of their interpretations reflect their beliefs and ideas, in many instances their primary concern is simply to explain what they have encountered in the text, which may be either difficult to understand or presenting some unacceptable contradiction or moral problem. But their interpretations typically start with the text itself, which has been examined in its every detail in search of hidden meanings. The meanings they find are, of course, relevant to the writer and to his communities as either a timeless moral truth or a law to be observed or a prediction of the future. But these interpretations typically flow directly from something seen *in the text*: an apparent contradiction, an unnecessary detail, a repetition, or an emphatic turn of phrase was seen by the exegete as an opportunity to explore the text to discover its real meaning. And very often the primary motivation remains making sense out of the biblical text, even its seemingly insignificant details, the confusing features and troubling passages. It was often these very things that were invitations for the exegetes to probe the texts more deeply.[18]

17. Kugel, *The Bible as It Was*, 17–23. J. Harris is largely of the same opinion as Kugel. He writes, "The relentless insistence on the exegetical foundations of Jewish practice that dominate *halakhic* discussions of the various rabbinic documents leaves little doubt that, in general, these documents are informed by the belief that many Jewish practices are to be derived from the Torah exegetically" (*How Do We Know This?* 3).

18. Ibid., 23–26.

Jewish Biblical Legends

Another scholarly position seeks to construe the *midrashic* texts as tightly constructed with a broad theological purpose. *Midrash* generally and *haggadic* traditions specifically were not snippets of isolated rabbinic exegesis but were collected as sustained arguments on various topics in which Scripture plays only a secondary role. William Scott Green argues that the rabbis' initial catalyst was not the canonization of Scripture but the destruction of the Second Temple and the manner in which the study of the Torah (or *Talmud Torah*) itself replaced the Temple cult as that which mediated divine presence.[19] Green claims that rabbinic Judaism is not exegetically derived, not the unfolding of scriptural hermeneutics, but the work of a small homogeneous group of pseudo-priests who sought to maintain Israel's daily life with God in the absence of the Jerusalem cult.[20]

Richard Sarason and Phillip Alexander present a median position. According to Sarason, what has led to such an intractable difference in perspective is the tendency to totalize certain elements of *midrash* at the expense of others. One must bear in mind at least three factors that are always at play in rabbinic *midrash*: the eisegetical factor, the exegetical factor, and the performative factor.[21] The rabbis are often careful readers of Scripture both in terms of its actual content (God's special relationship with Israel, messianic prophecies, eschatological hope of restoration) and of its textual details. Their commentary often serves "to deepen the biblical text through contemporizing paraphrase or dramatization."[22] Rabbis often struggle with the same kinds of interpretive/textual cruxes that have occupied the attention of modern interpreters, sometimes using similar techniques and patterns of interpretive analysis. "For instance, the rabbinic technique of *gezerah shavah*, interpreting a word in one context on the basis of its usage in another, is an artificial extension of what today is viewed as sound philological practice."[23]

The final impulse, the performative, involves the competitive spirit of the *beth midrash* according to which each interpreter gained status and praise for his ability to discover new insights from well-known passages of Scripture. This performative atmosphere stimulated novel and arcane

---

19. Neusner and Green, *Writing with Scripture*, 10.

20. Ibid., 10.

21. Sarason, "Interpreting Rabbinic Biblical Interpretation," 136. See also Alexander, "Midrash," 455.

22. Ibid., 138–39.

23. Ibid., 139.

Introduction

insight and accounts for the rather tongue-in-cheek nature of many rabbinic interpretations.[24] Even when the interpreter goes so far as to construct his own speculations using the Scriptures only as a resource from which to cut-and-paste snippets of language—what Neusner and Green have called "writing with Scripture"—he seeks to unlock meanings that have their ultimate source in the biblical text itself.

> The search for exemplary patterns of meaning in the text of revelation by ever more arcane means must be seen as a crucial part of the Rabbis' larger theological concern. That concern was to demonstrate to themselves and to other Jews that the world and human history are orderly, despite appearances and experiences to the contrary; that the paradigms of this order are to be found in Scripture; that God's providence still works in the present age on Israel's behalf as it did in the biblical past; and that it is therefore reasonable, on the basis of both scriptural promises and paradigms, to expect and to hope for God's future vindication of Israel's past and present suffering. This is a larger meaning that the Rabbis attempt to find in Scripture, but, of course, it also retraces some dominant strands of biblical thought that are "actually" there in the text.[25]

According to Sarason, these three factors or impulses are in constant dialogue with each other and the modern interpreter of the *midrash* must bear in mind all three components.

---

24. Ibid., 140–41.
25. Ibid., 143.

1

The Work of Creation

THE LIMITATIONS OF HUMAN KNOWLEDGE

"In the beginning..." (Gen 1:1).

THE RABBIS WERE CONCERNED about fanciful philosophical speculation, which was popular in their day; flights into imagination tended toward foolish and harmful notions. These speculations were motivated, in their opinion, by pride and an unwillingness to embrace divine boundaries appropriate for the natural limitations of human knowledge. They also believed that the Scriptures were resplendent with glorious significations that go far beyond obvious grammatical meaning. Modern interpreters of Scripture are naturally suspect of these deeper mysteries; we prefer to interpret on the historical critical level alone. For us, the first question is always, "What did this text mean to the original hearers?" which is the primarily locus of meaning the text bears.[1]

Rabbis enjoyed much greater freedom, and the schools of midrashic study encouraged interpreters to find deeper and deeper shades of meaning in texts following some general guidelines they called *middoth*. The historical critical meaning of Scripture had very little interest to rabbis. So

---

1. There are many more nuanced interpretive strategies than the historical critical method described here (canonical interpretations for instance, go beyond the historical critical meaning). Yet, modern interpretation, in comparison to the allegorical/midrashic readings common in the early church and synagogue, are very tame in comparison.

The Work of Creation

in sum, rabbis sought to suppress excessive philosophical speculation yet were enthused about a kind of *midrash* (biblical interpretation) that strikes moderns as quite speculative.

This tension comes into play in their interpretation of the first verse of Scripture. The Hebrew Bible begins with the word *bereshit* so the first letter of the Hebrew Bible is the letter "b" (or *bet* in Hebrew). A *bet* has this shape: ב. Please take a moment to examine the shape of the *bet*. To understand their interpretation it is also important to know that Hebrew is read from right-to-left rather than from left-to-right. That means that the open part of the *bet* is facing forward, not backward. Could there be any significance to the fact that the very first letter of the Holy Scripture takes this particular shape? Of course, for the rabbis the answer is a resounding *Yes!* The shape of the *bet* is intended to limit excessive philosophical speculation and to focus our attention on creation itself. These are their words.

> Why was the world created using the letter ב. Just how the *bet* is closed on the sides and open to the front, so it isn't permitted to investigate what is above, what is below and what is before and what is behind. But from the day the world was created and thereafter (it is permitted).[2]

Rabbis were primarily concerned here, more than likely, to limit the kind of neo-Platonic speculation that gave rise to heretical groups and ideas that today go by the title "gnostics" or "Gnosticism." Gnostics were a loose association of "Christian" folk whose beliefs orthodox Christians claimed to be perverse and heretical. For the gnostics, the true God is not the Hebrew god who created this world full of suffering as it is. No, the true God is the God of Jesus, and the God of Jesus is a more spiritual and much higher deity than the low-level deity proclaimed by Moses. The gnostic God is a God of pure spirit who had nothing to do with the creation of this world nor any interest in it; he was only interested in spiritual things. This deity sought to deliver humans from their enslavement not in Egypt but from their bondage to the capricious semi-deity of Moses. This was to be achieved through secret knowledge or *gnosis* given by the Christ, which provides secret access to the upper ethereal realms.

---

2. *Gen. Rab.* 1:10. Other *midrashim* describe an extended debate between all the letters of the alphabet as to which was worthy to be the first letter in sacred writ. In the end, the letter *bet* was chosen because through this letter (in Hebrew as in English) one says, "Blessed be the Lord forever" (Ginzberg, *Legends*, 1:19–21).

Jewish Biblical Legends

Whether this particular heresy is in view or not (and it very likely is), rabbis were concerned to limit the dangers of such speculative belief-systems, and they started by noting the shape of the first letter of the holy text. Nothing happens in Scripture haphazardly or accidentally; those of true sagacity serve by discerning deeper meanings of sacred writ.

The shape of the *bet* indicates certain limitations of human knowledge and provides direction for our spiritual inquiry. We should not inquire about what came before the creation of the world, what is above the creation, and what is below creation. Our focus must be on the created world and our inquiry must end when the world ends (where the arms of the *bet* end). There is no point speculating about the world to come other than what is based in Scripture. Rabbis thought a lot about the coming world—they called it *haOlam haba'*—but this speculation must be limited to *midrashic* biblical interpretation.

Not only would gnostics be guilty here of excessive speculation concerning the future, but within Judaism itself there existed apocalyptic groups (from which Christianity sprang), which worried the rabbis as well. For instance, in the *Apocalypse of Abraham* Abraham is envisioned to be swept into heaven by an angel named Yahoel where Abraham sees deep into the future and provides details about the end of all things.

Rabbis found this kind of literature troublesome and untethered to any biblical foundation. The letter *bet,* shaped as it is, provides a clue about the limitations of human knowledge and theological inquiry; our focus must be on this created world and the time of its existence. That should keep us occupied enough. Rabbis believed that their work was to be primarily focused on what they called the *halakah*, which is based on the Hebrew verb "to walk." *Halakah* is a legal work that intended to take what the Scriptures say (especially the 613 laws of the Torah) and spell out exactly how the godly are to walk through this life. The Talmud is essentially a commentary on an earlier collection of laws called the Mishnah. It is a very complicated collection of rabbinic legal opinions, but the point of all of it is to discern how to "walk" through this world in a way that gives honor to their good and loving Creator. Excessive speculations, enthralling though they might be, distract the community from its primary task.

The dangers of excessive philosophical speculation are echoed in Col 2:8: "See to it that no one takes you captive through hollow and deceptive philosophy, which depends on human tradition and the elemental spiritual forces of this world rather than on Christ" (NIV). Early Christian writers

The Work of Creation

like Irenaeus and Origin also expressed great concern about accommodating human philosophy too much as it gave rise to heresies.³ We must remember that what is in view here is not scientific inquiry but a kind of philosophical and apocalyptic speculation that lacks the controls of rationality and common-sense. While this kind of free-wheeling world-creation might dazzle the eyes and enthrall the imagination, the rabbis here call their disciples to live in the real world where decisions must be made about mundane things like eating dinner and plowing fields. The *bet* is a reminder to focus the energies of life in things of mundane yet practical value. What we need, rabbis believe, is not spiritual ecstasy and high-flying mind-bogglement. Rabbis sought to apply their genius to the present world and the Torah (which they often described as being almost the same thing—the world) and find contentment there. There we can speculate within *bet*'s boundaries and find delights enough.

CREATED OUT OF NOTHING?

"Now the earth was formless and empty and darkness covered the surface of the deep" (Gen 1:2).

The words in Hebrew translated above "formless and empty" (in Hebrew *tohu va-vohu*) could also be translated "waste and void." The text seems to indicate that the material from which God created the world was inferior and faulty.⁴ The reason Gen 1:1–2 posed such a challenge to the rabbis is because of the intellectual challenge presented by the gnostics. For gnostics,

3. See relevant chapters in Allen, *The Despoliation of Egypt*.
4. There are two viable translations of Gen 1:1. A) "When God began to create the heavens and the earth, the earth was *tohu va-vohu*" or B) "In the beginning God created . . ." If A is the case, then the formlessness and void appears to be co-eternal with God and possibly the stuff from which God fashioned creation. The B translations imply that God created the *tohu va-vohu*. The traditional Latin phrase for this is *creatio ex nihilo*. The *tohu* and *vohu* in B resulted from God's first creative act. In A, the provenance of the *tohu va-vohu* is unclear making it also unclear if God created the world out of nothing. In A, it is possible that God used pre-existing *tohu va-vohu* to create the world. What are the implications of God having created out of pre-existing matter? Gnostics were only too happy to provide their response: the *tohu va-vohu* was inferior chaotic matter, which the capricious and unqualified Hebrew god (or demiurge) used to create this world of sorrow. Because the world was made of such inferior matter, gnostics believed, it continually tends to revert back to chaos. This is the source of all human discomfort and suffering. Rabbis and Christian theologians both disliked this interpretation intensely and sought to explain things more positively.

17

the fact that the creator fashioned the world out of inferior construction materials (*tohu va vohu*) explains all the sufferings of the life. They claimed that the creator must be either malicious or weak and ignorant. If God didn't realize the pain caused by creating such an inferior world of degraded products then God is a fool. If God intentionally chose to create using the *tohu* and the *vohu* then God is malicious. Either way, the gnostics believed that the Hebrew Scriptures provided ample reason to reject the creator of this world and so worship the gnostic deity of pure spirit.

R. Eleazar responds by quoting a passage in Ecclesiasticus (or Sirach—abbreviated Sir), which encourages a humility that limits its own range of inquiry to questions of Jewish law and refrains from philosophical speculation. Sir 3:21–22 (NRSV) says: "Neither seek what is too difficult for you, nor investigate what is beyond your power. Reflect upon what you have been commanded, for what is hidden is not your concern.[5]" Eleazar illustrates Ben Sira's limitation of inquiry—and thus the critique of gnostic speculation—with the following parable.

> This is like a king who built a palace on top of piles of feces, sewers, and garbage dumps. Everyone who came along would say, "This palace was built on poop piles, sewage and garbage!" They wouldn't necessarily devalue the property, would they? That's the way it is when someone comes along and says, "The world was constructed on *tohu va vohu*!" They aren't necessarily likely to devalue the creation, are they?[6]

R. Eleasar's parable supposes, for the sake of the argument, that God *did* create the world out of or on top of pre-existent worthless matter. The rabbis would prefer to interpret the text so as to make creation *ex nihilo* its true meaning.[7] But the Rabbis knew that the Hebrew could naturally be read so that the *tohu va vohu* was at least coequal with God and the

---

5. This work was highly regarded by the rabbis and cited authoritatively in Talmud. Sirach did not achieve full canonical status yet the early church did consider it canonical and it appears in modern translations of the Apocrypha or Deuterocanonical writings. Because it failed to reach canonical status in Judaism, the Hebrew text was lost and complete versions of it survive only in its Greek, Latin, and Syriac. About two thirds of the Hebrew text has been recovered.

6. This passage found in both in *Gen. Rab.* 1:5 and in the Palestinian Talmud, *Hagigah* 2:1 (Bialik, *Sefer Ha-aggadah*, 5).

7. See footnote 4. It should be noted that the earliest translation of the Bible into Greek (around 280 BCE) translates the passage in the traditional fashion—as do most modern translations—with the words, "In the beginning, God created the heavens and the earth."

The Work of Creation

pre-existent building materials for creation (option A in footnote 4 above). They also realized that this translation did not necessarily mean that the formlessness and void were the source of human suffering, as nice as that argument may have sounded to the gnostics.

To limit just this kind of philosophical speculation, R. Eleazar provides the parable of the king who built his palace on a dunghill, sewers, and garbage dump. This does not *necessarily* demean its value. The palace must be judged on its own terms seeing a complete restoration could completely cover up and transform initial inferiorities of location. You cannot judge a palace simply because of its initial location. It must be judged as a finished product. If the king built upon a dunghill, yet the waste-dump was covered with earth and the whole complex had become transformed into a place of beauty, then even more praise must be granted. The original location may but doesn't necessarily devalue the property.

Unstated but assumed here is the notion that this complaint can also rebound to God's glory by illustrating how God can transform even a dunghill into the beautiful creation we experience. It all depends upon whether one wants to emphasize suffering or beauty in the created world. But the initial building materials or location do not necessarily devalue the completed product. That is Eleazar's point and for this reason one need not try to argue along these philosophically speculative themes.

Another saying appears in the context of the previous (*Gen. Rab.* 1:5) in which R. Huna confesses his frustration with the fact that the Genesis story is written so as to imply (at least in Hebrew—see note 8) that God built the creation of previously existing materials. He would have preferred the Scriptures to remove all ambiguity so that God's perfection would be guaranteed.

Rabban Gamaliel, in response to a pagan (gnostic?) philosopher, argues the world was indeed created out of nothing. He does this by citing texts that speak of God's creation of evil, darkness, and other similarly chaotic and unformed matter.[8] Since God created other chaotic features of the earth, God must have created the *tohu va vohu* as well.

---

8. *Gen. Rab.* 1:9. Texts cited are Isa 45:7 (evil), Ps 148:4 (waters), Amos 4:13 (wind), and Prov 8:24 (depths). Interestingly, the pagan philosopher—whose only access to the Genesis story would have been in Greek, Old Latin, or later the Vulgate—would not have assumed that the world was created out of *tohu* and *vohu*. This is only its possible meaning in Hebrew. These translations stress that God created the formless void as God's first creative act. We mentioned above that the Greek translation called the Septuagint translates, "In the beginning God created . . ." not "when God began to create . . ." This illustrates the imaginative nature of such discussions.

Jewish Biblical Legends

These discussions can be helpful to a Christian teacher in the following way. The discussions of creation *ex nihilo* were once a matter of life-or-death for the rabbis and early Christians in their debates with the gnostics. While Christians have traditionally understood creation as having come *out of nothing*, the Hebrew Bible is not as clear on this matter as we would like; a fact which we see caused the rabbis great anguish.[9] God could have created the *tohu va-vohu* and thus have created everything out of nothing (option B in footnote 4). But the text just doesn't make this as clear as we would like.[10] These *haggadic* traditions illustrate the complexity of the translation of Gen 1:1 where we catch a glimpse of the rabbinic struggles with these issues and some of their solutions.

JUSTICE AND MERCY

"The Lord God made earth and heaven" (Gen 2:4).

What captures the interpreter's attention is the fact that two names for God function here together as one, both Lord (*Yahweh* in Hebrew) and God (*'Elohim* in Hebrew).[11] According to standard rabbinic understanding, the ineffable and particularly holy name *Yahweh* was used by Moses when God's mercy was in view, and *Elohim* when God's justice was accented. Here we see mercy and justice kiss each other with the proximity of these two divine names. The following parable sheds light.

> Here's a story of a king who had fragile glass cups. The king said, "If I pour hot water into them, they will crack. If I pour cold water into them, they will shatter." What did he do? He mixed the water, and poured it into them, and the cups were fine. In this way the

---

9. Since Christian interpreters were reading the Septuagint or the Latin versions (Old Latin or Vulgate) that read "In the beginning," they often were not aware of the problems presented to readers of the Bible in Hebrew. Parenthetically, the mounting scientific evidence for the big bang theory provides an interesting source of support for creation *ex nihilo*.

10. The Christian doctrine of creation *ex nihilo* can be founded on the New Testament texts (Rom 4:17; Heb 11:3). This can be understood under the rubric of the progress of revelation.

11. LORD written in small capitals indicates in most English translations the Hebrew divine name is *Yahweh*. Because of rabbinic tradition that declared the pronunciation of this holy name verboten, typically the title *Adonai* (Lord) was pronounced instead. When the Hebrew itself has *Adonai*, the English specifies this with *Lord* (capital *L*, lower case *-ord*).

Holy One, blessed be He, said, "If I create the world with mercy alone, sins will abound. If I create the world with justice alone, how could the world survive? So I will create it with both justice and mercy and may it thrive."[12]

God's qualities of justice and mercy go to the core of the rabbinic understanding as seen in their understanding of the differing meanings of the divine names. The point of this parable is that God created the world with both justice and mercy in mind. The universe presents us with stunning beauty and agonizing pain. Sorrow and pleasure are both necessary elements of all human life. Just as the king in the parable mixed both hot and cold water so as not to break the glass, God designed the created world so that we experience both beauty and agony. If God only created with beauty, we would expand and explode with pride and sin would abound. If only with sorrow, all our hopes would be crushed and we would despair. If all was mercy, we would sin freely. If all was justice, we would despair.

This parable may again respond to gnostic opinion of Yahweh's inferiority and malicious nature. To them, human suffering indicates that the creator of this world must be inferior and untrustworthy. But this parable points out that suffering does not prove God's moral inferiority at all but it is a key part of God's plan for our welfare. God mixed both pain and pleasure in creation so as to encourage joy in living *and* discourage arrogance and self-dependence. God knew we need good doses of both pain and pleasure; opportunities for joy are everywhere present yet potential for pain can hardly be completely avoided.

This may foreshadow the theodicy of Irenaeus, who, also in arguing against the gnostics, claimed that the world was created with just enough suffering to force humanity out of its nascent childishness into the light of spiritual and moral maturity. Suffering in this view takes great importance in a world created to be the "vale of soul-making." God's purpose, even in allowing for suffering, is to force humanity into maturity and to provide opportunity for acts of compassion. John Hick's description of Irenaean theodicy is particularly apt.

> Irenaeus suggests that man was created as an imperfect, immature creature who was to undergo moral development and growth and finally be brought to the perfection intended for him by his Maker. . . . Irenaeus pictures [the fall] as something that occurred in the childhood of the race, an understandable lapse due to weakness

---

12. *Gen. Rab.* 12:15.

and immaturity rather than an adult crime. . . . Irenaeus sees our world of mingled good and evil as a divinely appointed environment for man's development towards the perfection that represents the fulfillment of God's good purpose for him.[13]

This rabbinic parable can be helpful for congregations coping with sorrow or rejoicing in the pleasures of life. It is by the fundamental combination of these two features of creaturely existence that we humans can live lives of sober and humble joy. Here the parable teaches that God fully intended for human life to be a mix of joy and sorrow to create an environment for human *moral* flourishing. Our created world itself crushes pride and nurtures joy. This duality goes back to God's attributes of mercy and justice represented by the divine names *Yahweh* and *Adonai*.

LET US MAKE MAN

"Let us make man in our image" (Gen 1:26).

Many of the issues with which modern readers struggle were also points of questioning for the rabbis of old. In *Gen. Rab.* ch. 8, we read of several rabbis debating over the meaning of the words in Genesis 1:26, "Let *us* make man in *our* image." Why the plural if God is one?

> Whom did He consult?[14] R. Ammi said, "He consulted His own heart. This is comparable to a king who built a palace with the consultation of an architect. When he saw the palace, it did not please him. At whom was he upset? Was it not at the architect? Hence, 'and *he* grieved His heart'" (Gen 6:6) [with which He had taken counsel at the making of man].
>
> R. Hanina said, "He took counsel with angels at his service."
>
> R. Berekhiah said, "When the Holy One, blessed is He, was about to create the first man, he saw the righteous and the wicked who were to be formed from him. He said, 'If I create him, wicked men will be formed from him; if I do not create him, where will the righteous come from?' What did the Holy One, blessed be He, do? He removed the way of the wicked from mind, partnered with his own merciful side, and then created him."

---

13. Hick, *Evil*, 214–15.

14. The Hebrew here is a *niphal* of the verb *malak*, which is derivative for the word for "king" and indicates a taking into counsel the way a ruler might consult with advisors who are clearly beneath him in authority.

The Work of Creation

Rabbis, while adhering to the highest form of monotheism imaginable, also believed that God's characteristics surpassed all human imagining. Out of this superabundance of divine substance, the rabbis could speak of differing aspects of God's nature as having some sort of conversation. They would never have accepted that the independent aspects of God's nature had hypostatic substance as the Christian doctrine of the Trinity claims. Yet, while God is one, different aspects of God's nature could be understood as being in conversation.

R. Ammi therefore answered that God was having a conversation with his own heart in saying, "Let *us* make humankind." For his case here, he looks to Gen 6:6, which speaks of the wickedness of the earth grieving God's heart. R. Ammi reads this verse as if the verb has "the Lord" rather than "the wickedness of the world" as its subject: thus he translates, "He [God] grieved his own heart."[15] He envisions God in conversation with his own heart and even angry with himself almost as a king might be angry at an architect who builds a palace not to his liking. In other words, since God is both king and architect, God was upset with what his own heart had constructed.

Admittedly, this answer is quite convoluted and other Rabbis look elsewhere for simpler answers. R. Hanina suggests that God was simply in conversation with the angels. R. Berekhiah believes that God (with mercy almost having its own personality) is in partnership with his own quality of mercy. He paints an imaginative mental experiment for us by describing God's internal debate as he looked forward into the future and knew that the humans he was in the process of creating would achieve both the heights of moral excellence and the depths of depravity. If God operated only on the basis of his own righteousness, he would not have created humans since they have done so much evil. God therefore chose to look to his own merciful nature in creating humans realizing that the glorious potential in creating free beings outweighed the risk.

Several elements of interest can be gleaned here for Christian interpreters. First, from a Trinitarian perspective, it is fascinating to read how close Rabbis actually are to a Christian understanding. Christians typically believe that the divine *us* describes an inner-Trinitarian discussion, and that Jesus is the ultimate personification of the mercy of God. The Holy

---

15. The subject of the Hebrew verb here is unspecified, so R. Ammi's reading is certainly a grammatical possibility. The verb is a *hithpael* (reflexive) of the verb *'atsav*. The fact that the verb is reflexive makes the notion of God grieving his own heart grammatically workable but not likely.

Spirit personifies the holiness or the righteousness of God: the *Holy* Spirit. While there is a difference between the Christian *one nature, three persons* rubric and what we encounter among the rabbis, it is remarkable just how comfortable this language is. The primary distinction for Christians is the confession of the incarnation of the mercy of God in the person of Jesus. While rabbis were scandalized at the notion of incarnation, their theological language and perspective makes some sense of the Christian development.

It is also fascinating to catch a glimpse of how these interpreters conceived of God grappling with indecision concerning what to do. Even though they adhered to the highest form of monotheism, their understanding of God is quite dynamic and personal.[16] Here is no Calvinistic sovereign who knows and manipulates every decision. This God, while not capricious, is struggling in his own mind as to the correct course of action. While this discussion may have been understood by them as anthropocentric (using human language to describe a deity who goes beyond our human understanding), even so, they do not conceive of God as utterly unchangeable and knowing the end from the beginning. In the modern categories of theological conversation, we would have to say that the rabbis come out on the "open theism" side of the theological divide. Open theism is a theological perspective that claims that God limits God's own knowledge of the future in order to secure the gift of human freewill, which is incompatible with absolute divine foreknowledge.[17]

THE CRAFTSMAN

"The Rock! His work is perfect" (Deut 32:4).

As we have seen, rabbis believed that the Bible was overflowing with meaning and that even random similarities of assonance or spelling were fair game and could be the source of mysterious signification. R. Simeon ben Yohai tells a delightful parable that illustrates the perfection of craftsmanship of the created world. In doing so, he playfully manipulates the spelling of the word "rock" in Deut 32:4 from *tzur* (rock) to *tzayyar* (craftsman). In

---

16. J. Neusner addresses the shocking degree to which the rabbis, especially in the Amoraic period of the composition of the Babylonian Talmud, conceived of God in incarnate terms, perhaps in response to the Christian doctrine of the incarnation of God in Christ (*Rabbinic Judaism*, ch. 3).

17. For an excellent introduction to this view, read the article by Greg Boyd in Beilby and Eddy (eds.), *Divine Foreknowledge*.

The Work of Creation

a non-vocalized text—that is, a text without vowels, as these readers would have been using—these two words look almost exactly alike.[18]

> The Craftsman who crafted the world and humans, His work is perfect. When a typical human king builds a palace, people entered it and said, "Had the columns been taller, how much more beautiful the palace would have been! Had the walls been higher, how much more beautiful it would have been! Had the ceiling been higher, how much more beautiful it would have been!" But does any man come and say, "If I only had three eyes, if I only had three arms or feet, how lovely I would be! If I walked on my head, or if my face were turned toward the back, how nice that would be for me!" Wouldn't that be strange![19] To assure that no one would say such a thing, the King of kings of kings, the Holy One and his court took a vote concerning every limb you have and set you up in a way that is best. For this reason we read, "He has made you and established you." (Deut 32:6)[20]

Again we may have the gnostic argument in the background here since the general purpose of the passage seeks to extol the perfection of God as master craftsman of the universe against gnostic arguments otherwise. Parables that compare the King of kings to human kings could hardly be more typical of *midrashic* interpretation. The logic usually works something like this: If the glory of human kings has a certain character, how much the more will God's glory be thus? But this parable functions not by way of comparison but by contrast. While we can always imagine a more beautiful palace—it can always have higher ceilings or more beautiful paintings—we can hardly imagine adding limbs to a human body with the result being anything but a sad mutation. When we read the words, "Let *us* make . . ." (Gen 1:26), we are reading of the Lord consulting with his ministering spirits.

This *haggadah* answers the question "Who is the *us* in Gen 1:26" with the answer, "God and God's ministering spirits." Why did God do this? God, as a master Craftsman, was polling the angels to determine the perfect

---

18. *Hatzur* (the Rock) and *hatzir* (the Craftsman). Note the only difference between the two is in the vowels. The consonants are identical.

19. Braude translates this word, "I wonder" (*Book of Legends*, 14). I thought "Wouldn't that be strange?" translated the Hebrew better. In the Soncino translation by Freedman and Simon (*Midrash Rabbah*), we read, "Surely not!"

20. *Gen. Rab.* 12:1.

designs for the created world so no one later could suggest improvements such as another arm or leg.

The idea of God polling the angels for design advice might strike moderns as a bit bizarre and unhelpful. But again we see the dynamism with which the rabbis understood God to be in cooperative engagement with the created world. Divine sovereignty and universal control for them didn't necessarily imply meticulous manipulation but powerful and wise engagement with a free creation of beings of almost godlike status.

In a similar vein, in *Gen. Rab.* 8:10, we encounter a humorous observation; if a human king were to build a palace, he would never place its rain spout right in front of its main entrance. Yet the Creator placed the human nose just in front of his mouth, "and that makes man's beauty, man's comeliness." We must imagine the rabbis chucking with each other and the text, yet there was a serious point involved. If a human had done the design job and put the downspout in front of the front door, we would fire him for such a stupid faux pas. Yet, the Master of the Universe can do the same thing while creating humans and we admire the perfection of the design plan as a thing of beauty. Thus, the rabbis affirmed the wisdom of the designer of this world with the reading: "The Craftsman! His work is perfect!"

ALL I HAVE CREATED

With increasing anxiety concerning the degradation caused by modern human life on the ecosystems in which we live, the following *haggadah* speaks in our day more potently than when the rabbis first proclaimed it.

> At the time the Holy One, blessed be He, created the first human, he took him for a walk and showed him all the trees of the Garden of Eden. He said to him, "Take a close look at all the things I have created. How beautiful and splendid they all are. Everything I have made, I made for your sake. Now take care lest you become corrupt and destroy my world. For if you become corrupt, there is no one else who will repair it after you."[21]

God is thrilled about the beauty of his creation and is calling on Adam to share in God's pleasure as if to say, "Just check out this great place I made! I hope you appreciate it as much as I do!" But then comes the challenge; "You had better not become corrupt and damage this lovely garden!"

21. *Eccl. Rab.* 7:13. §1.

The Work of Creation

Responsibility for its care is given over to Adam and his descendants. The saying thus encourages a kind of creation care that flows from both self-interest and obligation to care for what the creator himself loves.

What is fascinating here is the connection between human corruption and ecological disaster. The Hebrew verb for "to become corrupt" (*qilqal*) means "to disgrace yourself by immoral behavior." To become corrupt here implies a certain disgrace a person brings upon themselves through thoughtlessness concerning one's moral obligations. The word "repair" or "straighten" (*taqan*) is a very important verb in rabbinic thought even to this day. Many synagogues will have a page on their website devoted to *tiqun haolam* (sometimes spelled *tikkun olam*), which means "repairing" or "straightening the world." Any action of social righteousness that seeks to improve the world in any way qualifies as a *tikkun olam*. Jews tend to be very engaged in social justice issues as a primary locus of spiritual concern.

There is a specific biblical backdrop to this concept; rabbis believed that God intentionally created the world with work for humans to do to bring creation to greater perfection. God could have created a world without imperfections such as cancer or tuberculosis. But God knew that Adam (and all humanity by extension) needed work to do and God expected Adam to partner with him as something of a co-creator. Adam was tasked to care for the garden and to name its animals; God's work brought order to things but didn't order them completely. It was Adam's—and thus our—duty to bring further order and straightening to the created world.

But God also is concerned that human selfishness and corruption not degrade the created order of things. When it does, an act of *tikkun olam* can remedy the problem. Thus, these deeds of "world repair" are engaged in not only perfecting the world beyond its original creation, but to repair the damage of our own corruption. Rabbis were aware, much before their time, of the damage and destruction caused by human selfishness upon creation. This *haggadah* reminds us that God has no other partners to protect the beauty of his lovely garden. Angels will not swoop down and save us from ourselves. We must care for this garden motivated our own moral responsibility for our future and that of our progeny.

HAIL, LORD!

"In the image of God he created him" (Gen 1:27).

Jewish Biblical Legends

The *imago Dei* shapes rabbinic understanding of our humanity, human potential and sacred worth. Idolatry degrades and defaces the soul's ability to reflect the image of God into the world. Only in a state of holiness can humans reflect the divine image. The following rather humorous *haggadah* illuminates.

> When the Holy One, blessed be he, created the first man, the serving angels mistook him [for God Himself] and asked if they could proclaim him holy. What did the Holy One, blessed be he, do? He made him fall into a deep sleep so that everyone would know that he was a mere man. This can be compared to a king and a governor riding together in a state carriage. The people of the province were about to cry out, "*Domine!*" but did not know which one was king. What did the king do? He pushed the governor out of the carriage so that everyone would know that that one was no more than a governor.[22]

It is striking in the extreme that the rabbis, with all their high monotheism, were able to claim that humans are created with such divine glory and divinity, that Adam could be confused with God himself. In the above interpretation, God put Adam to sleep, not only to take a rib to create Eve, but to prove to the angels that Adam was a mere man and thus to discourage the angels from worshipping Adam! The idea that the angels would be tempted to worship Adam may stem from *haggadic* traditions in which Adam, when first created and before the entrance of sin, was of absolutely massive size and beauty; his body virtually reached from heaven to earth and spanned from east to west.[23] His size and beauty was like that of a god; angels nearly worshipped.

The tendency to portray God as almost human (called "anthropomorphism") represents a later stage in rabbinic thought when the Babylonian Talmud was being edited together (between when the Mishnah was edited ca. 200 to the completion of the Babylonian Talmud, ca. 500) in what is called the "Amoraic" period. God was increasingly depicted as a human personality—as in having a corporeal body—and having human traits doing deeds that humans do in the ways humans do them.[24] "When God participates as a hero and protagonist in a narrative, God gains traits of

---

22. *Gen. Rab.* 8:10.

23. Ginzberg, *Legends*, 1:55.

24. *Rabbinic Judaism*, 61. Chapter 3 describes the shocking degree to which rabbis understood God in thoroughly human terms.

personality and emerges into godlike humanity: God incarnate."[25] This seems to have been a response to the powerful God-made-flesh element central to Christian understanding of Jesus' incarnate nature. Now, for the sages, God and human beings share indistinguishable traits.

> Just as humanity feels joy, so does God, and just as humanity celebrates God, so does God celebrate Israel. . . . In the end, therefore, to be "in our image, after our likeness," the power of the powerless, the riches of the disinherited, the valuation and valorization of the will of those who have no right to will, is to be not the mirror image of God but very much to be like God.[26]

Crushed by the severities of the ancient (often "Christian") world, the rabbis created a world in which the powerless and disinherited found new liberating riches through an utterly unique relationship to an incarnate and interactive deity. Neusner claims that there is little indication, at least in this period, that these ubiquitous references to God's physicality are to be taken in some kind of spiritualized or this sense. Anthropomorphic language highlighted the potential to have genuine interaction with God; God speaks, laughs, and here, proves to the angels that Adam is a mere man by putting him to sleep.

So what theological insights can be gleaned from this parable? In being made in God's image, Adam (before the fall) was created with unique and almost godlike size and beauty so that even angels were tempted to worship. Certainly this speaks to the glory of our humanity as well. But we must remember that what is in view here is the glory of Adam before the fall. Rabbis had a distinct way of describing what was lost with the entrance of sin into the world; Adam (and all humans by extension) shrank in size and was disfigured in appearance. Angels are no longer tempted to shout out *"Hail, Domine!"* reduced and disfigured as we have become. On the other hand, as the next tradition teaches, a single soul—the effects of sin not withstanding—still is worth the world.

A SINGLE SOUL

"Let us make man" (Gen 1:26).

---

25. Ibid., 65.
26. Ibid., 81.

Jewish Biblical Legends

Some sages question why God chose to create a single human as the progenitor of the entire human race rather than a group of people all at once.

> Man was created alone in order to teach that anyone who murders a single soul (from Israel), Scripture treats him as if he was guilty of the destruction of the entire world. And anyone who saves alive a single soul (in Israel), Scripture treats him as if he established the whole world. Again, [man was created alone] in the interest of peace among men, so that one man might not say to his companion, "My father was more glorious than yours" and that heretics cannot say, "There are many ruling forces in heaven." Another purpose is to proclaim the greatness of the Holy One, blessed be He. For if a man strikes many coins from one die, they all look like the others; in fact, they are all exactly the same. But though the King of kings of kings, the Holy One, blessed be He, fashioned every man from the die of the first man, not a single one of them is exactly like his fellow. Hence, each and every person should say, "The world was created for my sake."[27]

It should be noted the words "from Israel" and "in Israel" are added in some manuscripts as if some rabbis limited this saying to Israel and others felt it applied to the whole human race. Many if not most Jews today would prefer reading the saying so its horizons expand to include the whole human race. Rabbis did believe that destroying a single life was commensurate to the destruction of the whole world. By this, they mean that when we destroy a human life, we erase from the earth all the benefits and influence that person and their descendants might have had. In so doing, we've destroyed the world that would have been with that person in it. As a result, the destruction of one person is a tragic loss far beyond what we can see. When you save one life, you have saved a complete world of potential existences from extinction. God chose to create only one human being so that we would always have a clear lesson of the impact of a single life; one life gives rise to the whole human race. God chose to create all humanity with one progenitor to illustrate the massive significance of each individual.

The second saying looks the opposite direction; God chose to create all from one not to glorify the individual but to humble the individual. No one can claim superior bloodline since all human ancestry goes back to the same person created by the same deity. While these two opinions have varying purposes, they are not actually in contradiction. God could wish to

---

27. b. Sanh. 38a.

The Work of Creation

help magnify the value of human life and still want to keep us all humble with the same creative act.

The third opinion is strikingly clever. It notes the superiority of God's creative power in comparison to our human creative powers. When humans strike coins, each coin coming from the press has an identical image. Yet, although God created all humans from the same template, every human being has a unique appearance (identical twins not withstanding, although their differences are not as visible on first blush). God isn't simply striking humans out of a dye like one might find in a mint. The uniqueness of our humanity and the glory of God's creative power are extolled.

Excursus: "I Don't Wanna Be a Pharisee!"

One of the things that surprised me in studying the Bible with rabbinical students was the degree to which they perceived the New Testament to be anti-Jewish. As a Christian, I found it troubling to hear the teachings of Jesus described as "anti-Jewish" and as contributing factors to Jewish suffering. Jesus' teachings in Matthew 23—in which he calls the Pharisees hypocrites, blind-guides, children of hell and much more!—are felt more deeply by Jews than Christians sometimes realize. They know that the Pharisees were direct precursors to the rabbis who shaped the Mishnah, which lies at the core of the Talmud.

This discomfort has been only accentuated when Christian children sing silly camp-songs like, "I don't want to be a Pharisee, 'cuz they're not fair, you see." To my rabbinical friends, this is the equivalent to saying, "I would never want to be a rabbi, because they are all a bunch of hypocrites." Imagine if Jews taught their children a camp-song: "I would hate to be a Christian since they are so stupid!" A woman once asked me if Jews tire of having a religion made up only of rules and regulations. "It must be so tedious to be legalistic and not have the Holy Spirit!" she said.

At Hebrew Union College I took a course with Dr. Ellis Rivkin on the history of the Pharisees. How differently Jews like Dr. Rivkin perceived the Pharisees! His book on the Pharisees, our class text not surprisingly, is called *A Hidden Revolution: The Pharisees' Search for the Kingdom Within*. On the back cover of the book we find a summary of Rivkin's view of the Pharisees that relates directly to the *haggadoth* discussed in the previous unit.

> Undergirding the hidden revolution of the Pharisees is a core teaching from one of the Mishnaic texts, summarized by Dr.

Jewish Biblical Legends

> Rivkin: "God so loves the individual that he created one person, not many. He so cherishes the individual that to kill an innocent person is equivalent to destroying the world; to save a person's life is equivalent to preserving the world. And God so commits himself to the uniqueness of the individual that he stamps out every person in his image and after his likeness, yet no individual is identical one with another."

It is often said, and worth remembering, that Jesus criticized his contemporaries as an *insider*, much as the prophets of old had done. The church that collected and cherished these teachings of Jesus did so as powerless underdogs. They could not have foreseen or imagined the triumphant Christianity that would later use such texts to justify acts of violence against Jewish neighbors, as sometimes occurred in the history of the church. Dr. Rivkin used to say that the New Testament is not anti-Jewish—and he was something of a minority opinion here—because Jesus didn't aim to destroy Israel but to purify it. The church that preserved these sayings had no power to persecute and didn't expect to ever have that power. The sayings were later perverted by Christians with meaner intentions.

But more could be said. Was Jesus really right about the Pharisees? Were they hypocrites who didn't practice what they preached (Matt 23:3)? Were they primarily concerned with spiritual showmanship but not spiritual authenticity (Matt 23:5–7)? Did they emphasize details of the law over the weightier issues like justice, mercy, and faithfulness? Did they strain at gnats and swallow camels (23:23–24)? A quick answer might be, "many did, many didn't."

The most famous rabbinic tractate of all, called *Pirke Avot* or "Ethics of the Fathers," illumines Jesus' teachings. We will discuss it more thoroughly in the last chapter of this book. The Mishnah lies at the center of the Talmud and *Pirke Avot* lies at the center of the Mishnah and is in many ways its ideological centerpiece. The fact that rabbinic teachers were called "fathers" (*avot*) is evident from the title. The absolute reverence for the fathers which Jesus sought to overthrow (Matt 23:8–12) is evident in *Pirke Avot* where Jose ben Joezer says, "Let your house be a meeting house for the sages, and sit in [literally "roll in"] the dust of their feet, and drink in their words with thirst" (*Avot* 1:4). Jesus, as Matthew tells us, sought to create a new egalitarian community of equals. Jesus is the New Moses whose interpretation of the Law is definitive in a way the rabbinic unending legal discussion is not. He is *the* Teacher. We call no one else "father."

The Work of Creation

Even the famous Rabban Gamaliel could be the object of Jesus' critique when Gamaliel says, "Do not accustom yourself to giving tithes by guesswork" (*Avot* 1:16). A whole tractate of the Mishnah is devoted to spelling out in exquisite detail how one is to offer tithes. Another tractate *Damai* is devoted to the question of giving tithes when there is some doubt as to its calculation. While the Mishnah didn't take its final literary form for about 170 years after Jesus lifetime, the laws of the tithes clearly are in development when Jesus criticized the Pharisees for their anxieties about tithing herbs correctly (Matt 23:23–25).

The early progenitors of the rabbinic movement were known to have commanded a fence to be built around the Torah: "Build a fence around the Torah" (*Avot* 1:1). The concept here is quite simple: in order to achieve covenant holiness, and to attain the true blessing of the covenant, we must interpret the law so as to insure that we keep it in all its detail. To illustrate, if the law says, "Don't drive over 65 mph," we will legislate a 55 mph speed limit. This is the secondary fence (rabbinic oral law) around the Torah (biblical written law). This theory, which lies at the core of rabbinic thought, had a tendency to lead to endless legal wrangling about exactly what was required by the biblical laws and what the rabbis should require to make certain that biblical laws were kept. The system also had a tendency to lead to casuistic special-pleading, as Jesus points out in Matt 23:16–22. For similar reasons, modern Reform Jews also de-emphasize the Talmudic law and seek social justice rather than legal purity.

The thing that many Christians do not see here is that while many of Jesus' criticisms of the Pharisees were valid in their own right, it is a fact that many other rabbis of Jesus' day were making similar points and were similarly concerned. Conflict within the rabbinic community between the Hillel (a more lenient interpreter) and the Shammai (a stricter interpreter) sometimes has Jesus sounding more like Hillelites and other times (notably on divorce) more like Shammai. It is common knowledge that Jesus sided with Pharisees against the Sadducees on the topic of the resurrection. Many rabbis at this time were aware of the dangers of hypocrisy and special-pleading the legal system enabled. Other rabbis felt the dangers of the system and sought to ground it in core values and warn against hypocrisy. Warnings against hypocrisy such as the following in *Pirke Avot* are easy to find: "Do His will as if it were your will. Then He will do your will as if it were his will" (*Avot* 2:4).

Jewish Biblical Legends

It is well-known that Hillel, who lived just a generation before Jesus, once told a would-be convert to Judaism that the primary rule of Judaism was not to do anything to a neighbor (Heb. *haber*) that one would personally find hateful (*B. Shab.* 31a). The rest, he said, was so much commentary. Some Jews claim that this, in fact, is a higher more challenging moral standard than the positive version of the Golden Rule taught by Jesus since it makes the effect of your actions on others the regulating principle.

Some have thought that Hillel's statement, in using Hebrew word *haber* for "friend," restricts the command to fellow Jewish legal sages (true friends) as the word sometimes means. But the context speaks otherwise; Hillel says these words to a would-be convert, who could hardly qualify as a *haber* in the advanced sense. In *Avot* 1:12, Hillel encourages the broadest kind of human sympathy with the exhortation to love your fellow creatures and bring them to Torah. The language he uses here clearly embraces all humanity.

Again, the point here is that there were differences of opinion in Israel already about how crucial the details of legal observance were. Some rabbis already realized that the heart of their faith could be lost in the blizzard of legal opinion and sought to prevent this. Many rabbis were aware of the need to clarify what lies at the heart of the law and to prevent hypocrisy. In words that lie at the beginning of *Avot*, and are sung to this day in many synagogue services, we read, "On three things the world is sustained: on Torah, on Temple service, and on deeds of loving-kindness" (*Avot* 1:2). A clearer statement of the legal centrality of love could hardly be imagined.

In a strange way, the New Testament illustrates this rabbinic interest to place love at the core of the law. In Matt 22:34, Jesus is asked by a Pharisee which was the greatest commandment. That Jesus' response was a fairly typical one in Judaism is proven by the Luke version (10:25–28). In this case, Jesus asks the legal expert how he understood the law's basic requirements. The response given sounds almost exactly like the opinion Jesus gave in Matt 22:34 (love God, love neighbor). What Jesus does with the following parable is somewhat unique: he makes absolutely explicit that "neighbor" is to be understood in a radically inclusive manner; we are commanded not only to love fellow Jews but even Samaritans (thus the following parable). What is unique is only the explicit inclusion of Samaritans, not the general principle.

The point of all this is quite simple. While Jesus certainly had abuses in the practice of Pharisaic piety and hypocrisy to condemn, he was not alone.

The Work of Creation

Other rabbis had similar criticisms of their fellows. As Christians often will notice, our faith also has a tendency to bring out the best and the worst in us. Modern believers can easily become hypocritical, legalistic, and petty just as the Pharisees of Jesus' condemnation. Jesus, in the best of his prophetic tradition, called Israel to a higher form of piety and covenant loyalty. He said, "Be perfect even as your heavenly Father is perfect" (Matt 5:48). He was not alone. On many topics, Hillel would have agreed with Jesus. Christians could do well to use the term "Pharisaical" more carefully and advisedly. We still casually use the term to mean "spiritually false" or "hypocritical." Let's be fair to these poor Pharisees or we're not being fair, ya see?

ADAM'S RIB

"And the Lord God fashioned the rib" (Gen 2:22).

The following *haggadah* deals with the creation of Eve from Adam's rib. As is quite typical, the rabbis experiment playfully with various ways of interpreting the text based upon assonance and other sound similarities. In this case, the rabbi notices that the Hebrew word for "fashion" (based on the Hebrew word for "to build"—*banah*) in the phrase sounds similar to the word *bin* (to understand). In some cases, the verb can mean "to ponder."[28] Thus with *bin* he gives the verse a new signification: "And the Lord God pondered the rib He had taken." For the rabbis, every verse in the Bible has a superabundance of meaning and from this vantage point the meaning is that God gave lots of thought to using Adam's rib instead of other body parts to create Eve. This, for the rabbis, is an invitation to put their creative genius into high gear and imagine why God chose to use a rib. Commenting on Gen 2:22, Joshua of Sikhnim wrote

> He pondered (*hitbonen*) from what to create her, saying, "I will not create her from Adam's head or she might be conceited, and not from the eye or she might be a flirt; or from the ear since she ought not be an eavesdropper. The mouth is out lest she be a gossip as is the heart lest she be prone to jealousy. Not the hand which might give rise to a shoplifter. The foot is not an option lest she become

---

28. Braude writes, "The commentator regards *va-yiven* as a form of *bin* (understand)" (*Book of Legends*, 19). The form assumed here is called in Hebrew a *hitpael*, which implies some form of reflexive action. This would give us the verbal form *hitbonen* with the meaning "to consider, to ponder."

a busy-body." So He made her from the rib, a place that is very modest in a man.[29]

I was a bit disappointed with this *haggadah* when I first read it. I was hoping for a different conclusion that said that the rib was used to create Eve since she was to be Adam's companion and to walk by his side. What we have here is really a list of the values to be admired in an honorable wife with an emphasis on chastity and modesty. The text goes on to remark how the ribs of a man always tend to be covered up. Similarly women ought to be chaste, modest, covered.

Women in the rabbinic world, as was the case in much of the rest of the world, were considered under the rule and protection of their husbands. While this kind of husband/wife relationship strikes moderns as an unacceptable patriarchy, let us not jettison the text too quickly. Chastity, modesty, and humility are qualities that, for the most part, the rabbis demanded of their disciples as well, and therefore the text is not necessarily a mechanism for the subjugation of women. It is against this backdrop that this saying can be best understood.

Rabbinic Judaism, as Neusner describes it, instructed its disciples concerning not only what the children of Israel were to do but also how they were supposed to feel. Their practical theology called for chastening of the emotions and a moderation of the spirit. "From beginning to end, the documents of Rabbinic Judaism set forth a single, consistent, and coherent doctrine: the true Israelite was to exhibit the moral virtues of subservience, patience, endurance, and hope."[30] Humility and forbearance were intended emotional outcomes that would themselves provide the spiritual foundations for a lifestyle of conciliation. "The hero was one who overcame impulses, and the truly virtuous person was the one who reconciled others by giving way before the opinions of others."[31] This was a method of survival in a hostile world.

What was required of the women in rabbinic communities was a reflection of what was demanded of all. Within their system, all ethical emphasis falls upon pleasing others and conforming to the will of the group for the survival of the group. Humility became the greatest mark of strength

---

29. *Gen. Rab.* 18:2. The text unfortunately continues on to say that all these undesirable qualities ended up in Eve in any case.
30. Neusner, *Rabbinic Judaism,* 129.
31. Ibid.

The Work of Creation

and the very avenue for the obtaining of God's approval. Virtue was found in attitudes of conciliation, restraint, and conformity to social norms.[32]

The rabbis can provide a model here for a feature of Christian faith that is often lost in the typical teachings and practices of the church. Perhaps due to the themes of grace and liberty in the Christian faith—or perhaps due to pressures from our culture—churches often fail to understand what these sages saw so clearly; faith is not only to inform the mind but also to shape the emotions. The impact of faith formation can be judged by the appropriation of new lifestyles characterized by these qualities. Certainly, Jesus and Paul both, as good rabbinical students, sought to shape human emotions. Jesus proclaimed blessing upon the poor in spirit, those who mourn, the gentle and meek (Matt 5:5), and Paul challenged believers to take upon themselves the mind of Christ by willfully assuming the role of a slave (Phil 2:3–8).

Modern Christian communities, contrarily, seek to develop Christians who are "wild at heart." Rabbis actively sought to shape the emotions toward humility, modesty, and chastity in ways that Christian ministry rarely does. This might strike many as a works-righteousness or excessive timidity unacceptable to our American swagger. Rabbis saw it as the harder road to salvation that liberates not just the mind but the heart from the many prides and pulls of life.

A PITCHER OF GOLD

"And the Lord God caused a deep sleep to fall upon Adam" (Gen 2:21).

Many rabbinic legends deal with conversations between their great rabbinic Torah scholar-heroes and various Gentiles. The celebrated Rabban—a title given to the head of the Sanhedrin during Tannaitic period cf. 10–220 CE—Gamaliel II is questioned by a Caesar concerning the moral qualities of the Jewish deity.[33]

---

32. Ibid., 141. Much more could be said of this quality of rabbinic thought. Chapter 6 of Neusner's *Rabbinic Judaism,* which is entitled, "Ethics: God and Virtue—The Doctrine of Emotions," provides an excellent overview.

33. Gamaliel II made at least two trips to Rome to represent the cause of the Jews in the emperorships of Domitian and Nerva. He was the grandson of Gamaliel I who is mentioned several times in the New Testament. Luke records Paul's claim to have been a Torah student of Gamaliel I (Acts 22:3; Acts 26:4) and describes Gamaliel as a celebrated Jewish leader who counseled the Sanhedrin to be tolerant of the early Christians (Acts

Jewish Biblical Legends

> Caesar said to Rabban Gamaliel: "Your God is quite the thief, for it is written, 'And the Lord God caused a deep sleep to fall upon Adam, and He took one of his ribs.'" His [Gamaliel's] daughter said, "Leave him to me so I may respond." She said [to Caesar], "Call the cops!" "What need could you possibly have?" he asked. She replied, "Thieves came to us last night and took a silver pitcher from us and left us one of gold!" "Would that we were robbed by that thief every day!" he exclaimed. "Ah!" said she, "was it not wonderful for the first man that his rib was taken yet a wife given to serve him?"[34]

While this story is likely not historical, it does represent the kind of Gentile/Jewish dialogue that likely occurred. These kinds of objections were likely experienced by Jews and the Jewish community sought to defend their faith and their God rigorously. Augustine, in his *Confessions*, describes how, as a Manichaean, he argued that the biblical deity was immoral and crassly physical. He rejected Christian faith for reasons that sound very much like the objections raised by Caesar.

Here, by having Gamaliel's daughter respond, the tradition seeks to communicate the superiority of their race as if to say, "Even our girls can answer these questions! Piece of cake!" The ubiquitous anti-Jewish bigotry of the ancient world had to be countered so the community could be nurtured in faith. Josephus at a very similar period of time also sought to counter the anti-Jewish rhetoric in the Roman world. We learn much about the kinds of slanderous things said about Jews from him. He quotes Manetho (*Against Apion* 1:228–51), the Egyptian writer for whom the exodus was led by a rebel priest of Heliopolis named Osarsiph who changed his name to Moses. Moses was initially victorious over Egypt, which he viciously pillaged (1:249) before he was expelled by Amenophis. Manetho goes on to describe the offensive behavior of the Jews under Moses saying that they defiled their sanctuaries, slaughtered sacred animals, and humiliated Egyptian prophets and priests. The same tradition seems to be operative when Lysimachus claims that Jerusalem was originally called "Hierosyla" ("temple robbery" in Greek) because of Jewish "sacrilegious propensities"

5:34–40). It would be tempting to try to determine whether the Caesar in question was Domitian or Nerva. However, the non-historical tenor of the story lies in the fact that a Roman Caesar would hardly have been able to ask detailed biblical questions such as he does here and Gamaliel would not have had his daughter at the ready to provide such a fetching response.

34. *b. Sanh.* 39a.

The Work of Creation

(*Ag. Ap.* 1.311). Similar anti-Jewish slanders and calumny floated about the Roman world.

This story illustrates a gracious engagement with a hostile environment. Caesar—if we can assume historicity for a moment and imagine him with a sense of humor—certainly was put in his place and yet may have enjoyed such a clever defense. Gamaliel's daughter defends her faith community with grace and dignity. We are reminded of the admonition of 1 Peter 3:15–16.

> Always be prepared to give an answer to everyone who asks you to give the reason for the hope that you have. But do this with gentleness and respect, keeping a clear conscience, so that those who speak maliciously against your good behavior in Christ may be ashamed of their slander. (NIV)

Gamaliel's daughter's point is that God's intentions in taking Adam's rib were for his welfare; that is, to turn the silver pitcher to gold. God is the best kind of thief imaginable because whatever he takes he replaces with something of greater value. God took a rib but left Adam with the gift of a wife and companion. This story both glorifies the gift of Eve (she is a golden vessel) and humbles her (she is Adam's servant). It illustrates the rabbinic view of women (which applied, ultimately, to all persons); true glory is found in service to others. While Eve's role is to serve her mate, it is one that provides her with great dignity and honor. The New Testament speaks of the wife as the "weaker vessel" (1 Pet 3:7), but Eve is here the golden pitcher.

2

The Serpent and Sin

EVE AND THE SERPENT

"This one shall be called *woman!*" (Gen 2:23).

TREMENDOUS INTERPRETIVE ENERGY WENT into explaining the serpent, Eve, and the first sin. What is the relationship between Satan and the serpent? Why did Eve fall for the serpent's wiles? Why didn't Adam do something to stop Eve? Who was truly responsible? The rabbis, from the beginning, appreciate Eve not only as the mother of the human race but as a submissive wife. They speculated about the reason why there seems to have been two wives created for Adam (one unnamed in Gen 1:27 and Eve in Gen 2:23) and decided that Adam must have been married twice. They came up with the name *Lilith* for Adam's first wife. She insisted on having equal status with her husband and was thus dispelled from the garden. Gen 1:27 implies that both she and Adam were equally made in God's image and she insisted on claiming her half. By calling out the ineffable divine name (Yahweh), she gained powers of flight and became a night demon.[1] In place of Lilith, God gave Adam Eve, made from his own rib. While a little gullible, Eve knew her place and knew not to rise above it. It is this duality—liking Eve because she isn't Lilith but finding her partly responsible for the fall—that shapes rabbinic thinking about her. In fact, in spite of how

---

1. Ginzberg, *Legends*, 1:31.

The Serpent and Sin

unsympathetic the rabbis are with Lilith, they, at least in this instance, give Eve every benefit of a doubt concerning her innocence and integrity.

> The Holy One, blessed be He, said, "For when you eat of it, you will certainly die" (Gen 2:17). She, however, didn't say this [to the serpent when asked] but said, "God said, 'You should not eat of it *or even touch it* or you will die (Gen 3:3).'" The serpent saw her speaking an untruth. He took her and threw her against the tree. "Did that kill you?" he asked. "Just as you were not killed by touching it, you won't be by eating it."[2]

The rabbis noticed that Eve, when she explained the prohibition against eating of the forbidden fruit, added the line "or touch it" (Gen 3:3). God had initially only told Adam not to eat of the tree (Gen 2:17) so Adam must have added the prohibition "or touch it" when he relayed the information to Eve. Rabbis speculate about why Adam included something God hadn't actually said. They supposed that Adam added the proscription against touching the forbidden tree out of zeal for God's law.

Yet the shrewd serpent was able to exploit this addition and execute his plan for their downfall. He tries two different tactics. In some legends, he appears as an angel and seeks to convince Eve that the tree's fruit is able to give its eater the power of creation. But in our text, the serpent takes a more direct course of action. The serpent knows God never said that touching the tree would evoke death. Yet Eve believes this is what the Lord said. In some stories, the serpent grasps the tree himself to prove it is not deadly. In our story, he shoves Eve up into the tree. According to the fuller *midrash* elsewhere, this caused Eve to say to herself, "All that my master (as she referred to Adam) has said to me is but lies."[3]

Another *midrash* appears in this context (*Gen. Rab.* 19:3) that is instructive. It contains a conversation between the rabbis as to what Adam was doing during Eve's interlocutions with the serpent. One rabbi claimed that they had just had sexual intercourse and he had fallen asleep! This is based on the fact that the last verse in chapter 2 speaks of the two of them becoming one flesh, which of course refers to sexual intercourse. This explains why Adam didn't do anything to stop Eve from eating the forbidden fruit. Genesis 3:6 specifically says that when she ate, she gave some to her husband who was with her, and he ate. Why didn't he say anything to stop

---

2. *Gen. Rab.* 19:4–5. See also *Abot R. Nat.* (A) ch. 1.
3. Ginzberg, *Legends*, 1:35.

her? They had had sex and he had fallen asleep! Then he woke up and ate the fruit Eve handed him.

Other rabbis hold that God had taken Adam on a tour of the entire world, and had shown him where he could plant trees and crops. Again, this explains the rather strange feature of the text that Adam did nothing to stop Eve. This explanation seems to go against the grain of the text, which claims that Adam had been at her side when she ate. Apparently he had been gone and had just returned when she handed him fruit to eat. Being hungry from his journeys, he ate immediately and asked no questions.

How can all this *midrashing* be helpful to modern Christian biblical interpreters? It does illustrate the various ways the rabbis have sought to understood Eve and her role in the story. Eve is a tragic figure, not to be disliked but to be pitied and yet appreciated. Satan appeared as an angel, and came with powerfully convincing and impressive arguments. Her confusion was in part based on Adam's addition to the divine command not to even touch the tree. Once the serpent had touched it, and forced her to touch it, and she didn't die, she began to doubt the commandment altogether. Adam wasn't around to be of much help to her. On the whole, their attitudes toward Eve would reflect their attitudes toward women generally; they are wonderful creatures when they know their place yet a good man knows to keep his eye on his wife lest she do something silly.

While these kinds of attitudes are completely unacceptable to us (as they are not acceptable to most modern Jews), there is a theological element of the *midrashim* that is worthy of our reflection. On the whole, according to the *midrashim*, the fall occurred not due to egregious wickedness or outright rebellion but from innocence, gullibility, and confusion. Evil is a present reality not because of our wicked nature as humans or the heinous nature of the original sin, but flows from their (and our) foolishness and immaturity.[4]

A MATTER OF TRUST

"You shall be like gods . . ." (Gen 3:5).

---

4. This view is more in line with the perspective of the church father Irenaeus but very much out-of-sync with the understanding of Augustine who believed Gen 3 to be a story of the beginnings of human evil and rebellion. The rabbinic position is quite in line with Irenaeus' perspective, which disappeared in the shadows after Augustine.

The Serpent and Sin

At its center, the biblical story of forbidden fruit in Gen 3 tackles the question: can God can be trusted? Is God's oversight loving or manipulative, gracious or overbearing? The serpent convinced Eve to wander astray by making her doubt the goodness of God's intentions. This is implied in 3:5 when the serpent says, "God knows that when you eat of it your eyes will be opened and you will be like divine beings who know good and evil" (NET). Eve's temptation begins with distrust and the fear that God wants to keep his new creatures on a very short leash. It is as if the serpent says, "God really doesn't want you to eat of the fruit because this is where the real power source lies and he doesn't brook rivals."

The rabbis expand on what is implied in Scripture. Here, the serpent elicits doubt in Eve using two different tactics. First, the serpent tells Eve that God created the world by the power of the tree and doesn't want Eve to create new worlds of her own lest she become his rival. In fact, the serpent claims that God created the world by the power of the tree and doesn't want Eve to create new worlds of her own lest she become his rival. Secondly, the serpent tries to frighten Eve by telling her that if she doesn't eat of the fruit and gain divine powers, God will continue to create. Because what is created last has dominion over what was created before it, God will create a being that will have authority over her. Eve can only save herself from slavery by eating the fruit and thus becoming God's equal. This is all *midrash* on the serpent's words, "You shall be like gods" (Gen 3:5).

Often rabbis created parables to illustrate their point. In one, a husband takes a cask and puts figs and nuts in it and seals it with a scorpion in the seal. He tells his wife that all he has done, including the scorpion. He assures her that all he owns is hers except for this cask. While her husband is away, an old woman visits his wife and asks how her husband treats her. She is effusive in her praise but says that her husband only keeps one thing to himself: a cask with figs, nuts, and scorpions. The old woman suggests that he is keeping jewels in the cask, which he intends to give to a new wife after he has divorced her. This thought compels the wife to open the cask and is bitten by the scorpion.[5]

This story is to illustrate Eve's temptation and fall. The serpent raised doubts about whether God can be trusted. Is he hiding something wonderful from us? Is he hoarding power for himself? Eve, in her immature state, lacks the ability to trust God just as the young wife of this parable was unable to trust her husband. God, the rabbis claim, is fully worthy of our

---

5. Braude, *Book of Legends*, 21, number 87.

trust, and we bring pain into the world when we doubt God's goodness and are seduced to live by our own resourcefulness.

Other opinions on this theme are worthy of note. Some interpreters surmise that Eve gives the fruit to Adam after she ate because she feared that she would die soon and didn't want God to make Adam another wife to replace her. She would rather have Adam dead than with another woman! Eve also continue to give the fruit to the other animals in the garden.[6] The purpose of this addition is to explain why all the other animals die after the fall when only man's death was guaranteed by the initial command (Gen 2:17). The rabbis use this feature of the story to explain the origins of the phoenix; it was the only animal in the garden that didn't eat of the fruit and thus lives a thousand years before it burns up and is re-constituted from the ashes.[7]

WHO IS TO BLAME?

"She also gave some to her husband . . ." (Gen 3:6).

The discussion of why Eve (and then Adam) chose to disobey God raises perhaps a more fundamental question: who is to blame here, Adam or Eve? In Eve's favor, Adam does appear to be directly beside her when she first eats. Genesis 3:6 simply says that she gave some of the fruit to her husband who was with her. The text clearly indicates that Adam was by her side all along. His full consent with Eve's actions is proven when he eats what she offered willingly. We also notice that when the punishments are meted out, the serpent is addressed first, Eve second, and Adam last. The fact that Adam came last could easily be read to imply his increased culpability for it was he who personally received God's command concerning the forbidden tree.

---

6. The biblical justification for this is found in the word "also" in "And she *also* gave unto her husband" (Gen 3:6). According to the rabbis, every word has a superabundance of meaning, and no words are irrelevant. Since the word *also* isn't absolutely necessary, its meaning is that she also gave the fruit to all the other animals.

7. The thousand years is significant in that the rabbis often used the text from the Ps 90:4 that a thousand years with humans is like only a *day* with God. This explains the statement, "In the *day* that you eat of it, you shall surely die." Since it is clear that Adam lived to be just short of one thousand years, he did die in the day of which he ate. It was, however, according to God's timing, not human timing. So the phoenix, according to the rabbis, lives just more than one full day with God since it didn't eat of the forbidden fruit.

The Serpent and Sin

Many texts from the ancient world pile blame on the soul of poor Eve. The Wisdom of Ben Sira says, "From a woman was sin's beginning, and because of her, we all die" (25:24). 1 Timothy 2:13-14 says, "I permit no woman to teach or to have authority over men; she is to keep silent. For Adam was formed first, then Eve; and Adam was not deceived, but the woman was deceived and became a transgressor."

We saw above an attempt to understand Eve's situation in the most positive manner possible. Again, this is based on the discrepancy between Gen 2:16-17, where God forbids eating of the tree (directed to Adam alone), and Gen 3:2-3, where Eve informs the serpent that they are forbidden not only the eating but the touching. Apparently, Adam added the proscription against touching the tree to the divine stipulation. The rabbis look to this situation to help read the text more positively so as to reduce the egregious nature of Eve's action.

In Louis Ginzberg's collection of *haggadic* texts, he has a section titled *Eve's Story of the Fall*.[8] Essentially, the rabbis take the exoneration of Eve to a new level; this section is written in first person as if Eve had a chance to write her version of the events of that fateful day. Eve first describes how Satan, smarting over being cast out of heaven, convinced the serpent to become his servant and do his bidding, which took some doing seeing how the serpent feared God's wrath.

The serpent happened upon her just when her two guardian angels were away and the serpent took the form of an angel and began to sing praises, which deceived Eve completely. He convinces Eve that she has nothing to fear and picks the fruit for her. But then he changes course and says he would rather she not eat the fruit. He then made her swear she would not eat of the fruit unless she gave some to her husband as well. He even made her take an oath to not eat the fruit unless her husband also ate, which she did. Then the serpent injected the fruit with the poison of evil inclination, and bent the branch down to the ground so Eve could take hold of its fruit. Having touched the fruit, she immediately believed she was stripped of the righteousness with which she had been clothed. She began to weep for this great loss and for the oath she had made.

The text goes on to tell of how they hid from God, were found, and punished.

What is striking to the modern reader, especially in light of the typical designation of Eve as the source of all evil, is how sympathetic and

---

8. Ginzberg, *Legends*, 1:80-83.

charitable these readings are. Eve is viewed as something of an ingénue, a woman tricked into distrust. In her version of the story, she was alone, deceived, and poisoned. Many rabbis felt quite free to fill in the gaps of the biblical story so long as it didn't contradict what was explicit. They here exemplify a certain spiritual value: don't condemn others as sinners until you've tried to see things from their perspective. The rabbis are applying to Eve what Paul asks of us all when he challenges us to a kind of love that believes all things, always protects, keeps no record of wrongs, and refuses needlessly to dishonor others (1 Cor 13).

3

The World after Sin

CAIN AND ABEL

"Where is your brother, Abel?" (Gen 4:9).

As we have seen repeatedly, rabbis love to fill gaps in biblical stories in order to explain why things occurred as they did, especially when the Bible leaves us with unanswered questions. The story of Cain and Abel in Gen 4 is particularly perplexing and begs several questions. Why does the Lord accept Abel's offering but not Cain's (Gen 4:5)? How did Cain and Abel know that God had accepted Abel's firstling of the flock but not the Cain's gift of grain? Other aspects of the story perked their curiosity, most of which would hardly raise an eyebrow today.

Some suggest that Eve's remark, "I have gotten a man with the Lord" (Gen 4:1) implies that Cain was born with abilities and skills that vastly exceeded his age (thus a "man"). What did Adam know when the text says that he "knew" his wife (4:1)? He knew, they surmise, she was already pregnant and he was not the father![1] Who then? Satan certainly! Others suggest the sacrifice of Cain must have been faulty in some way. The biblical "hint" of this is found in Gen 4:3–4, which say that while Abel brought the Lord the firstborn of his flock, Cain is said to have brought the "fruit of the

---

1. *Pirke R. El.* 21.

ground." Rabbis read this as if Cain picked up some leftovers actually off the ground for his sacrifice.[2]

In our selection, we find an extended story that the rabbis imagine might be the background for the biblical story. The passage to be cited here is quite extended and will be broken up into smaller portions for comment.

> "Cain said to Abel his brother" (Gen 4:8). What Cain said to Abel was, "Come and let us divide the world between us." Abel said, "Ok, lets." So Cain said: "You take the livestock and I will take land." And it was stipulated that neither should have any claim against the other about this division. Even so, when Abel proceeded to graze the flock, Cain said, "The land you are standing on is mine." Abel replied, "The wool you are wearing is mine. Strip!" "Fly!" said Cain. At that, "Cain rose up against Abel his brother" (Gen 4:8). [The meaning of "rose up" can be explained in what follows]: Cain proceeded to chase Abel from hill to dale and from dale to hill, until the two grappled. Abel overcame Cain, so that Cain fell underneath Abel. Cain, aware how badly it was going with him, began to plead aloud, "Abel my brother, there are only two of us in the world. What are you going to tell our father?" ... Abel, filled with compassion for his brother, let him go. At once Cain rose up against him and slew him. For the verse "Cain rose up against Abel his brother, and slew him" implies that at first Cain had been underneath Abel.[3]

The point of departure for this discussion is the mysterious lacuna in Gen 4:8, where the text strangely reads, "Cain said to his brother Abel . . ." What he said is not told and we more than likely have something missing in the text. Many English translations take from the Septuagint the words, "Let us go into the field" to tell what Cain said to Abel. But these words are not in the Hebrew text versions that we have; the Hebrew text has Cain say something to Abel but does not tell us what. A theory to explain this literary gap is that the word *said* in other Semitic languages could mean *to focus your attention upon*. With this implication, it refers to Cain's brooding fixation upon Abel and his blessing.

Again, the rabbis are happy to provide the explanation; they love filling in gaps! Imagine the rabbi before his students saying, "I think I might know what Cain said to Abel! He said, 'Let's make a deal!'" Cain encouraged Abel to make an impetuous agreement that divided the world

2. *Gen. Rab.* 22:5
3. *Tanhuma, Bereshit,* §9.

The World after Sin

between them. Abel took the cattle and flocks and Cain took the land itself. This inevitably led to difficulty because cattle can hardly exist without grazing on the land and agriculturalists need the wool of the sheep to wear. This foolish pact, which led to antagonism between the brothers, is what Cain "said"—as in "suggested"—to Abel. This pact explains why, as Gen 4:2 states, Abel kept the flocks and Cain worked the soil. It wasn't an accident but a contractual agreement.

The meaning of the Hebrew text in 4:8 comes into view: "And Cain rose up against Abel and killed him." The verb "rose up" in Hebrew literally means "to stand up." The rabbis take the literal meaning here and suppose that Cain stood up from a position below Abel. How did he get below Abel? Cain had attacked Abel after their foolish argument over their ill-advised contract. Cain, being bested by his little brother, pleaded for mercy, which Abel granted. Then Cain arose and slew his brother.

The purpose of this passage is more than to magnify the wickedness of Cain and glorify the goodness of Abel. The story told here is not a mere fabrication meant to give a chuckle. The rabbinic tale has implications and lessons. The biblical story gives the impression the first murder arose almost out of the blue. We don't know why God is not favorable towards Cain and we don't know what Cain said to Abel. We don't know why Cain is angry at Abel instead of God and we don't know how Cain goes about killing Abel. Things just seem to careen along without clear causation.

But while things can appear that way on the surface, a deeper causation drives the story forward. Darkness and malice, anger and envy simmer for days like a witch's brew. A recipe of evil intent is spiced and stirred, simmered and stirred over a slow fire. A tragic school shooting isn't the result of one insane flash of evil intent no matter how things may appear on the surface. The rabbis want to re-tell the story so we get a sense for the time involved, the motives evolving, and the outcome that resulted. While things can seem haphazard on first blush, we find more complex self-interests and machinations below the surface.

BLASPHEMOUS CAIN

"Am I my brother's keeper?" (Gen 4:9).

Rabbis are troubled by the Lord's question to Cain, "Where is your brother, Abel?" The Lord knew perfectly well that Abel was dead. God responded to

Cain's arrogant question, "Am I my brother's keeper?" with the unsettling defamation, "The voice of your brother's blood cries out to me from the ground" (v. 10). So why did God ask? God asked, according to *midrash*, because he wanted to give Cain opportunity to judge himself.

The rabbis provide a series of parables or comparisons to explain this story. It is like a person who catches someone stealing mulberries and eating them out of their garden. When the owner demands, "What is in your hands?" the thief replies, "Nothing." The owner then responds, "But why are your hands stained?" The stained hands proved their guilt just as the blood crying from the ground proved Cain's guilt. The question was asked, not because God didn't know, but because God wanted to see how Cain would respond and to give Cain some rope to hang himself with, which of course he does.[4]

Another story illustrates the guilt of Cain.

> Cain said to God, "Am I my brother's keeper? (Gen 4:9). You are the keeper of all creatures, yet you are seeking him from my hand?" Here's a parable to illustrate what this is like. A thief stole some items during the night and was not apprehended. The following morning, the gatekeeper did catch him and asked, "Why did you steal these items?" The thief replied, "I, thief that I am, didn't slack off at my vocation, but you, your job is to guard the gate! Why did you do such a poor job?" So we see that Cain really said, "I murdered him but you created in me the evil impulse. But you are the keeper of all things so is it my responsibility to lay off killing him? You really killed him. If you had accepted my offering the way you did his, I would not have been jealous of him." Immediately the Holy One countered, "What have *you* done? The voice of your brother's blood cries from the ground!" (Gen 4:10)[5]

This interpretation draws attention to the word *you* in Gen 4:10: "What have *you* done?" What is the deeper meaning of that word? Cain, the rabbis imagine, has been trying to justify his actions by claiming that God is the one who is fundamentally responsible. God, as the maker and keeper of all things, was responsible on two levels for the murder. God, according to Cain, is responsible because God made Cain with an evil impulse and because God did not stop Cain from murdering as he was compelled to do by his evil impulse. Just as the negligent gatekeeper was responsible for the

---

4. This is a paraphrase continuing from *Tanhuma Bereshit* par. 9.
5. *Tanhuma, Bereshit*, §9.

The World after Sin

theft in his garden, so God is responsible that Cain killed Abel because he is the keeper of the world.

The text explores how Cain might have shifted responsibility off his own shoulders and onto God's. Cain's blasphemy examines wonderings that arise in us all periodically: if God made everything, and made us to be the way we are, why isn't God ultimately responsible for the evil in the world? Couldn't God have made the world any way he wanted? Why didn't God make us more prone to good? Since God made us to be inclined to darkness, God can hardly blame us when we commit the deeds and actions of darkness. As clever as this line of thinking might be, it must be resisted at all costs. God's response—characterized by the word "you"—is one that draws attention back to ourselves as the responsible agent. Ultimately, our freedom does not constitute God's criminality but our irresponsibility. Our impulse to shift our evil actions upon God's shoulders amounts to psychotic self-rationalization.

M. Scott Peck, in his insightful book *The People of the Lie*, describes evil as "malignant narcissism" that is characterized by a psychotic need to rationalize wrongs done, to do everything possible to protect one's self-image, to find ways to blame others for wrongs done, and to refuse to experience feelings of empathy. Cain, for the rabbis, is a test-case for our evil impulse, not only to murder, but to shift the blame for that murder onto God himself. Evil, according to Peck, is the desire to appear good without being willing to do the hard work of actually being good. The first step in the process of healing human evil is recognizing and owning up to our responsibility for the harm done. This is something Cain is here desperately trying to avoid.

Paul pronounces the purpose of the law as, "Now we know that whatever the law says, it speaks to those who are under the law, so that every mouth may be silenced, and the whole world may be held accountable to God" (Rom 3:19, NRSV). Humans have an impulse to shirk responsibility even to the point of making God the author of evil, an attempt that God thwarted by the giving of the law.

C. S. Lewis, in *Mere Christianity*, points out that there is a sense in which God is responsible for evil, having given us our freewill. Anyone in a position of authority knows that sometimes things are in your will in one sense yet not in another. Imagine a mother who says to her children, "I'm not going to clean your room every day. You have to start doing this yourself." If she goes to their room and finds it a mess, she's responsible in

Jewish Biblical Legends

the sense that she handed over responsibility to the children. She would prefer the children to be tidy and disapproves of the mess. Yet, her choice made the mess possible. Lewis says,

> It is probably the same in the universe. God created things which had free will. That means creatures which can go either wrong or right. Some think they can imagine a creature which was free but had no possibility of going wrong; I cannot. If a thing is free to be good it is also free to be bad. And free will is what has made evil possible. Why then, did God give free will? Because free will, though it makes evil possible, is also the only thing that makes possible any love or goodness or joy worth having.[6]

While the rabbis certainly didn't have all these things in mind, their *haggadic* treatment of the Cain story indicates that they were aware of some of these kinds of objections and sought to emphasize the absolute necessity of personal responsibility for our actions. Cain exemplifies the beginnings of the dark human tendency to shift blame and scapegoat—even to the point of blaming God!

CAIN'S PUNISHMENT

"You will be a fugitive" (Gen 4:12).

The rabbis also sought to explain the fact that God seems to let Cain off the hook for his murder. One would expect a capital sentence for the capital crime. If there are sufficient witnesses, premeditated murder is indeed a capital offense in biblical law (Num 35:30). God, instead, allows Cain not only to wander the earth freely but to have a mark of protection to prevent anyone from putting him to death. He was able to live out his days in the land of Nod (Gen 4:16).[7] Cain was the first to get away with murder and God was supposed to be the judge and jury!

In one rabbinic explanation for this mild sentence, Cain received a lighter sentence because he didn't have murderous intent. Cain had no way of knowing what would be the outcome of his striking Abel, and thus was judged more lightly (*Gen. Rab.* 22:12). The biblical story therefore does not

---

6. This quote may be found toward the beginning of Book 2, chapter 3, "The Shocking Alternative."

7. Alan Dershowitz has written provocatively on the fact that Cain seems to walk after having committed a capital offense in chapter 2 of *The Genesis of Justice*.

indicate God's lack of legal evenhandedness but God's ability to adjudicate each case according to intent. In other rabbinic explanations, when Cain cries out, "My sin is too great to bear!" (Gen 4:13), he is essentially admitting that what he had done was in fact a sin. He didn't initially realize he would kill Abel by striking him, but after God's pronouncement in verse 12, Cain comes to terms with the enormity of his crime and confesses his sin. God therefore lightened his sentence from capital punishment to exile due to Cain's repentance.[8]

Rabbis also wondered who the Lord had to protect Cain from if he and his immediate family are the only souls alive. The answer is that the animals, both wild and tame, knew that Cain was a murderer and condemned to wander, so they surrounded him to kill him. Cain cried out to God and God responds with the mark of protection and the curse against any who kill him.

THE BIRTH OF NOAH

"This one shall bring us relief" (Gen 5:29).

Stories abound that playfully imagine what the birth and childhood of Noah might have been: he was born circumcised, his skin was as red as a rose, his hair as white and full as wool, and his eyes like the rays of the sun. When he opened his eyes, he brightened the whole house with rays like the sun. He opened his mouth directly after birth and praised the Lord. His father Lamech was frightened and ran to his father Methuselah, who in turn consulted the deceased Enoch, who appeared to him from the presence of God. Enoch informed Noah's grandfather of the coming destruction upon the earth and of Noah's calling to be the savior of the family. Enoch gives Noah his name, which according to the biblical writer, means "relief from our work and from the toil of our hands" (Gen 5:29 NJPS). For Enoch, the relief or consolation of Noah stems from knowledge that Noah will deliver his family from coming destruction.

Lamech prophesied in the biblical text that Noah would provide relief from toil and from the curse of the soil. This causes great concern for the interpreter because there is no discernible relief in the biblical story from the toils of life that can be accredited to Noah; the life of the farmer is just as tedious and harsh after the flood as before. Again, the rabbis have

---

8. *Tanhuma, Bereshit*, 9.

an answer: God did provide a temporary reprieve from the curse of the soil immediately after the birth of Noah. After Noah's birth, all things returned to their state preceding the fall of man. Another way in which Noah brought agricultural relief was by inventing the plough, the scythe, the hoe, and other implements to aid in agriculture. Before Noah, the rabbis say, farmers turned the soil with their bare hands![9]

As a result of Noah's achievement, the rabbis suppose that a period of ideal conditions for agriculture and human prosperity ensued; a single harvest was sufficient to feed them for forty years, children were born after a few days pregnancy and could walk and talk immediately like Noah. Even demons could do them no harm. In one charming story, a newly born child met the chief of demons and a combat ensues in which the demon is easily bested by the child who cries out that if it hadn't been for its uncut navel cord, it could have killed the demon!

Yet for all their prosperity and natural dignity and strength, they were lulled into moral laxity due to excessive time for leisure. Here rabbis are simply imagining what kinds of relief Noah may have brought since the Bible doesn't specifically say. But they tell the story with an awareness that every blessing comes with its attending curse; the higher the income, the more pride. The greater the wisdom, the greater the self-reliance. The larger the herds, the greater the risk of disease and theft. So with all the benefits Noah achieved, things turned back to moral turpitude and laxity fairly rapidly.

THE ARK AND THE FLOOD

"The Lord said to Noah, 'Go into the ark'" (Gen 7:1).

The rabbis imagine the completion of the ark according to the specifications of what was already an ancient book of knowledge (called the *Book of Raziel*) dating all the way back to Adam. On the day they boarded the ark, there were severe earthquakes and lightning storms as the world had never seen. Yet sinners remained unrepentant. When the flood actually broke loose, 700,000 people had surrounded the ark and cried out for protection. Noah refuses with the taunt, "Are you not those who rebelled against God saying 'There is no God!'?" When the sinners tried to storm their way into the ark, the animals that remained around the ark set upon them and

---

9. Ginzberg, *Legends*, 1:115–16. We have here two explanations as to how Noah can be connected to the relief from the curse of the soil as described in Gen 5:29.

The World after Sin

kept them from entering. God then made the waters, which fell pass first through Gehenna so they were scorching hot and scalded the skin, as was befitting to their crimes.[10]

The rabbis imagine in great detail what it must have been like to care for so many animals for a year's time. Lions suffered fevers because they had to live on dry food. The rocking motions of the ark put the animals into great agony, and they made such a racket as to drive Noah and family to despair. But they cried out to God and God gave them relief from the treacherous waters. The rabbis imagine a conversation between Eliezer, Abraham's servant, and Shem, Noah's son.

> Eliezer asked Shem, Noah's oldest son, "How were you able to care for so many kinds of animals?" Shem replied, "We actually had a lot of trouble in the ark. The animal that habitually would eat during the day, we fed by day; the ones that were nocturnal consumers we fed at night. As for the chameleon, my father didn't know what it ate. One day, as my father was sitting and cutting a pomegranate, a worm fell out of it and the chameleon ate it. After that, he would rub prickly reeds infested with worms and feed it with them. . . . Our master said, "During the twelve months Noah spent in the ark, he did not enjoy sleep—neither he nor his sons—neither by day or by night since he was so preoccupied with feeding the creatures with him."[11]

Rabbis continue to describe the recession of the waters from the face of the earth, which left it so miry that the dwellers in the ark had to stay inside for a while year. When Noah sent out the raven, it didn't return for it had been feasting on the dead carcasses. The dove returned with a leaf plucked from the Mount of Olives at Jerusalem, since that Holy Land had not been ravaged by the flood.[12]

---

10. Ginzberg, *Legends*, 1:123–25. Rabbis add these warning signs (earthquakes, lightning storms, etc.) to the biblical narrative to highlight God's justice in executing this colossal act of judgment. By this reading, no one could have been taken off-guard by the flood; they all received abundant warning of the judgment to come yet they remained unrepentant. In the eyes of the Gentiles, the Israelite God appears willing to destroy the world without warning. The rabbis fear that Gentiles might use the Noah story to justify their belief in the misanthropic nature of the Jews and their god. See "The Social Background of the 'Fair-Wage' Interpretation," in my *The Despoliation of Egypt* (137–48). By adding what the text lacks—that is, warning signs of divine displeasure—they can claim that God's judgment did not come out-of-the-blue.

11. *Tanhuma B. Noah*, par. 3.

12. Ginzberg, *Legends*, 1:126–28.

Another legend says that when Noah stepped out onto the open ground, he began to weep at the sight of the immensity of destruction. He cried out to God asking why God, being merciful, had shown no mercy. God responded that Noah should have wept earlier when God first threatened to bring a flood upon the earth. God asks Noah how it is that he spent all his effort on escaping the flood with his family yet he didn't lifted a finger to avert the ruin that he knew would come upon the earth. Noah has no business complaining at the devastation when he didn't seek to stop it in the first place. Noah realized he was wrong and offered his sacrifice to the Lord (Gen 8:20–22).[13] This interpretation ties Noah's sacrifice after his exit from the ark to his apparent lack of concern for the devastation of the earth!

The *midrashim* concerning Noah trend in two opposing directions simultaneously; some magnify his righteousness while others point out his failures. On one hand, his observation of duty and detailed observance of God's command find their praise. Noah works night and day to care for the animals, and he not only does not enter the ark until God give the green light, but after a year's time, he refuses to leave until God gives him the go-ahead. Yet, God finds fault with Noah for not doing more to avert the devastation of the flood. God expected Noah to do more than build an ark; God expected him to cry out for the salvation of those destined to die while there was still time for their salvation.

In the *midrash*, God's initial proclamation of upcoming judgment was intended to be, for Noah, an opportunity for him to intercede for his neighbors. The rabbis are troubled by his lack of concern for the suffering humanity around him even if they were guilty of sin and under the judgment of God. Rabbis admire Noah in many ways but look dimly on the "fortress" mentality displayed. While he was a righteous man, his righteousness did not extend beyond the confines of his family. Somewhat like the modern survivalists who pack away food and weapons in a bunker to protect their families from a feared apocalypse, Noah spends years seeking to save his own family. This kind of isolation and self-interest is out-of-whack with rabbinic communal values.

Other rabbinic texts go a different direction and imagine Noah preaching righteousness to the crowds gathered watching him build (*Pirke R. El.* 22). Interestingly, we find a similar theme in 2 Pet 2:5, which refers to Noah as a "preacher of righteousness." The underlying value system

---

13. Ibid., 1:128.

The World after Sin

remains: great revelation brings with it heightened responsibility. To whom much is given, much is required. God's gifts are to be shared, not hoarded.

NIMROD THE MIGHTY HUNTER

"Like Nimrod, a mighty hunter before the LORD" (Gen 10:9).

The rabbis tied together the story of Nimrod and his wickedness to the story of the tower of Babel, making Nimrod, about whom the Scriptures say precious little, the summation of all the evils of the world, which continued unabated after the flood. They told typically outlandish stories about him. He (Nimrod) had the good fortune of receiving from his father Cush the clothes made of the skins that God had given initially to Adam and Eve after they had fallen from grace. The clothes made the wearer invincible and irresistible, which is why Nimrod was such a mighty hunter since he could walk up on animals without their sensing his presence. He was equally powerful in battle and became king. Nimrod fashioned idols and not only led a godless life himself but tempted everyone under his influence to do the same.

As a result of his great success, people ceased trusting God and, encouraged by Nimrod, began to rely on their own powers and abilities. Therefore people said of him, "Since the creation of the world there has been none like Nimrod, a mighty hunter of men and beasts, and a sinner before God." Nimrod wished not only to turn others from God but to have himself worshipped as a god. He established for himself a tower and throne, and his arrogance eventually motivated him to sponsor the building of the tower of Babel in his honor.[14]

The glory and divine status Nimrod achieved was a hoax empowered by a stolen magical garment that was God's gift to Adam in the Garden of Eden. Every good gift, even a good gift directly from God himself, when used outside of its intended purpose, has evil possibilities and ramifications. This power was used by Nimrod to conquer the world and to achieve a status of "mighty hunter before the Lord." But he was, if one knows the rest of the story, a great sinner before the Lord who led a whole movement of sinners away from their trust in God. Nimrod represents the glory of self-centered human achievement which, while empowered by arrogance and violence, produces wonders that enthrall the imagination.

14. Ginzberg, *Legends*, 1:37–38.

Jewish Biblical Legends

THE TOWER OF BABEL

"Come, let us make bricks" (Gen 11:3).

Rabbis spun out tales associated with the building of the Tower of Babel as well. The building of Babel required many years and became so tall as to require a year's climbing to scale to the top. Brick became so precious at the top of the tower that if a person fell from the top no one noticed but if a brick fell the workers wept because it would take a year to replace it. Bricks were so important that even a woman about to give birth would be required to continue laboring on the construction of the tower to not lose time. As soon as a child was born, it would be strapped to her back and she would go back to work.

God and the angels descended upon the makers of the tower. "Angels" are implied in the biblical text by the "us" in "Let *us* go down" (Gen 11:7). God and the seventy angels with him cast lots to determine the distribution of languages. Each angel represented a nation and the language it would receive. God also participated and Israel's lot fell to God. Since God had received the "Israel" lot, God designated Hebrew—God's own language—to be the language of God's people. How did the rabbis know Hebrew was God's personal tongue? Hebrew is the language used by God in the creation of the world.[15]

The following explores the poetic justice of the Babel story. The Lord's judgment was exactly what the people of Babel feared; dispersal.

> And they said . . . "[Come, let's build ourselves a city with a tower that reaches up to the heavens] . . . Otherwise we will be scattered over the face of the earth. . . ." So the Lord scattered them over the face of the earth (Gen 11:4 and 9). R. Levi said, "In its foreboding, the generation that was to be dispersed was like a woman who said to her husband, 'In a dream I saw you divorcing me.' The husband replied, 'Why only in a dream? Here is your bill of divorce—a real one!'"[16]

The generation of the tower feared being dispersed over the earth and built the tower to prevent this from coming to pass. God responds as if to make their dreams come true, but with this ironic twist; their dreams were nightmares that came to life. The rabbis do not try to downplay the

---

15. Ginzberg, *Legends*, 1:138–40.

16. *Gen. Rab.* 23:7. Braude's translation (*Book of Legends*, 30) is explanatory; there is no "a real one" in Hebrew.

glory of human achievement. Humans, apart from God's mercy and grace, manage great things, even if they do so through the abuse of God's gifts and mercy. The height of the tower, made by persons who completely rejected divine aid of all types, reached overwhelming height. They may have had in mind the glories of the Roman Empire: wondrous yet dehumanizing and violent. The tower was a construction zone in terms of human glory but a destruction zone in terms of human dignity. Women were not even allowed to give birth under normal circumstances, and people were unconcerned about the human deaths that occurred. Brick became more prized than human life. Rabbis are particularly aware of this evil potential of unrestricted power seeing that they, as the underdogs of human history, were typically on the suffering side of the equation. Jews were commonly viewed in the ancient world as people who contributed nothing of value to society and who cared only for their own and not for the whole. Jews themselves felt dehumanized by the power-systems and these stories reflect their critique of the "empire." God's justice is truly just and God's law is designed to limit human sin and to counteract evil.

In the last *haggadah*, we see Rabbi Levi reading the Babel story with a view toward the irony that the people of Babel did everything they could to prevent their dispersal. Yet their effort to prevent dispersal motivated God to bring it about; that is, if they hadn't built the tower they would have feared dispersal but would not have been dispersed. Having built the tower to prevent their scattering, they perhaps feared dispersal less but were in fact dispersed. R. Levi's interpretation reminds us that often we can bring about what we fear almost because we fear it. This is the lot of our human frailty and the underlying reason we are cast upon divine mercy.

4

Abraham, Our Father

ABRAHAM'S BIRTH AND CHILDHOOD

"When Terah had lived 70 years, he became the father of Abram" (Gen 11:26).

ONE OF THE BIBLICAL difficulties facing the rabbis in their understanding of Abraham is that Scripture provides no explanation why God acted as the Bible describes. Why did God choose Abraham and not his brothers Nahor and Haran or anyone else for that matter? God must have had reasons, and the diligent reader can prize them from the text with enough training. In one of the most famous documents of all Rabbinic Judaism, *Pirke Avot*, the answer is found in the genealogies.

> There were ten generations from Adam to Noah—to make known God's patience, for all those generations kept provoking Him until finally [in the days of Noah] He brought the waters of the flood upon them. There were ten generations from Noah to Abraham—to make known God's patience, for all these generations kept provoking Him until our father Abraham came and received the reward [saving] all of them.[1]

---

1. *Avot* 5:2.

Abraham, Our Father

Implicit here is the notion that Abraham saved the whole world because he is the father of all Israel. It is due to the righteousness of Israel alone that God refrains from destroying the whole world for its wickedness. R. Berekhiah told a parable to explain why, in the Scriptures, in the ten generations between Noah and Abraham, God only spoke to Abraham.[2] It was as if God were sifting through the generations until he found someone worthy of addressing. It is as if a king lost a pearl from his crown while in transit. He halts the whole retinue and piles up the surrounding soil in heaps, and sifts through the soil until he finds the pearl he is looking for. God, like this king, sifted through the generations until he found someone worthy of his blessing.

There is actually a biblical (according to rabbinic thinking) justification for this interpretation. It is found in the first few words of Gen 12 where the Hebrew uses a rather common idiom that cannot be translated directly into English but literally would be rendered, "Go to you."[3] It emphasizes the importance of the command and directs it specifically to an individual. We might say, "Go, you!" in a similar way. But in this *midrash* it means something like, "Go, I've been waiting for you." Since God doesn't spare any words in Scripture and everything has deep meaning, this is the biblical clue as to the vastness of Abraham's value and worthiness of his calling.

Perhaps the greatest rabbi of all time, R. Judah the Prince, explains Abraham's greatness from Gen 14:13, which refers to Abraham as a Hebrew (*ha-'ivri*). This designation is based on the Hebrew verb *'avar* (to cross over) and so the Bible—as Judah is interpreting it—is hinting that Abraham is to be understood as one who is on the other side in terms of his qualitative excellence. Abraham is on one side of reality and the rest of us are on the other. Why pay Abraham such honor? Because of all humans, he alone perceived the one true God.[4]

Stories of Abram's childhood border on the absolutely fantastic. Much like Moses and Pharaoh, he was sought after by the evil Nimrod, who ruled at that time as a god. By astrology, Nimrod knew that one who would give the lie to his false religion was about to be born, and much like Pharaoh and

---

2. Rabbis do not call Abraham "Abram" when speaking of his earlier career but use the name "Abraham" throughout. I will follow that practice.

3 The grammatical feature is called the *ethical dative* or in Latin the *dativus ethicus*. This passage is found in *Gen. Rab.* 39:10. The rabbi also refers to Neh 9:7–8, which claims Abraham was chosen because of his faithful heart. Already the process of expanding on Abraham's worthiness had begun in the days of Nehemiah.

4. *Gen. Rab.* 42:8.

Herod, Nimrod did all he could to kill his potential rivals and slaughtered 70,000 children in the process. Abraham's mother miraculously was able to hide her pregnancy and when the child was born, she hid him in a cave where he was miraculously cared for by the angel Gabriel or by God himself (depending upon the tradition).

The cave itself was filled with light from the glory of the child's countenance. As a baby (traditions vary as to how old exactly) he, because he had no pagan influence and was gifted with extreme intelligence, discovered on his own that there was only one God. He tried praying to the sun, the moon, and the stars, but they each disappeared from sight, and he surmised that one force must control them all. "There is One who sets all them in motion!"[5] Abraham becomes something of an evangelist for his new belief from that day on, and soon convinces his mother (with his miraculous power of speech), when she comes to check on her baby, that there is but one God.

Word eventually gets back to Nimrod of Abraham's existence, and Satan himself counsels Nimrod to make all haste with all his weaponry and have Abraham killed. Abraham called out to God, and Gabriel heard and covered the baby with a thick cloud too dark to penetrate. Nimrod and his princes fled in terror to Babylon, and Abraham pursued them there to proclaim the one true God to them. On one occasion, Abraham seized Nimrod's throne and shouted at the top of his lungs that there was only one true God. While doing so, all the idols around Nimrod fell on their faces and Nimrod became unconscious for two days in shock. When he came to, he pleaded with Terah to take his son from their region.[6]

The speculation as to why God chose Abraham finds its solution in Abraham being understood as the first real monotheist. He must have "figured this all out" in some way and for this reason God called Abraham to himself, but only after he had already had quite a background in evangelism for the monotheistic understanding. The articulation of the magnificence of his persona highlights a distinction between Jewish understandings and the Christian thinking shaped by Paul. Paul argues in Rom 3 that confidence in one's relationship with God is based on trust in Christ and not in membership in a chosen race. We are not saved through works of the law, but all persons, law-abiding (Jews) and those apart from the law (non-Jews),

---

5. Ginzberg, *Legends*, 1:145. This is directly tied to the opinion above that Abraham stands in a whole different qualitative zone; he was the first to discern that the earth has only one God. Even Moses has been taught by Abraham in this regard.

6. Ibid., 146–48.

Abraham, Our Father

are justified on the basis of faith alone (Rom 3:3). But this is not a new idea according to Paul; it has been God's plan all along. Paul uses the story of Abraham to make his point.

For Paul, the story of Abraham shows, from the beginning, that God's desire has been for all humans to base their relationship with God "on trust that he will keep his promises. Thus the true descendants of Abraham are those who share not his gene pool but his trust in God (Rom 4:9–13). It was Abraham's faith, not his ethnicity, that allowed him to stand in a positive relationship with God (Rom 4:22)."[7] Paul looks to Abraham with a completely different perspective; Abraham did nothing other than trust in God to be made right with God. For him, the fact that the biblical narrative says *nothing* about Abraham's inherent virtue or spiritual magnificence before his calling, the fact that he is an ordinary human who struggles to understand and stumbles along the way, and the fact that Abraham does not perfectly fulfill the law of Moses (especially when he lied about Sarah being his sister), are central to his interpretation of this great patriarch of *faith*. Abraham did nothing but trust in God and this was reckoned as sufficient for the declaration of righteousness (Gen 15:6).

It is certainly an intriguing possibility that Paul knew some of these traditions of Abraham and not only ignored them but interpreted strongly against them. The sparseness of the biblical depiction, so uncomfortable for rabbis, was of interpretive significance for Paul as proof of Abraham's inherent unworthiness. For the rabbis, the vacuum before Abraham's calling in Gen 12 is an interpretive challenge and something to be filled with imaginative *haggadoth* that creatively read the context to expand the narrative structure and fill in the lacunae.

ABRAHAM AND THE HOUSEHOLD GODS

A whole series of stories, well-known in the Jewish world, concern Abraham's destruction of the household gods. In rabbinic imagination Abraham's father Terah was an idol maker by trade. It was Abraham's task to take these idols into the market for sale and his conversations with the buyers

---

7. Achtemeier et al., *Introducing the New Testament*, 314. Paul, remarkably, never mentions Abraham's almost-sacrifice of Isaac. James, whose purposes are very different than Paul's, refers to the sacrifice of Isaac immediately upon mentioning him (2:21), noting that by this deed his faith was demonstrated by acts.

end up being opportunities for Abraham to spread his belief in the one true God. Abraham ends up pedaling monotheism more than idols.

> Abraham's father's home used to produce images for sale in the market. One day, on Abraham's turn to sell, his father Terah gave him several baskets of household gods and situated him in the marketplace. A man came and asked him, "Do you have a god for sale?" Abraham said, "Which god do you wish to take?" The man said, "I am a powerful man. Give me a god as powerful as I am." So Abraham took an image that was standing on a shelf higher than all the others and said, "Pay the money and take this one." The man asked, "Is this god as mighty as I am?" Abraham replied, "You nincompoop! Don't you know the way it is with gods? The one who sits above all others is more powerful than the rest." As the man was about to leave, Abraham asked him, "How old are you?" The man answered, "Seventy years." Abraham said, "Woe to a man who is seventy, yet prostrates himself before this thing which was just made." At that, the man flung that god back into Abraham's basket, demanded the return of his money, and went his way.[8]

Clearly Abraham was not very good for the family business. But he was passionate, in rabbinic imagination, about monotheism and the foolishness of pagan idolatry. Similar stories follow so that Abraham's career as an idol-salesman is short-lived and completely unsuccessful. His family decides that since he is so incapable of selling gods, he would do better as priest. He is instructed to wait upon the gods, to offer them sacrifices and serve them food and drink. So Abraham puts out food and drink, and when the gods do not eat or drink, he quotes the Psalm, "They have mouths, but cannot speak, eyes, but cannot see; they have ears, but cannot hear, noses, but cannot smell; they have hands, but cannot touch, feet but cannot walk" (Ps 115:5–7).

At one point, a woman came to offer flour to their gods. Abraham seized a stick, smashed all the images, and placed the stick in the hand of the biggest of them. When his father came, he asked, "Who did this to the gods?" Abraham told him that a woman came with a bowl of fine flour. When he offered it, one god said, "I will eat first," and another said, "No, I will eat first." Then the biggest of them rose up and smashed all the others. His father replied, "Are you making sport of me? They cannot do anything!" Abraham answered essentially by saying, "Listen to what you are saying and think about it!"[9]

8. *Gen. Rab.* 38:13.
9. Ibid.

Abraham, Our Father

At that point Abraham was brought by Terah to Nimrod again. After Abraham again argues for the irrationality of the worship of idols, Nimrod determines to have him burned to death. He commanded Abraham to bow down to the fire if he would be spared. Abraham suggested that perhaps it would be more appropriate to bow to water, which quenches fire. Nimrod agreed, but Abraham thought better; perhaps he should bow to clouds, which carry water. Or perhaps to the wind, which moves the clouds. Or to a man, who withstands the wind. With that, Nimrod had him bound and thrown into the fire, but God saved him from the flames much like Daniel.

Arguments excoriating paganism here reflect a whole tradition of similar arguments in Scripture (Pss 115:3–8; 135:15–18; Isa 40:18–20; Jer 10:1–16; Letter of Jeremiah, Tobit) and elsewhere. We encounter an especially extensive argument in Isa 44:9–20, which through a detailed review of the manufacture of idolatrous objects pours scorn upon the idolater and nature worship. Deutero-Isaiah describes in detail how the idol maker fashions an image from wood cut from a tree. With some of the wood he heats himself, with the rest he makes a deity for worship. The irony of the process leads him to say, "He feeds on ashes; a deluded mind has led him astray" (Isa 44:20).

The author of Wisdom of Solomon directed similar arguments with more philosophical refinement. Not only does he argue that idolaters ought to realize the irrationality of placing trust in images, which are patently powerless, he claims that worshippers take on the status of what they worship, and because images are accursed by the one true God, the worshipper of images lies under the curse of the true God (Wis 14:8–11). Because idols are a perversion of God's initial intention and design, they will ultimately be destroyed (Wis 14:12–21). Drawing upon the Greek philosopher Euhemerus (ca. 300 BCE), the author contends that gods were little more than human kings who became glorified to the point of deification upon their deaths (Wis 14:17–20).

Another passage of comparable interest is Clement of Alexandria's *Exhortation to the Greeks*, a writing by a second-third-century Christian presbyter from Alexandria in Egypt. Clement appeals to those followers of traditional Greek religion to consider the folly of their ways. After describing the moral inferiority of Greek myths and religion practice, he points out, again following Euhemerus, that the gods were originally men and what are now temples were originally tombs. Even philosophers such as Heracleitus scoffed at image-worship. Images have no life, and sacrifices offered to them are a waste. Even the lowest life-forms such as worms have more sense than images made of inanimate materials. The fact that the images are impotent is proven when thieves steal them or earthquakes destroy them. Birds regularly nest in images and defecate on them. Sculptors often are known to make an image of a deity appear like someone they love. Fascination with art causes people to fall in love with statues and leads them to worship them. Image-making is off-limits for Christians, who are living images of God. Persons should seek after God and not worship any created thing as God.[10]

It is difficult to say just how effective such arguments may have been. Arguments such as this had a ready answer among the pagans. Images were not understood to actually *be* the deity but to represent the deity in a ritualized way so as to invoke the deity's interest, presence, and favor. Special prayers consecrated the image made of wood or iron and transferred it from the world of the mundane to the world of the sacred. Images gained special association to the deity in this way, as is reflected in Hab 2:19, "Alas for you who say to the wood, 'Wake up!' to silent stone, 'Rouse yourself!' Can it teach? See, it is gold and silver plated, and there is no breath at all in it" (NRSV). Habakkuk here is almost certainly mocking the actual ritualistic prayers by which the priest would ceremonially call the image to "Wake up! Rouse yourself!" in the ritual of consecration. In other words, while priests are going through the protocols to transform the wood or stone into an image, they would cry out to the image to awaken into the deity. But in doing so, they (idolatrous priests) understood that the object did not actually become the deity but was rather consecrated into the sacral realm due to its proclaimed deity-association.

Again, worshippers of images didn't believe that the image *was* the deity. They believed the image only conveyed the sacred presence of the deity through its ritually-transformed status. The actual deity, who may be flying around in the clouds, was duty-bound to heed worship and prayers directed toward or before their image. In this way, the deity protected their honor and encouraged the worshipper to continue in bringing sacrifice.

---

10. This summarizes chapter 4 (pages 101–43) in the Loeb Classical Library text *Clement of Alexandria*. The whole book is fascinating as a highly advanced Christian argument against paganism, which at the same time affirms and accepts, as a preparation to the gospel, all the best of the knowledge of the Greeks. Primarily Clement affirms the wisdom of Plato, but many other Greek witnesses to the oneness of God and the wisdom of holiness he also affirms.

Abraham, Our Father

So would Abraham's arguments and those like it have succeeded? They may have in the sense that, by pointing out the inability of the image to protect itself and feed itself, they highlighted the general incapability of the deity to protect its own image. However, as these arguments appear, they seem to be straw-men since worshippers of images didn't actually worship the image but that which the image represented.

But we also do well to point out that the biblical text gives us no real reason to believe that Abraham was ever a full-bred monotheist much less a passionate evangelist for monotheism. God shows up in Abraham's life and says something like, "Let me take you on a trip to a new place. I'll bless you there. Just trust me" (a loose paraphrase of Gen 12:1–3). There is no theological information or legal requirement involved at all. Abraham's faith is impulsive and intuitive; it is not theological or philosophical. He probably thought this deity calling him was some local deity interested in his particular family as was commonly perceived in the ancient world. This may be the implication of God's title, "God of Abraham, Isaac, and Jacob." We must assume God worked through the cultural background and situation in which he found Abraham initially. God always works with us from the point where God finds us.

And ironically, instead of being faithful and devout, Abraham doubts God's promise of blessing almost immediately; when a famine occurs he abandons the land of promise and heads for Egypt where he lies about his wife (Gen 12:10–20). Abraham in Scripture strikes a marked contrast to the Abraham of *midrash*. Abraham of Scripture is a doubting, bumbling, confused liar who somehow trusts God through it all and is used of God, almost in spite of himself. Abraham of *midrash* is something else indeed; a model of passionate monotheistic piety. The Abraham of Scripture stands much closer to the daily reality of our faltering human existence.

The value of knowing something about the *midrashic* Abraham, for Christians, is that against the backdrop of the Abraham of *midrash* we can see anew the humble humanity of the biblical Abraham; chosen for no clear reason, not clear on exactly who was calling him, faithful only to a point, willing to lie to save his skin, believing yet doubting. Yet in all these things, God's plan succeeded, Abraham soldiered on, and the redemptive purpose of providence moved forward.

The rabbinic conception of Abraham is based on the observation that God seemed to expect Abraham to know there was only one God when Abraham was called. Rabbis figure that when God said to him, "Go . . . to

Jewish Biblical Legends

the land I will show you" (Gen 12:1), Abraham knew who the "I" in view was. Abraham must have figured this out before Gen 12. Abraham's faith and knowledge of God must have been magnificent enough for God to notice him, choose him, and to begin redemptive story with him. Rabbis see their work as merely filling in the narrative gaps and providing a fuller narrative structure to the story. They read the story looking for hints of his great faithfulness. Their *midrashic* imaginations work in their world but are very much out-of-sync with the Christian understanding of the story whereby the vacuum surrounding his calling has deep theological meaning; he was—and we are—called by grace.

ABRAHAM AND HOSPITALITY

"Go forth from your native land" (Gen 12:1).

Abraham's calling in Gen 12 is a key moment in the scriptural narrative since Abraham, as progenitor of the nation, stands at the very beginning of Israel's story as a unique and called people. As we would expect, the rabbis magnify Abraham here as at every point in the biblical narrative. Abraham was severely tested by the calling itself, reluctant as he was to leave his family. He pled with God to let him stay because by abandoning his family he would destroy his reputation. God commanded him to leave all his family since their only desire was to ruin him.

God's promise (Gen 12:2) to make of Abraham a great nation, to bless him, and to make his name great, was focused directly upon Abraham's specific fears. He was reluctant to leave his family and move because he feared first that by emigrating, and moving from place to place, the growth of his family would be restricted. God promised to make of him a great nation. Second, he feared that a move would decrease his ability to produce wealth and he would be impoverished. So God promised to bless him. Third, he feared that his status as a migrant would diminish his esteem in the eyes of those around, so God promised to make his name great.

> When the Holy One said to Abraham, "Get out of your country and from your kindred" (Gen 12:1), what was Abraham like? He was like a vial of perfume with a tight-fitting lid put away in a corner so that no one could smell the aroma. As soon as it was moved from there, its fragrance began to dissipate. So the Holy One said to Abraham, "Abraham, many good deeds are in you. Travel about

from place to place, and the greatness of your name will go forth in my world."[11]

The commentator here recognizes that it was only with Abraham's act of obedience—to follow his Lord into a place unknown in the face of all doubt and reluctance—that the fragrance of his life was able to be unleashed. Before he was perfume in a bottle; afterward, an aroma on the breeze. The statement, "many good deeds are in you" probably refers not only to his proclamation of the Lordship of the one creator, but to Abraham's reputation as a man of magnificent hospitality. Certain biblical stories highlight Abraham's hospitality (e.g., the story of Abraham and the three visitors in Gen 18). Yet the rabbis found even more reason to see in Abraham a paragon of the generous hospitality so necessary in the ancient world, which lacked a lodging industry. The *midrash* focuses on a phrase in Gen 12:5, "Abram took . . . the persons [literally *the soul* or *souls*] that they had *acquired* in Haran." There is here a rather odd use of the Hebrew verb *'asah*, which is a common verb that normally means "to do" or "to make." It is translated by the NJPS as *acquired* above but this is not its normal meaning at all! How could anyone "make" a "soul"? This midrashist, understanding the phrase quite literally as, "The souls that they had *made* in Haran," claims it implies the following.

> The verse implies: Our father Abraham would bring people into his home, give them food and drink, befriend them, and thus attract them, and then convert them and bring them under the wings of the Presence. Hence you learn that a man who brings a single creature under the wings of the Presence is accounted as if he had created him, shaped him, and articulated his parts.[12]

This is how Abraham made souls in Haran. Abraham's generosity and hospitality were an avenue for proclamation of the "gospel." Other traditions expand on this notion. In the following, the sage reinterprets Gen 21:33 as follows.

> "And he called there on the Name of the Lord, the [everlasting] God of the world" (Gen 21:33). Resh Lakish said, "Don't read this as, 'And he called,' but, 'And he caused to call,' meaning that our father Abraham caused the name of the Holy One to be called by the mouth of every passerby. How did it come about? After

11. *Gen. Rab.* 39:2; *Song. Rab.* 1:3.
12. *Sif. Deut.* par. 32; *Gen. Rab.* 39:14.

travelers [whom he made his guests] had eaten and drunk, they stood up to bless him. He said to them, 'Was it mine that you ate? You ate of that which belongs to the [everlasting] God of the world. Thank, praise, and bless Him who spoke and the world came into being.'"[13]

While it may seem brash to English readers to alter the meaning of the text in such a way, in Hebrew this interpretation makes sense and is reasonable. The original text of the Hebrew Bible contained few vowels (or *nikud*, which are vowel points made under the consonants). The vowel points were actually added in the medieval period by scribes called the *masoretes*. To this day, unpointed texts are read in synagogue services. The text being read by this rabbi almost certainly had no vowels so his interpretation is simply saying, "When you read this passage, assume a few different vowels and the verb changes from a *qal* to a *hiphil*" (from a base-verb to a verb-form that emphasizes causation, as in "caused to call").

In a similar legend (*Gen. Rab.* 49:4; 43:7; 54:6), Abraham, after giving food and drink to wayfarers, would bid them say grace to the everlasting God of the world. If they did so, he let them have their food and drink for free. If they refused, he would give them the bill for his services. Most, after hearing the terms, would say grace to the God of the world as bidden.

Parenthetically, Job was also known for his great hospitality in the Jewish literature, especially the *Testament of Job*, where Job's liberality as a host is vastly exaggerated. For instance, his house is built with doors in every direction so travelers could enter with minimum hindrance (*T. Job* 9:4). One legend says, "And why did Job make four doors to his house? So that the poor should not have the trouble of going round the entire house" (*Abot R. Nat.* 7:1).[14]

In the case of Abraham, while making people pay for their food if they don't pray to the one Creator God strikes modern readers as manipulative, the Abraham of rabbinic imagination has a lesson to teach in the witness

---

13. *b. Sotah* 10a. Reading from an unpointed text—that is, a biblical text to which the vowels had not yet been established in fixed tradition—the rabbis sometimes change the vowels in their reading, and thus the meaning, as is the case here.

14. Parenthetically, Job is also an iconoclast like the Abraham of Jewish legend who purges his area of idolatry, throws down idols, and closes idol temples (*T. Job* 4.2–5). His struggle is entirely against Satan and not against God (*T. Job* 4.6–8). This Job suffers not because of a pact between God and Satan but because he has destroyed Satan's idol and has thus raised satanic ire. Yet, he was forewarned that if he destroyed the idol this action would bring upon him immeasurable suffering (*T. Job* 4.5–6). Still he believed that God would restore him in the end and would raise him up at the day of resurrection (*T. Job* 4.6–8).

of faith. Rather than approach the unbeliever as an object to be converted, Abraham focused upon their "felt needs" so that when they naturally would want to express thanks, he could direct that thanks toward his Creator. In this way he won glory to his God. Perhaps, Abraham grew in his understanding of the nature of witness. The earlier Abraham was argumentative, confrontational, and attacked the gods of those around him. The mature Abraham had learned a better way to proclaim the message on the basis of their needs rather than direct confrontation and iconoclasm.

In the rabbinic presentation of Abraham we learned that by bringing souls into the care and worship of their creator, it is as if those souls are created anew. Resh Lakish taught us above that a man who brings a single creature under the wings of God "is accounted as if he had created him, shaped him, and designed his parts." The idea here is that we humans become like what we worship. If one worships images of created things, one's soul is diminished and destroyed, in the end becoming like the soul of an animal. If we worship God, our souls increasingly reflect the divine image. If one helps another person worship the true God, it is as if you have created a person in the image of their creator. This principle—"You become like what you worship"—is a commonplace in *midrash*; all persons are intended to reflect the *imago Dei* and thereby to be true bearers of divine glory in this world. However, genuine worship makes what is true legally true in fact.

These Abraham stories also potentially motivate and encourage modern methods of faith-witness. We should live so that our witness flows directly from the quality of our lives and by our concern for the needs of others. By bringing others into a true worship of their creator, we are building their souls not just feeding their bodies. Hospitality was highly prized in the ancient world in ways that are hard to appreciate in our modern world replete with hotels and restaurants on every corner. Most of us can hardly imagine asking a complete stranger for a place to spend the night and a meal. We can less imagine complete strangers asking for food and lodging on a moment's notice. One's decency as a human being was judged by how well you cared for those who needed a place to stay. There is a solid biblical tradition that remembers Abraham as a person who knew how to care for the traveler and even provides a model for how a good host treats the uninvited guest (Gen 18). However, the Abraham of *midrash* is more than a good host, he is an evangelist.

Jewish Biblical Legends

George Hunter writes of something like this in *The Celtic Way of Evangelism*. Hunter's thesis is that Christians in the West have much to learn from St. Patrick's version of non-Roman, Irish Christianity, which swept through Ireland in the fifth century with transformational effect. In a nutshell, the Roman methods of evangelism emphasize belief; one must believe before one can belong. The Celtic method of evangelism affirms that one must belong in order to believe. Rather than preach, call for decision, and invite into community, the Celtic way is to invite into community, meet needs, engage in conversation, and explain the gospel conversationally and in response to their questioning.[15]

The Celtic method has advantages, especially in a day and age when many persons resent church hierarchy and are suspicious of institutions that claim unique authority. The genius of the Celtic way is that, by allowing seekers into their communities of faith (typically monasteries), they presented the gospel as a part of a friendly two-way conversation rather than a top-down "I'm right and you're wrong" proclamation. Further, the Celtic monks encouraged expression through storytelling, poetry, art, dance, music, and oratory. These artistic activities often found their mark in ways that sermonizing could not. While the rabbis certainly don't have all this in mind, they do present Abraham as someone whose methods of proclamation were based around home and hearth, a meal shared, a need met, and dinner conversation. St. Patrick, at least in part, would have understood and approved.

ABRAHAM'S JOURNEY TO EGYPT

"Now there was at that time a famine in the land" (Gen 12:10).

The last half of Gen 12 tells of Abraham's journey to Egypt, due to a famine in Canaan, during which Abraham urged Sarah to lie about being his wife. He feared that the Egyptians would covet her so greatly they would put him to death. This famine, according to the rabbis, was a special test of Abraham's faith—one of ten—to see if he would murmur against God for bringing him to a new land only to encounter a famine so soon after his arrival. Abraham passed the test and did not murmur against God nor did he show any indication of becoming impatient with God. The famine also provided him with opportunity to travel down to Egypt to learn the

15. Hunter, *The Celtic Way*.

wisdom of their priests and to provide them with instruction in the truth (undoubtedly concerning monotheism).

According to the rabbis, when Abraham asked Sarah his wife to lie about being his wife because of her great beauty, this was the first time he had ever noticed just how beautiful she was! How could they claim this? Genesis 12:11 has Abraham say, "I know what a beautiful woman you are." This is the first time the Bible mentions Sarah's beauty, so it must be the first time Abraham noticed just how beautiful she was. Again, the rabbis seek to magnify Abraham's great piety; he was so holy he didn't notice Sarah's glorious beauty and this wasn't because she wasn't very good looking. Her beauty outshone all others. Abraham notices her beauty shining—like the brilliance of the sun—in the water of the river as they pass through it. All other women were like apes in comparison.

Abraham did his best to hide Sarah from the Egyptian officials, but they finally found her and they determined that her beauty should not be the property of a private individual but should be on display. Pharaoh sent an army and brought her to his palace while Abraham and Sarah cried out to God for deliverance. Pharaoh gave great wealth to both Abraham and Sarah, and even gave Sarah his own daughter Hagar as a servant. Pharaoh was so impressed with Sarah, he would rather see his daughter as Sarah's mistress than reigning as mistress in another harem.[16] When Pharaoh tried to approach Sarah sexually, an angel would strike him on the forehead with each attempt. Then Pharaoh and his nobles were smitten with leprosy such that he could not indulge his natural desires. This occurred on the 15th of Nisan, the same night when later God visited the death angel upon the Egyptians during the exodus.[17]

When Pharaoh had experienced these strange events, he called upon the priests to explain them. They informed him of Sarah's married status, and he immediately returned Sarah to her husband undefiled. He again gave them gifts and excused himself claiming that he had full intentions of marrying her and becoming associated by marriage to one he thought her brother. Abraham's sojourn in Egypt had great value to the inhabitants of the country since he had been able to convince them of the futility of their religion. He also taught them astronomy and astrology, fields unknown to the Egyptians before his time!

---

16. In Gen 16, Hagar is an Egyptian but not a daughter of Pharaoh.
17. Ginzberg, *Legends*, 1:165–69.

Jewish Biblical Legends

THE COVENANT OF THE PIECES

"Fear not, Abram, I am a shield to you; your reward shall be great" (Gen 15:1).

In Gen 15 God reaffirms his covenanted promise to Abraham. Abraham physically expressed his entrance into the covenant by splitting apart several sacrificial animals and walking through the severed pieces. The rabbis note first off that God addressed Abraham initially with the "Fear not" command. What would Abraham have feared? His love for God was greater than his fear, and he had no need to fear God just as he was. The rabbis found their answer in the previous chapter where Abraham had organized and led a military campaign to rescue his nephew Lot. Because of the great sensitivity of his spirit, he was in anguish over the possibility that he had caused the spilling of innocent blood. God assuaged his anxiety and promised him that God would cause other pious men to come after him who would also be a shield to their generation.[18] He also has noticed that, according to his astrological reading of the stars, he can expect no fruit from Sarah's womb. God objects saying, "You are a prophet, not an astrologer!" Abraham demanded no signs to believe but trusted in God's promise fully and without reservation. Because of his simple faith he was rewarded with a share in this world and in the world to come; that is, riches in this life and a place in the eternal kingdom. Furthermore, the redemption of his descendants from exile (Gen 15:13–14) was assured as a payment for Abraham's assurance and faith.

Even though his faith was strong and abiding, Abraham still wanted to know by what merit his descendants would maintain themselves. In the biblical text, directly after he was counted righteous by faith (15:6), God reminds Abraham again that he will inherit the land of Canaan. Abraham asks in the next verse, "Sovereign Lord, how can I know that I will take possession of [the land you just promised to me]?" (15:8). The rabbis interpret this question not as an expression of continuing doubt or unbelief but rather as a need for further information as to how his great faith will be able to be continued in coming generations. The sacrifices that God requires at this point in the biblical text are an answer to that request. In other words, by asking for sacrifices (v. 9), God teaches Abraham the various sacrifices

---

18. The biblical text has God promise Abraham to be a shield to him (that is, his source of self-protection). The rabbis interpreted this to also mean that Israel's presence in the world was a source of protection for the whole world. That is, because of their righteousness God would refrain from judging the rest of the human race.

Abraham, Our Father

that will be brought forward in the temple of Israel to atone for the sins of the nation and thus maintain their faithful status with God. This is an answer to Abraham's question. How can Abraham, through his descendants, maintain their possession of the land? By the offering of sincere sacrifices in the temple, their place is secure.

In the *midrashic* imagination Abraham asks God for further information. What will become of his people if and after the temple is destroyed? God responds, "If they read the order of sacrifices as they will be set down in the Scriptures, I will account it unto them as though they had offered the sacrifices, and I will forgive all their sins."[19] In other words, it would seem that the destruction of the temple would make faithful sacrifice—as required by biblical law—impossible; you cannot offer sacrifice according to the law without the Jerusalem temple. God here is saying that, in the case of the temple being destroyed, they have another way of offering the required sacrifice; by study of the law of sacrifice, in God eyes, they keep the law.

This principle, called *Talmud Torah*, became one of the central tenants of rabbinic Judaism; the study of Scripture and Talmud replace the actual temple after its destruction. By studying Torah (oral and written)—especially the texts dealing with temple sacrifice—one can recreate or re-encounter the *Shekinah* presence of God and receive all the benefits of temple sacrifice. Study therefore replaces sacrifice for the rabbis; study is a sacred duty that transforms the *beth midrash* into a spiritual temple for communion with the God of the temple. Understanding this theory can help Christians appreciate how Jews have continued with their religious devotion after the loss of the temple, which, in its time, was the center of all their sacrifice and service.

This notion of *Talmud Torah* had a biblical precedent in Ezekiel's vision in chapter 1 of the mobile glory of the Lord. While some of the Jerusalem priests conceived of God's glory as bound to Mt. Zion (Ps 125:2), Ezekiel's revelation sets God free and explores God's willingness to "hit the road" on an amazing set of wheels! If there ever was a "pimped ride," this was it! God (or God's glory set atop a magnificent wheeled chariot) met Ezekiel in Babylon by the river Chebar, coming from the north; that is, from the opposite direction of Jerusalem (Ezek 1:4)! While weeping and the hanging of harps on the willow trees was understandably part and parcel of the exile experience (Ps 137), the hopefulness of Ezekiel's message of their God aboard a "pimped ride" let the exiles know that they were not exactly leaving God behind.

19. Ginzberg, *Legends*, 1:177.

Jewish Biblical Legends

Rabbis built on this theory, especially after the temple was destroyed again in 70 CE, and came to understand the act of Torah study as the ultimate gateway to the *Shekinah* experience; study Torah and God's *Shekinah* will come rushing back in. God was not bound to the temple! Christians similarly have been taught that God's presence can be known in the simple act of unified prayer while gathered in Jesus' name (Matt 18:19–20).

THE BINDING OF ISAAC

"Take now your son, your only son, whom you love—Isaac" (Gen 22:2).

The story of the sacrifice of Isaac found in Gen 22 is called by the rabbis the *Aqedah* or the "Binding" of Isaac. Isaac was not actually sacrificed but was indeed bound to the altar in preparation. The conversation between Abraham and God in the biblical text is blown up like a balloon by these interpreters. Again, the biblical text is remarkably terse and rabbis are eager to fill in the gaps, usually in ways that play creatively with features in the biblical text.

> "Take now your son" (Gen 22:2). Abraham said, "I have two sons." God said, "Your only son." Abraham said, "Each are the only son of that particular child's mother." God said, "The son whom you love." Abraham said, "Master of the universe, are there gradations of one's innermost being? I love both of them!" God said, "Very well, then—Isaac." Why did God drag out His command to such length? This happened so that his mind might not be stunned [by such a heartrending demand].[20]

It is something of a commonplace in rabbinic thought; the truly wise know how to break hard news to a loved one so as to soften the blow. The tragedies of Jewish existence and the general harshness of ancient life gave rise to this cultural phenomenon. The reason the rabbis slow down the conversation, which in the Bible is only a few words long, is to emphasize God's tender compassion for Abraham's terrible task ahead and to break it to him slowly.

As the story continues, Abraham tells Sarah that he is going to take Isaac away to be taught about his creator and she agrees, thinking they are going to study Torah. The commentators ponder on the words, "And he saddled his ass" (v. 3), noting, "Love disregards dignity! How many

---

20. *b. Sanh.* 89b.

menservants, how many maidservants did that righteous man have, yet he himself saddled his ass in his eagerness [to do God's will]."[21]

The rabbis suppose that the two young men brought along (v. 3) were Ishmael and Eliezer. Somehow the two of them knew that Abraham was expecting to sacrifice his own son, and they begin to argue as to which would be the heir of Abraham's estate. The Holy Spirit responds and puts the argument to naught with the words, "Neither will be the heir."

The rabbis envision Satan attempting to hinder Abraham from his task of sacrificing Isaac. First Satan appears in the guise of an old man who tries to convince Abraham that he is losing his mind. "Old man, you are out of your mind. A son who was given you at the age of one hundred—and you are setting out to kill him!" Satan claims that God will consider Abraham a murderer for killing his own son. Abraham responds with the words, "Even so," and continues his journey to Moriah.

Satan tries several other ways of putting Abraham off-task. Finally Satan decides to simply tell Abraham the truth! Satan tells Abraham that he heard it from the very throne room of God himself that God intends to stop him and provide a lamb in Isaac's place. Abraham assumes Satan must be lying since Satan is always lying, and goes on his way. Abraham, when he saw the mountain in the distance (v. 4) asked Isaac what he saw. Isaac replied, "I see a mountain glorious in majesty." He asked the other two with him if they saw anything but they did not. Abraham said, "O people like donkeys! As the donkey sees but does not comprehend, so it is with you. Stay here, people who are like a donkey."[22] The biblical text reads that Abraham said to the servants, "You stay here with the ass." But with a very simple change of vowels (the vowels still are not present in scrolls) one can understand it to mean, "Stay here, people like an ass."[23]

The rabbis imagine that Isaac suspected he was to be sacrificed when he realized they still lacked a lamb for the offering. He asks his father and Abraham tells him openly what God had commanded him to do. Isaac's first concern is for his mother's grief yet they continue on their way, "one to slaughter and the other to be slaughtered." Isaac asks his father to bind his hands and feet lest he flinch involuntarily, causing the knife to cut

---

21. Ibid.

22. Ibid.

23. ʻim (with) has been read as ʻam (people), which would render "people of the donkey." Therefore, the people who were like asses stayed behind with the asses.

improperly. If that happened, he would be impaired and disqualified as a blemished sacrifice.

As Abraham lifted his arm to strike the blow, Satan shoved his arm aside so the knife fell to the ground. Yet Abraham fetched it and continued his task crying to God with the words of Ps 121:1, "I lift mine eyes to the mountains; whence will my help come?" Isaac was able to look into the heavens and see myriads of angels weeping as they watched the scene. They cried out to God and remind God of his oath that Abraham's seed should be as the stars of the heavens (Gen 15:5). The Lord then commanded Michael to stop Abraham. "Then the angel of the Lord called unto him out of heaven and said: 'Abraham, Abraham'" (Gen 22:11). The angel said his name twice as one does when in distress.

> When Abraham turned his face toward the angel, the angel said again, "What are you about to do? Do not lay a hand on the boy!" (Gen 22:12). Abraham asked, "Who are you?" Michael replied, "I am an angel." Abraham said, "When the Holy One told me to offer my son, he himself spoke to me. So too, if he now wishes something else, he himself should speak to me."[24]

The Lord then personally declared, "By myself I swear, the Lord declares . . ." There is a feature in the biblical text that explains Abraham's demand to hear from God himself. The Hebrew text has here the rather confusing yet not uncommon feature of an angel speaking as if it were God himself. In verses 12 and 15 the text says an angel addresses Abraham, yet the angel says, "By myself, I swear . . ." (v. 16). The rabbis are creatively reading the text so that, at first, the angel addresses Abraham. Abraham demands to have God's personal word on the matter. Then God addresses Abraham individually saying, "By myself I swear." The creative reading solves the awkwardness of the text (an angel speaking as if it were God himself) and portrays Abraham's absolute devotion to do God's will; he refused to back down until he heard from the Lord himself.

It is only after God commands Abraham to spare his son and sacrifice the lamb in his place that Abraham registers his complaint against God. He asks God what anyone under the circumstances would ask: How could God promise progeny through Isaac and yet command Abraham to kill Isaac? He even indicates that he should have brought his complaint to the Lord previously. But Abraham requests that God would consider the whole event to provide redemptive grace to Isaac's descendants.

24. Ibid.

> When Isaac's children shall sin and find themselves in distress, be mindful on their behalf of the binding of Isaac; let it be reckoned in your presence as though his ashes were in fact heaped upon the altar. Be then filled with compassion for his children, forgive them, and redeem them from their distress.[25]

God replied that Isaac's descendants will indeed sin and be in danger of judgment. To avert God's wrath, God commands that every New Year's Day (on *Rosh Hashanah*) Isaac's descendants should remind God of the binding of Isaac by blowing the horn of a certain creature. Abraham asks, "Which creature?" God said, "Turn around." At once, "Abraham lifted up his eyes, and looked, and behold a ram" (Gen 22:13). To this day, the *shofar* or ram's horn is blown especially on *Rosh Hashanah*.

According to the rabbis, this blowing of the shofar on *Rosh Hashana* was intended to remind God of the binding of Isaac and re-activate God's redemptive grace and continuing forgiveness. Surely the rabbis didn't believe that *God* needed the reminder, but that the practice of blowing the shofar during *Rosh Hashanah* was a reminder to the community. Abraham's act of faithfulness was their spiritual heritage and source of blessing. To Christian eyes, this story feels quite similar to Calvary and may in fact have functioned in the rabbinic community as a Jewish alternative.

It is very worthwhile for a Christian to notice in this Abraham tradition something critical about this *haggadic* tradition and the spirituality that underlies is. Judaism is not "legalistic" in the way Christians mean when they bring this charge.[26] First, when Jews use the word "Torah" they don't typically mean "law" but "instruction" or "a way to live." *Halakah*, another word for rabbinic law, actually comes from the Hebrew word for "walk" and doesn't so much mean "law" as "lifestyle."

Second, Judaism is not man's attempt to work their way to God by human efforts. Of course, Judaism is much more interested in law as "instruction in a way of living" than Christianity, but this is not a method to attain divine favor so much as *a response to divine favor*. Traditions such as the one we just encountered show that within the very heart of the Jewish religion is an understanding of the importance of divine grace and mercy. The yearly blowing of the shofar at *Rosh Hashanah* is a reminder of their need for mercy and of God's promise of it.

---

25. Ibid.
26. See "I don't wanna be a Pharisee" above.

5

Jacob and Esau

THE SURPRISING RENDEZVOUS

"To see your face is like seeing the face of God" (Gen 33:10).

THE RABBIS TOLD A clever and humorous parable describing Jacob's meeting with Esau in Gen 33. As the Bible tells the story, when Jacob was returning to Beer-Sheba, after his Haran sojourn, he encountered Esau for the first time since he tricked Esau from his birthright. While Jacob expected the worst, Esau was completely forgiving and hospitable. There was no attempt at vengeance as one might expect under the circumstances. The Bible itself presents Esau as an amiable oaf and Jacob as a conniving shyster. Yet rabbis have consistently described Esau as the worst of sinners and Jacob as the most righteous man imaginable. Esau, for the rabbis, had come to represent the brutally oppressive Roman government. Of Jacob, the very scent of heaven clung to his garments.

This meeting goes against all the rabbi's expectations. Jacob prepares a large gift for Esau in hopes that Esau would be forgiving. But Esau rejects the gifts and simply welcomes his long-lost brother home. Jacob insists that Esau accept the gifts he has prepared saying, "for to see your face is like seeing the face of God" (Gen 33:10). How could Jacob say anything so kindly and complimentary to this paragon of wickedness? The rabbis' answer is quite clever and yet troubling.

Jacob mentioned God's Name to Esau in order to intimidate and frighten him. What parable illustrates Jacob's mention of God? A man invited his friend to eat dinner with him. When the guest realized that the host planned to murder him, he said, "This dish tastes like a dish I had in the palace." "This means he knows the king!" the host thought to himself, and seized with fear, he did not go through with his murderous scheme. This is how it was with Jacob. As soon as he said to Esau, "Seeing your face is like seeing the face of God," wicked Esau said to himself, "Since the Holy One brought him to such honor, I stand no chance against him."[1]

Here we see a typical example of how rabbis can transform the meaning of Scripture. Especially in light of later associations of Esau with Rome, the rabbis cannot allow Jacob to say Esau's face is like the face of God. The Rabbis find ways of reading into the story meaner intentions for Esau and greater virtue for Jacob. Esau isn't welcoming Jacob home, he's inviting him over to prepare to murder him. In the *midrash*, Jacob wants Esau to think, "Jacob is so familiar with God's face that he can recognize a likeness of it elsewhere! Then he has friends in high places indeed. To kill such a one would incur great retribution." For this reason, Esau allows Jacob to proceed unharmed.

The rabbis may be simply having fun with the biblical text as they often did. While they were serious Bible scholars, they also knew how to have some fun in the process. But they also wanted to paint Esau in the darkest colors since he had come to represent all that was wrong with the world. As we said above, Esau in the Bible itself is something of a kindly dim-whited oaf. Jacob is a wily trickster. Things are very different for rabbis. So I also share this story as something of a cautionary tale. We all have certain patterns of thought and habits of the mind that impact our biblical interpretation. Each community of believers shares certain assumptions about what the Bible means and what it cannot mean. While these shared traditions can be helpful "wisdom of the ages," they can also be intellectual blinders. For the rabbis, Esau simply had to be worse than the text indicated. These intellectual habits are a blessing and a bane, and something we need to know when to cherish and when to chuck. Perhaps I share this *haggadah* as a cautionary tale; sometimes our own tragedy and negative experience can make us overly suspicious and unable to recognize a smile and hand stretched out in friendship.

---

1. *b. Sotah* 41b.

Jewish Biblical Legends

JOSEPH AND HIS BROTHERS

"... with their camels carrying gum, balm, and resin" (Gen 37:25).

Rabbis often would focus their interpretive attention on aspects of Scripture that could appear unnecessary. They believed the smallest features of Scripture were endued with deep meaning and that nothing in the Scriptures is accidental or meaningless. In the Joseph story the biblical text gives what seems to be an unnecessary detail when it divulges exactly what the Ishmaelite caravan was carrying (Gen 37:25). These were the Ishmaelites who purchased Joseph and carried him down to Egypt. The verse reads, "and looking up they saw a caravan of Ishmaelites coming from Gilead, with their camels carrying gum, balm, and resin, on their way to carry it down to Egypt" (NRSV).

> R. Tarfon and the elders were sitting in the shade of the dovecote in Jamnia, and someone asked, "What is the meaning of Scripture's saying, 'With their camels bearing gum, balm, and resin?'" "It is to make known how very much the merit of the righteous helps them," he said. "For if this person [Joseph], who was both chosen and loved, had had to go down with an ordinary caravan of Arabs, would they not have suffocated him with the reeking stench of their camels laden with foul-smelling resin? But for his sake the Holy One arranged that the sacks be full of spices and fragrant balm. In this way he should not be suffocated by the stench of the camels and the foul smell of resin."[2]

Here the interpreters are reading Scripture to find hidden signals of God's providential care for the righteous. The sweet-smelling spices were God's provision to keep Joseph's gentle soul from suffocating from the stench on his trip down to Egypt. While this may come off as wildly speculative, they are reading the text with a creative interest in finding indications of God's character and care. In a world that was convinced that the Jews were inferior and their God was worse, they sought to find every excuse to praise and magnify God's providential purpose and plan.

Here is what we can learn from the rabbis: it is better to err on the side of excessive faith and hope than be beset by excessive skepticism and cynicism. Rabbis here come off as almost ridiculously enthused with the goodness of their God. They knew, as we have described above, that in the broader public it was commonly believed that the Jewish God was morally

---

2. *Mek. Be-shallah.*

Jacob and Esau

duplicitous and the Jewish people were untrustworthy. Rabbis are looking for every opportunity to believe the best about their beloved "Master of the Universe." They had had their belly full of malicious anti-Jewish calumny. They chose to live by believing the best about the trustworthiness of God and by seeing it everywhere they were looking. We daily encounter people who have moved from faith to skepticism, from belief to doubt, from discipleship to denial. This is often accompanied by a major disappointment with the church or a personal tragedy that has left them angry at God or the synagogue/church. They often take an extremely negative tone about everything the Bible says and focus on its violence or contradictory themes. These are issues that have challenged my faith, and I've sought long-and-hard to come up with reasonable understandings. In the main, I'm satisfied with my understanding and find there to be good reason to continue in faith and discipleship.

But when I try to speak to a person who has left the faith, I often find a kind of spiritual blindness and willful rejection as if they have said, "I've given up on faith and that is all there is to be said about it." What surprises me is how, when I've tried to share some ideas for dealing with specific problems and questions, they are completely uninterested and sometimes perturbed. Their "been there, done that" attitude leaves them spiritually inoculated. They have chosen the easier downward trail of doubt rather than climbing the mountain of seeking and finding.

There are good reasons for faith, but real faith always seems to involve a struggle upward that can be arduous. All relationships involve times of misunderstanding and frustration, especially if they are meaningful and long-lasting. But just the way we should never jump to believe the worst about an old friend, we ought also to strive to believe the best when we are grappling with doubt. Caving too soon is a disloyalty of sorts; there is such a thing as intellectual loyalty.

In my own case, when I was going through a period of serious spiritual struggle, I made the choice to fight for my faith by planning a retreat to a Trappist monastery near Bardstown Kentucky. I brought along some books that could help me through the specific problems I was having.[3] I came away from that experience ready to serve God again. If I had just

---

3. My primary issues surrounded the belief in the Bible as "God's Word." Two books I heartily recommend on this topic are both by professors at Eastern University: Peter Enns, *Inspiration and Incarnation*, and Kenton Sparks, *God's Word in Human Words*.

thrown in the towel when I began to encounter serious problems with the Bible, I would likely be an agnostic today.

This, in a sense, is what rabbis are seeking to prevent. They have opted for the faith-preference and have chosen to believe the best about God come hell or high water. They find the goodness of God in all kinds of odd places in Scripture. This is especially remarkable seeing how they had suffered for their faith. May we walk boldly in the light they shine.

JOSEPH IN POTIPHAR'S HOUSE

"The Lord made all that he did to prosper in his hand" (Gen 39:3).

Once in Egypt, the writer of Genesis says that Joseph prospered in everything he laid his hand to do. The rabbis explain this as follows.

> When Joseph served his master spiced wine, the master would ask, "What have you served me?" When Joseph replied, "Spiced wine," the master would say, "But I want bitter wine," and it became bitter wine. When the master said, "I want mulled wine," it became mulled. The same things happened with water, and in fact, with everything he did. As is said, "The Lord made all that he did to prosper in his hand." When his master became aware of it, he turned over all the keys to Joseph, so that Joseph was able to say, "My master has no concern about anything that is in the house" (Gen 39:8).[4]

This legend appears to seek to explain Joseph's meteoric rise from slavery to the heights of power in Egypt by imagining how God made him prosper in every way. The biblical hook here are the words "in his hand"; that is, something remarkable must have happened to the things he held in his hand that caused him to prosper.

But Joseph is not beyond reproach for the rabbis, and they imagine him taking on an aura of vain pomposity.

> When Joseph found himself comfortably situated, he began to eat and drink well, to frizz his hair, and to say, "Blessed is He who is everywhere and who helped me forget my father's house." Then the Holy One said to Joseph, "Your father is mourning for you in sackcloth and ashes, and you eat and drink well and frizz your hair! You spoiled brat! Just you watch! I'm sending a she-bear to

---

4. *Tanhuma, Va-yeshev,* par. 8; *Gen. Rab.* 86.5.

Jacob and Esau

get you." At once, "it came to pass that his master's wife started taking an interest in him" (Gen 39:7). Here's a parable of a strong man who stood in the marketplace, made eyes at the ladies, kept combing his hair and walking with a swagger. He said, "How fit I am! How well-endowed I am! How strong! How handsome I am!" He was told, "If you are so strong and so fit, here is a she-bear. Try to give it a thrashing!"[5]

Joseph clearly, in the rabbinic imagination, has fallen prey to the luxurious life of Egypt. On one hand, he's become something of a dandy. And as judgment for his arrogance, God decided to set a she-bear on him in the person of Potiphar's wife. Yet even in this morally weakened state, Joseph does not succumb to her wiles as the next legend exemplifies.

Joseph was seventeen and had all the charm of youth. Each and every day his mistress, Potiphar's wife, tried to seduce him by various enticements. Every day she would wear three different dresses. The dresses she wore in the morning she did not wear at noon, and those she wore at noon she did not wear in the evening. Why all this? So that he might gaze at her.[6]

Potiphar's wife was not only madly in love with Joseph, she was scheming and wily in her seduction. The rabbis are clearly having fun with the biblical story, and they continue to imagine Potiphar's wife not only manipulating Joseph but other women who are equally smitten with Joseph's looks.

Once some Egyptian women gathered [in Potiphar's house] eager to see Joseph's handsomeness. What did Potiphar's wife do? She took citrons, placed them before the women, and gave each of them a knife. Then she called Joseph and had him stand before them. As they peeled the citrons they were gazing at Joseph's physique and they cut their fingers. The Potiphar's wife said, "You saw him only for one instant and are still overcome! How much more am I, who see him all the time." And though each and every day she sought to seduce him with her wiles, he nevertheless stood strong against his desires.[7]

Apparently, these dizzy ladies were so enamored with Joseph's beauty that they had trouble peeling a citron with a knife while gazing on his handsomeness. The point was that they ended up cutting themselves even after

---

5. Ibid.
6. *Tanhuma, Va-yeshev,* par. 5.
7. Ibid.

their first encounter with Joseph. She, being in his presence day after day, was much more enamored than even they were. Still, Joseph was able to withstand her wiles. How could a young man manage to be so self-controlled? It is one thing for a monk to take and keep a vow of celibacy by remaining in the monastery away from temptation, but for a young man continually tempted by his master's wife to remain vigilant in righteousness seems almost beyond belief. One legend tells of those who asked just this question.

> A Roman noblewoman asked R. Yose, "Is it possible that Joseph, at seventeen, with all the sexual desire of youth, could act with such self-control?" R. Yose brought out the book of Genesis and began reading to her the story of Reuben and Bilhah and the story of Judah and Tamar, and said, "If Scripture does not cover up for these, who were full-grown and still under their father's authority, how much less likely is it to cover up for one who was a minor and on his own?"[8]

Gen 35:22 tells the story of Reuben sleeping with his father's concubine Bilhah and Gen 38 describes Judah sleeping with his daughter-in-law Tamar who was playing the prostitute. R. Yose's comment is quite sagacious; he claims that it is much more forgivable for a young man who is yet a minor to have sexual indiscretions than for married adults. Yet the Bible is honest about the more egregious indiscretions of Reuben and Judah. If Moses was willing to expose the more culpable sins of their ancestors, it is not likely that he sought to cover up the relatively minor infraction of the young unmarried Joseph. Since there is no good reason to believe that Moses is hiding Joseph's sins, Joseph must have indeed been as self-controlled as the Scriptures indicate.

JOSEPH BEFORE PHARAOH

"... and Pharaoh had a dream" (Gen 49:1).

The rabbis also enjoy imagining what might have stood behind the biblical statement, "But there was none that could interpret them unto Pharaoh" (Gen 41:8). When Pharaoh had his dreams, apparently Egyptian wise men tried to interpret his dreams without success. What could have been the circumstance here?

8. *Gen. Rab.* 87:6.

R. Joshua of Sikhnin said in the name of R. Levi, "They did interpret them, but Pharaoh did not like what they said. For example, they said, 'The seven fat cows mean that you will have seven daughters. The seven lean cows mean that you will bury seven daughters.' Or, 'The seven full ears of corn mean that you will conquer seven countries. The seven thin ears mean that seven countries will arise in rebellion against you.'"[9]

Pharaoh could hardly have appreciated the prognostication of the birth of future daughters—fat cows all! But then to imagine that they would all die of starvation! Pharaoh clearly had problems accepting this interpretation. Was this because it offended him? Or that he found it too demeaning or defeating? The rabbis don't say. They are probably just having some fun. But they do tell us what the purpose of this all was.

> Why did this come to pass? So that Joseph would follow and be raised to high rank. For the Holy One said, "If Joseph were to come right away and interpret the dream, he would not receive the accolades that should come his way. The magicians would say to Pharaoh, 'If you had you asked us, we would at once have interpreted the dream for you the same way.'" Therefore He waited for the magicians to exhaust themselves in trying to provoke Pharaoh's spirit until Joseph would come and restore it.[10]

This is another example of rabbis supplying background details to fill out suggestions in the biblical narrative. The text simply says that no one could interpret the dreams to Pharaoh, so someone must have tried. If they did try, how did God work to bring about the purpose through their vain attempts? These unsuccessful interpretive efforts helped to highlight Joseph's wisdom and skill in dream interpretation and help launch Joseph into the heights of Egyptian power. They also illustrate Joseph's political savvy; his interpretations where not personally offensive to Pharaoh. The rabbis admire Joseph not only for his ability to interpret dreams but for his practical wisdom. They knew that their survival, then as at present, was dependent upon both faithful devotion to God *and* skillful negotiation of the capricious powers of the state.

---

9. *Gen. Rab.* 89:6.
10. Ibid.

Jewish Biblical Legends

THE DEATH AND BURIAL OF JACOB

"Joseph's brothers saw that their father was dead" (Gen 50:15).

After the death of Jacob, the Scriptures say that Joseph's brothers became increasingly anxious about their relationship to him. "When Joseph's brothers saw that their father was dead, they said, 'What if Joseph still bears a grudge against us and pays us back for all the wrong that we did him!'" (Gen 50:15). The commentator notices the brother's anxiety follows the burial of Jacob in Canaan, which they always saw as a hint of an association. Joseph and a rather large entourage of mourners made the journey from Egypt to Canaan to bury Jacob in the "cave of the field of Machpelah" (Gen 50:13). What happened after this to cause Joseph's brothers to be frightened of Joseph?

> What did they see that frightened them? As they were returning from burying their father, they saw that Joseph turned off the road to look at the pit into which his brothers had thrown him. When they saw this, they said, "He still bears a grudge in his heart. Now that our father is dead, he will act on his hatred." But in fact Joseph's motive was a holy one—he wanted to thank God for the miracle for him that happened there.[11]

This interpretation may be loosely associated with an odd feature in the biblical text at exactly this point. Jacob died in Gen 49:33, and a rather long description of the burial entourage and mourning process has already consumed the first fourteen verses of Gen 50. It strikes the reader as quite odd that the brothers are only now in 50:15 noticing that their father was dead. This rabbinic interpreter might well read the passage with a slightly different emphasis and explain the oddity. The word "saw" here not surprisingly means "realized" or "pondered upon." The rabbis take it literally as if something was actually seen. In Hebrew the word "that"—as in "*that* their father was dead"—could be translated "when." Thus we could read, "When the brothers of Joseph saw [something unspecified], *when* their father was dead, they said . . ." This rather awkward reading is grammatically possible and begs the question, "What did the brothers see?" The advantage of this awkwardness is that it allows for the brothers to have realized that their father had died earlier. They now, after his death, have seen something else. What? They saw Joseph looking at the pit into which they had cast him.

11. *Gen. Rab.* 100:8.

Jacob and Esau

This ominous sight brought fear to their hearts, but Joseph's motivations were altogether harmless and pious.

What kind of insight arises from what the rabbis have here supposed might have happened? As people whose motivations and behaviors, pious though they were, were often considered suspect and dangerous, they imagine the same with their great ancestor Joseph. This *haggadah* relates something of the danger that arises when a guilty conscience suspects the worst in others. This is a situation the Jewish community often found itself in; their simple acts of piety were viewed by the broader Gentile world as deeply disturbing.

Interestingly, Josephus, Joseph's namesake, wrote the book called *Against Apion* in the first century to combat many of the calumnies leveled against his people. For instance, Josephus says that Apion (an anti-Jewish writer) claims that Antiochus Epiphanes IV, when he conquered Jerusalem and entered into its temple (in 171 BCE), found an imprisoned Greek man who claimed he was being fattened by the Jews to be offered as a sacrifice (*Apion* 2:8). Apion conveys the following description.

> After a while, he inquired of the servants that came to him and was informed by them that in order to fulfill a law of the Jews . . . they used to catch a Greek foreigner every year and fatten him up, and then lead him to a certain wood, and kill him, and sacrifice with their accustomed solemnities, and taste of his entrails, and take an oath upon this sacrificing a Greek, that they would ever be at enmity with the Greeks; and that then they threw the remaining parts of the miserable wretch into a certain pit.[12]

Josephus can hardly find words to express his dismay that so many Greeks and other Gentiles believe such dreadful things about their Jewish neighbors. The eating of any human flesh would be an absolute abomination to the Jews, yet many Gentiles believed that Jewish law required just this. Jewish people lived in an environment in which the worst was commonly believed about their laws and practices. Jews are particularly aware of the fact that even the most pious act, by an outsider armed with hateful misinformation and a guilty conscience, can be interpreted as something sinister and dangerous.

---

12. *Ag. Ap.* 2:8.

6

Israel in Egypt

ENSLAVED IN EGYPT

"Then a new king came to power in Egypt who didn't know Joseph" (Exod 1:8).

RABBIS ARE INTRIGUED BY the comment of Exod 1 that there was a new king in Egypt who didn't know Joseph (v. 8). How could such a savior of the land of Egypt become unknown to the following king? Some rabbis thought this perhaps might be the same king but that such new decrees were issued by him that he was declared a new king; that is, he was new in that he acted as if he didn't know Joseph. The text never describes the death of the old king. Therefore, this was really the same king as before who is yet being described as "new" in some sense. Some challenged this interpretation claiming that the text should be taken at face value; a new king meant a new king. Yet, how could it be that he did not know Joseph who had saved Egypt from devastation?

> The sages asked, "Why then is he called a new king? Was he not the same pharaoh?" What occurred is that the Egyptians said to Pharaoh, "Come, let us attack this people." He replied, "You are fools. To this day we are eating what one could say belongs to them. How can we attack Joseph's people? If it were not for Joseph, we would not have survived." When Pharaoh refused to listen to them, they

removed him from his throne for three months until he said to them, "I'll comply with your wishes." Then they restored him. For this reason, "There arose a new king."[1]

By creating this tale, the rabbis do two things. They explain why the text does not observe that the previous king had died and they magnify the greatness of Joseph by having the Pharaoh declare such allegiance to his memory that only after he was deposed from the throne would he issue new decrees against the Hebrew people. In this case, the claim that the "new" Pharaoh didn't "know" Joseph implies he acted *as if* he didn't know Joseph or no longer honored Joseph's memory.

The rabbis seek other ways to discover how the goodwill that Joseph had gained toward the end of Genesis could have been so squandered that the next king didn't know Joseph or honor his memory in any way.

> When Joseph died, the Israelites were saying, "Let's be like the Egyptians!" They abolished the covenant of circumcision. After they did this, the Holy One turned the love the Egyptians had for them into hatred, as the Scriptures say, "He turned their heart to hate His people, to deal craftily with His servants" (Ps 105:25).[2]

What could have motivated God to have done such a thing? Why make the Egyptians hate them? They had tried to become like the Egyptians by abolishing the covenant of circumcision. What could be the biblical reason for making such a claim? There actually is something. The covenant of circumcision is first mentioned in Gen 17 where Abraham is commanded to circumcise his whole household. Yet, besides the very opaque reference to circumcision in Exod 4:26, the ceremony is never mentioned again until Josh 5. There, just before the Hebrew entrance into the land of promise, it appears that the people are all in need of circumcision. What happened? Why wasn't the covenant of circumcision being kept in the days in Egypt? The rabbis have an answer here that becomes a life-lesson in what we might call "peer-pressure." The Israelites had ceased to circumcise their children to order to fit in with Egyptian culture and custom. The lesson? Accommodating one's surroundings to avoid persecution only produces greater hatred. That seems to be the message the rabbis are finding in Scripture, one which certainly had great applicability to the Judaism of the Greco-Roman or Christian world.

---

1. *b. Sotah* 11a; *Exod. Rab.* 1:8.
2. *Exod. Rab.* 1:8.

Jewish Biblical Legends

Another observation treats Pharaoh's mistreatment of the Hebrew slaves differently. Concerning the verse, "Let us deal shrewdly with *them*" (Exod 1:10 NJPS), they notice that in the Hebrew the object of the preposition is actually singular; "Let us deal shrewdly with *him*." This is typical in Hebrew; a singular suffix can and often does bear a plural force. But the rabbis are experts at divining deep meaning from the details of the text.

> "Come, let us deal craftily with *him*" (Exod 1:10). The text does not say "with them," but "with him," which implies, so asserts R. Hama son of R. Hanina, that Pharaoh said, "Come, Let us deal craftily with Israel's deliverer [or God]."[3]

There is no good contextual or grammatical reason to suppose the object of the preposition could be God. The Lord's name has not yet appeared in the book of Exodus at this point. But their animosity against the children of Israel ended up being a declaration of war against Israel's God. The interpreter here supposes that Pharaoh knew what he was doing, and that he intended to pick a fight with Israel's God as much as with the children of Israel themselves. This interpretation underlines the egregious nature of Pharaoh's intention and its foolishness. To attack Israel is to attack God.

Interpreters were often willing to find humor in cases where words in Hebrew sounded something like something else. In Exod 1:13 the text says that the Egyptians made the children of Israel serve with rigor (Heb. *beparek*). In non-vocalized Hebrew this looked like it could mean, "with a soft mouth" (*be peh rakh*) which meant for them "gentle speech."

> R. Eleazar said, "The word means 'with gentle speech' (*peh rakh*). After pharaoh said, 'Let us act craftily,' he gathered all Israel and, affecting gentleness, said, 'I beg you, as a special favor, work alongside me today.' Then Pharaoh picked up a basket and a shovel. Everyone who saw him pick up the basket and shovel came and worked at the making of bricks alongside him. Thus it came about that Israelites worked to the fullness of their strength and with great eagerness alongside Pharaoh. But when it grew dark, he stationed taskmasters over Israelites and said, 'Reckon up the number of bricks.' After the taskmasters counted them, the Israelites were told, 'This is to be the number you are to provide me each and every day.'"[4]

---

3. *b. Sotah* 11a.
4. *b. Sotah* 11b.

Israel in Egypt

This legend envisions a grand trick whereby the Pharaoh works alongside the Hebrew slaves for a day and gently (with *soft mouth*) urges them to help. The result is that the workers labored with such enthusiasm that they produced a terrific amount of brick. Then this became the required quota for the following days.

Rabbis perhaps intended this story to encourage listeners to be wary of gentile overlords who seem excessively kind and forbearing. They may have a trick up their sleeve. But a less sinister interpretation and lesson may well be in view; this as a reminder to lead by example and kindness rather than by cruel brutality. In this case, the kindness itself was a cruel ruse.

THE BIRTH OF MOSES

"Now a Levite man married a Levite woman . . ." (Exod 2:1)

How does one respond to oppressive evil in government? When does our resistance to evil so complicate matters as to become more problem than solution? The rabbis, by envisioning this story set in ancient Egypt, remind themselves of the problem of unintended consequences to good intentions. Before reading this *haggadah,* a comment about the biblical text in Hebrew should be of assistance. The Hebrew of Exod 2:1 literally says, "Then a man from the house of Levi went and took [that is, "married"] a Levite woman." They find the first verb "went" (*halak* in Hebrew) redundant. Why not just say, "A Levite man married a Levite woman"? Since nothing is actually redundant in Holy Scriptures, there must be a reason the text stands as it does. What is the background story? We find that the man (whose name is "Amram") didn't actually go anywhere. He had previously divorced his wife—not wanting to bring children into the horrible circumstances under which they lived—and was now returning to take her back again as his wife.

> "And then a man from the house of Levi went and married a Levite woman" (Exod 2:1). Did Amram, the man mentioned in the verse, go anywhere? No, nowhere. R. Judah bar Zevina taught that Amram went and acted upon his daughter's advice. He, as is well known, was the most eminent man of his generation. Aware that Pharaoh had decreed, "Every son born you will be thrown in the river" (Exod 1:22), he said, "We labor in vain," and was the first to divorce his wife. At that, the others divorced their wives. Then his daughter said to him, "Dad, your decision is crueler than Pharaoh's, for Pharaoh has decreed only against the males, while

your decision impacts both males and females. Pharaoh decreed only about this world, while your decision affects both this world and the one coming. Now, since Pharaoh is an evil man, there is doubt whether his command will or will not be fulfilled. But you are a righteous man so your decision is sure to be fulfilled." At once he went and took back his wife, and so did all the others. "And he took" (Exod 2:1). Scripture does not say, "And he restored," but "He took," [as in "married"] implying, said R. Judah bar Zevina, that he took her back in a formal wedding ceremony, seating her in a bridal litter, Miriam and Aaron dancing before her, while the ministering angels said, "The mother of children will [again] rejoice" (Ps 113:9).[5]

The observation that the verb translated *went* (*halak*) doesn't imply he actually went anywhere is not surprising. It is a commonplace that the verb signify something other than an actual change of location; here he went forward with his plan. We have the same meaning variation in English: "A certain man of the house of Levi *went* and married a Levite woman" (Exod 2:1 NJPS). "Went" has little to do with going anywhere, but proceeding as planned.

Yet R. Judah imagines a more complicated background to explain the non-locational meaning of "went." As stated above, Amram had decided to divorce his wife rather than to give birth to children when there was the chance they would be males and thus killed by Pharaoh. Because he was such a man of influence, many others follow suit. His daughter realizes that this will devastate their population. She talks him out of this decision claiming that his decision was more destructive than Pharaoh's ruling. Pharaoh's ruling snuffs out male lives in this world alone. Amram's decision eliminates the lives of both men and woman in this world and the next. She argues that Pharaoh's decree only affects this world since the children killed will live again in the world to come. Amram's decision de-populates not only this world but the next as well.

R. Judah is thus creatively reading the verse so as to add a whole new narrative into the space he creates. When the text says, "a man went" it means he went from hearing his daughter's words to find his wife and re-marry her. The words, "and married" (literally, *he took* in Hebrew, which is the typical expression for marriage) mean that he re-married his wife in a full marriage ceremony with all the nuptial song and dance. The typical marriage language of the biblical text is now imbibed with new meaning.

5. *b. Sotah* 12a; *Exod. Rab.* 1:19.

Israel in Egypt

This marriage celebration is in expectation of the birth of a deliverer Moses (Ps 113:9).

The daughter's argument fully persuades and Amram changes course and as a result, Moses is born. If it weren't for Miriam's courage and moral-sensitivity, Moses' birth would have been prevented. Amram's foolish divorce almost cost the nation its salvation. The morale of the story: when you are beaten down by evil, just keep doing the good you can do. Don't change course. Salvation might well arrive in the normal sequences of life. Don't let the evil take from you the routines and blessings of your life. This might be comparable to what we hear people say after a terrorist attack: The best response to an act of cowardly violence is always to go on living freely and fully. If we stop doing what we normally do, we have relinquished to them power over us. That should always be avoided.

MOSES IN PHARAOH'S PALACE

"When the child grew older..." (Exod 2:10).

The Jewish interpreters of Scripture imagine all sorts of happenings as Moses is being brought up in Pharaoh's palace. The following is both charming and instructive.

> "And she brought him unto Pharaoh's daughter" (Exod 2:10). Pharaoh's daughter used to kiss and hug Moses. She loved him as if he were her own son, and would not allow him out of the palace. Because he was so handsome, everyone wanted to see him, and whoever saw him could not turn their eyes away from him. Pharaoh also used to kiss and hug him and Moses used to grab Pharaoh's crown and put it on his own head. The Egyptian magicians seated there said, "We worry that the one who grabs your crown and puts it on his own head may be the one, as we have been saying, who will steal your kingdom from you." Some of the magicians suggested that he be slain, others that he be burned alive. But Jethro, who sat among them, said, "This child has no understanding yet. Let's put him to the test! Place before him a basin with a gold piece and a burning coal in it. If he reaches for the gold, he has understanding, and you may kill him. But if he reaches for the coal, he has no understanding, and a sentence of death is not called for." The items were brought at once. Then, as Moses put out his hand to grab the gold, Gabriel came down and shoved his hand toward the coal, so that Moses not only seized the coal but also put

the hand with the coal into his mouth and burned his tongue. As a result he became slow of speech and slow of tongue."[6]

There is, of course, no biblical reason to believe Jethro, who later became Moses' father-in-law, a priest of Midian, would have been an advisor to Pharaoh. For some reason, rabbis often understand him playing this role. But the advice he gives, along with the intervention of Gabriel, saves Moses' life and underlies Moses' reluctance for public speaking. This story is devised to explain a question the biblical text begs us to ask. If Moses was God's special child and God's chosen messenger, why did God create him slow-of-speech? Why couldn't he have been perfect as a child? The answer is that he *was* a perfect child! He was perfect, adorable, and intelligent to such a degree that Egypt's magicians became suspicious, especially after they have seen Moses grasp at Pharaoh's crown. The story also plumbs out Moses' reluctance concerning his call. How could such a gifted and inspired leader have been so reluctant to respond to God's invitation to service? Why be so reluctant to seek deliverance for his people. Moses' problem, this *haggadah* supposes, wasn't just a bit of a stammer. It was an actual injury that was caused by a severe facial burn.

This story highlights God's providential guidance and intervention in Moses' life. The rabbis sense that the biblical story only scratches the surface in telling of God's powerful ways of guidance and empowerment. Even as a small child, Moses had a compelling and winsome way, and he was so impressive the Egyptian magicians began to suspect he was more than a boy and his grasping the crown was more than child's play.

Even in Moses' speech impediment, we see the hand of God at work. When Gabriel intervened, he saved Moses from the suspicious magicians and also laid the groundwork for the deliverance of Israel by the combined leadership of Moses and Aaron. If it weren't for this event, Moses would have delivered Israel from Egypt alone. Aaron's leadership ended up being critical and, in spite of his rebellion with Miriam in Num 12, he was a key player in Israel's deliverance from Egypt. These may be some of the thoughts that underlie why the rabbis told the story as they did.

MOSES AS A YOUNG MAN

"One day, after Moses had grown up . . ." (Exod 2:11).

6. *Exod. Rab.* 1:26.

Israel in Egypt

Exodus 2 tells of how Moses as a young man murdered an Egyptian taskmaster who had been beating a Hebrew slave. The rabbis are quick to decide the identity of the man Moses killed. Leviticus 24:10 tells of a half-blooded blasphemer whose mother was Israelite and whose father was an Egyptian. Rabbis surmise that Moses killed the father of this blasphemer. They also imagine an even greater intrigue and justification for his actions.

> What preceded the Egyptian beating the Hebrew? The taskmasters were Egyptian but the foremen were Israelite. One taskmaster oversaw ten foremen, and one foreman oversaw ten Israelite workers. The taskmasters used to go around early in the morning to the foremen's homes to get them to work at the crack of dawn. Once an Egyptian taskmaster noticed an Israelite foreman's wife, Shelomith daughter of Dibri. She was beautiful, lacking any blemish, and he ogled her. Early the next day, he went to that foreman's home and told him quietly, "Go, gather your team of ten." Then he hid himself behind the staircase and the moment the husband left, the Egyptian got into the bedroom and raped the girl. When it happened that the husband turned back, he saw the Egyptian leaving the house. The husband reentered his house and asked his wife, "Did the Egyptian touch you?" She responded, "Yes, but I thought it was you!" When the taskmaster became aware that the husband knew what he had done, he put the husband back to heavy labor and beat him all day long, saying, "Work harder, work harder," trying to kill him.[7]

This story identifies the woman as Shelomith daughter of Dibri. It is not accidental that this is the very name of the women mentioned in Lev 24:11 who fathered a child with an Egyptian and whose son was a blasphemer. By tying these two stories together in such creative fashion we have explained a problem. How could an Israelite woman be married to an Egyptian man as Lev 24 could be taken to imply. The text does not say Shelomith and the Egyptian were married but only that they had a child together. The text supplies our answer: the Egyptian taskmaster raped Shelomith and then tried to work her husband to death. The story continues.

> "And he saw what had happened and what was now happening" (Exod 2:12). Through the holy spirit, Moses saw what the Egyptian did to the Hebrew in his home and what he intended to do to him in the field, and said, "Not only has this lecher defiled the wife, he also intends to kill the husband." "He looked around and saw no one" (Exod 2:12) means that he saw that there was no one who

---

7. *Exod. Rab.* 1:28–29; *Lev. Rab.* 32:4.

> would be zealous for God and slay the Egyptian. Therefore, "he killed the Egyptian" (Exod 2:12). Taking a shovel used for mixing clay, [he split the Egyptian's skull] so that his brain spilled out.[8]

The interpreter wants us to read the phrase that is typically translated as "he turned this way and that" (Exod 2:12) in a new light. In its biblical context, it means that Moses looked about to make sure he was alone before he killed the Egyptian. But in the eyes of the rabbi, this means that Moses looked at what had happened (the rape) and what was happening (the attempt to murder Shelomith's husband by beating). The Hebrew literally says, "and he turned here and here," which the sage understands as turning to past events (seen by the power of the spirit) and present events. Also, when the text says "and he saw there was no one" (Exod 2:12) it means (in the *midrash*) that he saw there was no one zealous for God like he was zealous. Thus his action is not only morally justifiable but honorable and exemplary.

On one level, a text like this has a very prosaic point; to exonerate Moses as a murderer. He wasn't someone who lost his cool and did something foolish; he was a man whose actions were justifiable under the circumstances and who was led by the spirit. But if we remember that Moses was commonly believed, by their gentile neighbors, to be a murderous leper and thief, we can understand why the rabbis seek to airbrush any moral duplicity and murder out of the story. The story celebrates a man who stood up for a poor raped woman and who prevented the murder of her poor husband. In a sense the rabbis here encourage other Jews to similar acts of righteous resistance to evil.

MOSES IN MIDIAN

"But Moses fled from Pharaoh . . ." (Exod 2:15).

Rabbis are understandably concerned by the narrative that describes Moses' marriage to the daughter of Jethro, a priest of Midian. Their explanation of how Moses could have had such truck with idolatrous folk follows.

> "Now the priest of Midian had seven daughters" (Exod 2:16). Does not the Holy One reject idolaters? Yet He seems to have allowed Moses to take up residence with an idolater. The truth is that Jethro had been a priest for idolatrous worship but when he realized that

8. Ibid.

it had no substance, he rejected it. He thought of turning to God in repentance even before Moses came. So he called his townsmen and said, "I have been ministering to you until now. But I am old. Choose another priest for yourselves." And then and there he brought forth all the accoutrements used in that worship and turned it over to his townsmen. They excommunicated him immediately and declared that no man should associate with him or work for him. When he asked the shepherds to tend his flock, they would not hear of it. That is why his daughters had to go out and tend it: "And the shepherds came and drove them away" (Exod 2:17). Jethro's daughters said, "An Egyptian delivered us" (Exod 2:19). Was Moses an Egyptian? Of course not. He was a Hebrew but his dress was Egyptian.[9]

This whole story hangs onto the biblical statement that Jethro's daughters were tending sheep. Why were daughters of a man of such high standing doing such menial male-oriented labor? This imaginative story provides the answer and solves the problem of how Moses could be so closely related to an idolatrous family. Jethro was a recent convert to monotheism and had been rejected by his own people as a result and thus could not hire laborers to shepherd his flocks. There is another possible biblical hook on which the story may hang. In Exod 3:1, Mt. Sinai (also called Mt. Horeb) is called "the mountain of God." If it had already been called this before Moses arrived, Jethro must have been already worshipping God there. One biblical problem they seem to ignore is that Jethro is still being called a priest of Midian in Exod 18:1. But undoubtedly interpreters of this level of ingenuity could provide an answer.

Rabbis are also curious about the fact that Jethro's daughters say that they were delivered by an Egyptian after Moses saved them (Exod 2:19). We saw the rather obvious (and ho-hum) explanation above; Moses still looked like an Egyptian because he had just come from Egypt. A more creative explanation follows.

> This parable explains the reference to an Egyptian in the daughter's account of their deliverance. A man was bitten in the foot by a lizard and ran to soak his feet in water. When he got to the river, he saw a child drowning in it; he reached out and pulled the child out. The child said, "If it weren't for you, I would now be dead." The man replied, "I didn't save you. It was the lizard who bit me and from whom I was escaping. It saved you." So, too, when Jethro's

---

9. *Exod. Rab.* 1:32; *Tanhuma, Shemot,* § 11.

> daughters said to Moses, "May you be blessed! You saved us from the shepherds!" Moses replied, "It was the Egyptian whom I killed. He saved you." That is why, in speaking to their father, Jethro's daughters mentioned an Egyptian. They meant, "Who caused this man Moses to save us? The Egyptian he had slain."[10]

The rabbi responsible for this interpretation clearly was avoiding Moses being called an Egyptian in any fashion. It begs the question: How did Jethro's daughters know about the Egyptian killed by Moses in Egypt. But the story he tells recognizes that good deeds are often at least partially a result of chance and unintended outcomes. Perhaps the interpreter also wants to urge the congregation to recognize the role that chance and happenstance plays in the good we do. If the lizard had not bitten the man who happened upon the drowning child, the child would have drowned for certain. We also do the good we can when we happen upon someone's tragedy but we mustn't take all the credit.

SHEPHERD IN MIDIAN

"Now Moses was tending sheep" (Exod 3:1).

Moses' forty years as a shepherd in Midian stirred rabbinic interest. What was God's purpose in such an extended sojourn? How could such a holy and revered prophet be assigned to such menial labor?

> "Now Moses was tending the flock" (Exod 3:1). The Holy One tested Moses by means of the flock, as our masters explained. When Moses our teacher was tending Jethro's flock in the wilderness, a lamb scampered off and Moses followed it until it approached a shelter under a rock. As the lamb reached the shelter, it came upon a pool of water and stopped to drink. When Moses caught up with it, he said, "I didn't know that you ran away because you were thirsty. Now you must be tired." So he picked up the lamb on his shoulder and started walking back with it. The Holy One then said, "Because you showed such compassion in tending the flock of a mortal, as sure as your life, you will become shepherd of Israel, the flock that is mine."[11]

---

10. Ibid.
11. *Exod. Rab.* 2.2.

Israel in Egypt

Thus, Moses' devoted and tender care even for a lost sheep belonging to another moved God to call Moses to shepherd God's own flock. God claims that such a caring shepherd is fit to guard and guide God's own flocks from bondage to liberty. One cannot help but think of the teaching of Jesus, "Whoever can be trusted with very little can also be trusted with very much and the one who is dishonest with very little will be dishonest with much" (Luke 16:10).

MOSES AND THE BURNING BUSH

"I will go over and see this strange sight" (Exod 3:3).

We thoughtlessly walk over pebbles in this story that for rabbis were stones of stumbling to be transformed into golden nuggets through good interpretation. In what follows, the burning bush was thought to be a thorn bush with all kinds of implied meanings.

> A heathen asked R. Joshua ben Korhah, "Why did the Holy One see fit to speak to Moses out of a thorn bush and not out of another kind of tree?" He replied, "Had he spoken to Moses out of a carob tree or out of a sycamore tree, you would have asked me the same question; but it wouldn't be right to dismiss you without a reply. So I will tell you why; to teach you that no place on earth, not even a thorn bush, is devoid of the Presence."

While one might expect God to appear in something more impressive than a lowly thorn bush, the bush teaches an important lesson. God's presence is to be found everywhere, not just in the mighty and majestic. Another lesson rabbis draw from the thorn bush: God shares in the distress of God's people. He continues.

> The Holy One said to Moses, "Don't you realize that I live in distress whenever Israel find themselves in distress? Take notice of the place where I speak to you, a thorn bush. I [if you dare attribute such words to God], fully share in their distress, as implied in the words "In all their affliction, He is afflicted." (Isa 63:9)[12]

The lesson here from the thorn bush is that, just as God was in the burning thorn bush, God shares completely in Israel's distress. Just as the thorn bush was not destroyed or consumed by the fire, so Israel will not

12. *Exod. Rab.* 2:5.

Jewish Biblical Legends

be destroyed by sorrow. Rabbis also pondered the intimacy Moses enjoyed with the Holy One, which developed into a face-to-face relationship (Exod 33:11). How did that kind of affection come about and can we see signs of it in this first encounter between the two of them?

> R. Joshua the Priest bar Nehemiah said, "When God revealed Himself to Moses, Moses was but a novice in prophecy. The Holy One said, 'If I reveal myself to him in a thunderous voice, I will scare the wits out of him. If I reveal myself in a whisper, he will take little note of prophecy.' What did God do? He revealed Himself in the voice of Moses' father, whereupon Moses answered, 'Here am I. What does my father wish?' God said, 'I am not your father. I am the God of your father. Because I wanted to win you over, I addressed you in a familiar voice so that you would not be afraid.'"[13]

This idea of God speaking in the voice of Moses' father is an extrapolation on the first words God spoke to Moses at the bush, "I am the God of your father" (Exod 3:6). More specifically, the dual use of Moses' name in verse 4 has the ring of a parent calling a child. By taking the voice of a parent, God introduces God's self to Moses in a non-threatening manner that allowed Moses to respond without fear or anxiety. God's practical concern for Moses' mental well-being laid the groundwork for the success of their relationship.

THE NAME OF THE LORD

"They will ask me, 'What is His name?'" (Exod 3:13).

The name for God given Moses, "I am that I am," in Hebrew could hardly be a more unusual name. Other possible translations are suggested by rabbinic interpreters. Because the word "that" (Heb. *asher*) in verbal form can mean "confirm, make abide," some understood it to connote *forever*.[14] Thus we have the following explication based on this understanding.

> "I am forever I am" (Exod 3:14). The Holy One said to Moses, "Go tell Israel, I am he who is with you in this servitude, and I am also he who will be with you during servitude under other kingdoms." Moses replied, "Master of the universe, sufficient for the hour is

---

13. *Exod. Rab.* 3:1.
14. Braude, *Book of Legends*, 63.

its own affliction."[15] The Holy One said, "Very well, just tell them, "I-am hath sent me unto you." (Exod 3:14)

One can hardly notice (and Braude points out) the similarity of Moses' words ("sufficient for the hour") to those of Jesus in Matt 6:34; "Do not worry about tomorrow, for tomorrow will worry about itself." The biblical phenomenon the interpreter is toying with is the repetitive nature of Exod 3:14. God reveals God's own name as "I am that I am" but God then commands Moses to divulge to the people a shortened form of the name (only "I am" or *'Ehyeh*). The interpretive tale explains the shortening of the name based on a creative translation for *'asher*. Moses realized that the longer name (I am "forever" I am) would have reminded Israel of future sufferings in which God's presence will be known. Moses suggests God not overload the people with anxieties about the future. A lesson intended for the Sabbath sermon listeners perhaps is the same; don't let tomorrows worries ruin today's joys.

MOSES BEFORE PHARAOH

"This is what the Lord, the God of Israel says" (Exod 5:1).

The dynamic encounter between Moses, representative of an enslaved people, and Pharaoh, ruler of the world's greatest empire, couldn't help but stir the imagination. When Moses demands that Pharaoh let the people go, Pharaoh responds with the proud question, "Who is the Lord that I should heed Him and let Israel go?" (Exod 5:2). The rabbis imagine Pharaoh going on to demand a crown from Moses. He was too proud to respond to mere words. He asks for something more tangible. Then Pharaoh demands his aids check the archival lists of gods to see if the Egyptians have any information on the Lord. The rabbis imagine this response from Moses. "You are a complete idiot? Are the living to be sought among the dead? The gods in your records are dead. But our God is a living God! He is the King of the Universe."[16] Pharaoh should also have known that Israel's God would not be in the Egyptian archives listed as if the Lord were a local deity with all

---

15. The implication is something like this: What is the point of picking a name that continually reminds Israel of their future sufferings. In saying, "I am the God who will be with you," they cannot help but think of their coming servitude to foreign nations.

16. *Exod. Rab.* 5:14.

the rest. Pharaoh, seeing that the children of Israel had lived in Egypt for 400 years by then, should have known this.

Pharaoh goes on to ask all sorts of foolish questions about Israel's God. Is he old or young? How many cities has he subdued? Moses' response is typically monotheistic; God is none of those things and the creator of all things. Pharaoh asks for a list of the Lord's notable deeds. God's great and notable deeds, Pharaoh is informed, are quite impressive: the creation of the whole universe, and oversight of the whole cosmos. Moses concludes with the words, "He removes kings and sets up kings."[17]

> Pharaoh replied, "From the very outset you have spoken lies. I am lord of the universe. I created myself as well as the Nile." Then and there he gathered all the wise men of Egypt and asked them, "Have you ever heard the name of the God of these two?" They replied, "We did hear that He is 'a son of the wise, a son of ancient kings'" (Isa 19:11). At that, Pharaoh told Moses and Aaron, "As for your God, I have no idea who He is. Who is the Lord that I should hearken to His voice?" (Exod 5:2)

Rabbis suppose that when Pharaoh asks, "Who is the Lord that I should heed Him and let Israel go? I do not know the Lord, nor will I let Israel go" (Exod 5:2 NJPS), the reason for his question is that he considers himself to be the Lord. He isn't really asking to gain information out of any sincere curiosity but only because he sees Moses' God as a possible threat to his own God-status. He is so stupidly arrogant as to suppose he created both himself and the Nile. When he inquires of his wise men about Moses and Aaron's god, they quote Isa 19, which is a prophecy against Egypt that they foolishly misunderstand. They think it has something to say about Moses' God, but the passage really is a condemnation of these famed Egyptian sages themselves. Providing a bit more of the context, we read.

> 11 The officials of Zoan are nothing but fools; the wise counselors of Pharaoh give senseless advice. How can you say to Pharaoh, "I am one of the wise men, a disciple of the ancient kings"? 12 Where are your wise men now? Let them show you and make known what the Lord Almighty has planned against Egypt. 13 The officials of Zoan have become fools, the leaders of Memphis are deceived; the cornerstones of her peoples have led Egypt astray. (Isa 19:11–13)

This whole comedy of errors flows from the dumb arrogance of those who are deceived by their own wealth and power into thinking they are

17. Ibid.

masters of the universe. Just as Isaiah condemns the foolish short-sightedness of these Egyptian sages who couldn't perceive the unity of God or the impending end of their own worldwide dominance, so all of us are endangered by our own success and the arrogance that often attends it.

OF STAFFS AND SNAKES

"Take your staff and throw it down before Pharaoh!" (Exod 7:9).

By one tradition, Pharaoh belittles the magical skills of Moses and Aaron when his staff is turned into a snake. He called Egyptian children who were also able to do similar tricks. Pharaoh quotes the dictum, "Who in their right mind would bring fish brine to Apamea (a city known for fish brine)?" Moses replies with a proverb of his own: "People do say, 'Take your best herbs to Herbville!'" The specialized market town can be just the place where the best products should be brought for sale because there the finest quality product is appreciated. Thus, Moses and Aaron's magical arts, resulting from the command of the highest deity, will be shown to be superior right there in Egypt.[18]

In Exod 7:12, when Aaron cast down his staff, it turned into a snake and consumed the snakes produced by the Egyptian magicians. However, the text oddly says that Aaron's staff consumed the Egyptian staffs. Why does the Bible not say that Aaron's snake ate the snakes produced by the Egyptians? As we might expect, and perhaps with a chuckle, we are supplied with an answer we would never have thought up on our own.

> At that time the Holy One said, "If Aaron's serpent were to swallow up the serpents of the Egyptians, there would be nothing remarkable in that, for a serpent usually swallows another serpent. Therefore, let the staff that turned serpent first resume its original form and only then swallow the serpents of the Egyptians. . . ." R. Yose son of R. Hanina said, "In addition, another great miracle happened to that rod, for although it swallowed up all the rods that had been cast down, enough to make ten heaps, still that rod did not become any thicker, and all who saw it recognized it as Aaron's rod."[19]

---

18. *Exod. Rab.* 9:6–7; Braude, *Book of Legends*, 66.
19. Ibid.

Jewish Biblical Legends

Rabbinic imagination is able to magnify the miracle so as to explain its superiority to any magical arts of the Egyptians. Aaron's rod turned into a snake and back into a rod. This is why it is referred to as a rod in 7:12. Not only did his rod consume all theirs as a wooden staff consuming other wooden staffs, it did not expand in size. The biblical justification for this is that Aaron's staff appears later in the story apparently unchanged. Again, the purpose of this interpretation is to explain the odd feature of the biblical text and to magnify the grandeur of the miracle in order to underline its superiority to Egyptian magical arts.

THE HARDENING OF PHARAOH'S HEART

"But I will harden Pharaoh's heart..." (Exod 7:3)

One of the most perplexing aspects of the exodus story is the hardening of Pharaoh's heart. Why does God harden Pharaoh's heart? If God didn't harden his heart, would Pharaoh not have released the Hebrews sooner and spared everyone no end of sorrow? The following story illuminates their understanding.

> The sages wondered how to understand the hardening of Pharaoh's heart? Here's a story that sheds some light on the matter. A lion and all kinds of animals, including a fox, were about to sail on a ship. The donkey was collecting the fare for the trip saying to each animal, "Pay me the fare." The fox said to the donkey, "How foolish you are! You know that the king of animals is with us and still you demand the fare." The donkey replied, "After I take it from the king, I will put it back in his treasury." [Upon hearing these words], the lion ordered, "Bring the ship to." He then got off, ripped the donkey apart, and told the fox, "Lay out the parts of this fool's carcass for me." The fox laid them out. But when he saw the donkey's heart, he ate it up. When the lion came back and saw all the parts cut up, he asked, "Where is the fool's heart?" The fox replied, "My lord king, he had no heart. If he had had one, he would not have presumed to collect the fare from the king." So, too, if wicked Pharaoh had a heart, he would not have said to the King who is King of kings, "Pay me my due."[20]

While this story is rather opaque, we can assume that the donkey represents Pharaoh and the lion the Lord. The fox is a voice for wily wisdom. The

---

20. *Exod. Rab.* 5:14.

Israel in Egypt

tale seems to be saying something like the following; there is a sense in which Pharaoh's heart was hardened by the Lord, and another sense in which Pharaoh had no heart to be hardened. By exacting slave labor from the children of Israel, God's firstborn, Pharaoh shows he has no heart at all. So while the Lord might be blamed for hardening Pharaoh's heart in one sense, there is another sense in which Pharaoh has already proved himself to be heartless.

The rabbis also justify God's actions by pointing out that God seems to bend over backwards to help Pharaoh.

> "Behold God is so great in power! Who dares to instruct as He does?" (Job 36:22). In human custom, when a man wishes to bring sudden disaster upon his enemies, he will maneuver to surprise him. God, however, forewarned Pharaoh before each and every plague to give him an opportunity to repent.[21]

The Gnostic interpreters who claimed the Hebrew God was a bully pointed out that if he hadn't hardened Pharaoh's heart, the same ends could have been achieved with much less suffering. God's behavior exacerbated Egyptian suffering unnecessarily and unjustly. Rabbis saw in the text the exact opposite. God bent over backward giving Pharaoh ample opportunity to repent. Moses and Aaron appeared before Pharaoh to warn him of each coming plague; thus God was giving Pharaoh an opportunity to repent. Clearly the rabbis did not see the hardening of Pharaoh's heart as something that negated his will completely but only that which confirmed his own choice. God's mercy exceeds that which is typical in human behavior.

THE PLAGUES OF EGYPT

"I will send the full force of my plagues against you" (Exod 9:14).

The rabbis were curious about the fact that the plagues of Egypt seem to be directed not only against the people of Egypt but also against their gods. This feature has often been noted by modern commentators and opinions vary concerning the degree to which the biblical story implies a "war of the gods" motif. But the following supports this reading.

> Why did God begin by bringing the plague of blood upon the Egyptians? Because Pharaoh and the Egyptians worshipped the Nile. Therefore the Holy One said to Moses, "Go, and in their

21. *Exod. Rab.* 9:9.

very presence smash their gods," which follows the saying "When idols are smashed, their priests are abashed." God will not punish a people until He first punishes its gods.[22]

This text goes on to imagine (rather humorously) how Israelites profited from the plagues.

> R. Avun the Levite said, "The Israelites became rich from the plague of blood. How did that happen? If an Egyptian and an Israelite dwelled in a house where there was a vat full of water, and the Egyptian went to fill a kettle from it, the water turned into blood, but the Israelite would continue to drink water from the same vat. When the Egyptian said to him, 'Give me some water with your own hand,' and was given water, it still turned into blood. Even if he said, 'Let us both drink from one vessel,' the Israelite drank water, but the Egyptian drank blood. It was only when the Egyptian bought water from the Israelite for money that he was able to drink water, and this is how the Israelites became rich."[23]

Braude points out that this passage explains how Gen 15:14 can predict that the Israelites can come out of Egypt with great substance.[24] Clearly, a reader of Scripture can hardly wonder how the gold used to build the wilderness tabernacle could have been in the possession of a group of escaped slaves.

The Jewish sages imagined the whole plague episode in terms of poetic justice; each plague corresponded to a particular kind of sorrow the Egyptians planned against Israel. Since they intended their Hebrew servants to draw their water, God turned their water to blood. Egyptians expected the Hebrews to carry their cargo, so the Lord sent frogs upon Egypt to defile and destroy their wares. Egyptians intended the Israelites to till their soil, so the Lord filled their soil so that it swarmed with gnats. Egyptians intended the Israelites to tend their vines so the Lord sent locusts that consumed their vines. Egyptians intended to slay the Israelite children so the Lord smote the firstborn of Egypt. Egyptians intended to drown them in water so the Lord hurled their army into the Red Sea.[25] Interpretations such as this are likely meant to counter the feeling of many readers that the God of the Exodus story should have achieved the exodus with less human suffering.

22. *Exod. Rab.* 9:10.
23. Ibid.
24. Braude, *Book of Legends*, 67.
25. *Tanhuma, Bo*, §4; Braude, *Book of Legends*, 68.

Israel in Egypt

The interpreters seek to bring out the justice of God and the righteousness of their salvation story.

A humorous story attends to the plague of frogs. The story jumps off from the fact that in Exod 8:2, the Hebrew literally reads "the frog come up and covered the land of Egypt."

> R. Akiva said, "It was only one frog, but it bred so rapidly that it filled the entire land of Egypt." R. Eleazar ben Azaria said to him, "Akiva, what business have you with *haggadah*? Stop trying to preach and turn to *Negaim* and *Ohalot* [legal tractates in Mishnah]. True, at the beginning there was only one frog, but this one croaked for the others, and they came in swarms.[26]

Akiva, known as the Father of the Mishnah, was renowned for his expertise in the law. Eleazar suggests that he go back to the tractates of *Negaim* (which deals with leprosy and blemishes) and *Ohalot* (dealing with defilements). These are both very complicated bodies of legal material and were Akiva's expertise. He was not known to be a preacher, and *haggadic* matters (dealing with non-legal matters) were associated with preaching. Akiva pre-dated the inscription of these traditions into written form (Mishnah); we ought to think here of oral not written traditions. But Akiva's interpretation is not feasible because it would require too much time. Eleazar suggests the other frogs came when the first one summoned them with its croaking.

Pharaoh is described in Scripture as at times softening to the pressures brought by Moses' God, but then changing his mind when the plague was over. The rabbis, of course, comment on the verse, "When Pharaoh saw that there was relief, he became stubborn and would not heed them, as the Lord has spoken" (Exod 8:11 NRSV). "This is just like the wicked; when they are in trouble, they affect humility, but as soon as they have respite, they return to their perversity."[27] In the next verse, the Lord tells Moses to tell Aaron to stretch out his rod and strike the dust of the earth. The rabbis wonder why God told Moses to tell Aaron rather than have Moses use his own rod. "According to R. Tanhum, the Holy One said to Moses, 'It is not proper that the earth, which protected you when you slew the Egyptian, should now be smitten by you.'"[28] The earth protected Moses when he murdered the Egyptian and hid his body in the sand (Exod 2:12). Again, rabbis are always quick to read the text with a heightened sense of God's poetic justice.

26. *b. Sanh.* 67b.
27. *Exod. Rab.* 10:6.
28. *Exod. Rab.* 10:7.

Jewish Biblical Legends

The Bible raises its own interpretive questions in Exod 9:24 where it describes a plague of hail that had fire flashing in the middle of the hail. They tell an interesting interpretive and explanatory tale.

> R. Hanan went on to say that this brings to mind a crystal lamp in which water and oil work together to keep the flame of the wick burning. "The interaction of the water and the oil may be illustrated by the parable of two fierce legions that were bitter rivals. When the time came for the king to wage war, what did he do? He made peace between them, and they both marched out and executed the king's orders together. So, too, fire and hail are bitter rivals, yet when the time came to wage war against Egypt, the Holy One made peace between them, and together they smote the Egyptians. Hence the verse is to be read, 'There was fire flashing up within the hail,' so that when an Egyptian sat down, he was scorched by hail, and when he stood up, he was scorched by fire."[29]

While the biblical description describes hail falling during a severe thunder storm, the rabbis enjoy imagining hail and fire cooperating to scorch the Egyptians on both ends, sitting or standing. The biblical hook is quite obvious; the text says that this kind of storm had not occurred since Egypt had become a nation. This was not a typical storm and the rabbis have enjoyed themselves imagining just how atypical this storm was.

They go on to imagine the Egyptians seeking to make the best of a bad situation by making use of various features of the plagues.

> R. Yohanan taught, "When the locusts came, the Egyptians, endeavoring to find some joy in their plight, said, 'Let us gather the locusts, pickle them, and put them up in casks.' The Holy One retorted sharply, 'Scoundrels, do you expect to find any joy in the plague I bring upon you?' Immediately 'the Lord turned an exceeding strong sea wind'—the westerly wind—'which took up the locusts,' etc. (Exod 10:19). What is signified by the words that follow, 'There remained not one locust'? That even those that had been pickled in the Egyptian's pots and casks took wing and fled."[30]

This interpretation is based on the apparently repetitive nature of the Hebrew. The text cited says that the locusts were hurled into the Sea of Reeds first. Then the text states that not a single locust was left. If *God* had hurled them into the sea, obviously none were left. Why repeat what the

---

29. *Exod. Rab.* 12:4; *Num. Rab.* 12:8.
30. *Exod. Rab.* 13:7.

previous sentence said? Because God hurled first the living locusts into the sea and then took care to remove the pickled locusts. A less thoughtful and creative reader might not have noticed.

In a very similar text we read,

> "But all the children of Israel had light in *their* dwellings" (Exod 10:23). Scripture does not say, "in the land of Goshen," but, "in their dwellings," to show that wherever a Jew entered, light entered with him and illuminated for him what was in casks, chests, and hidden depositories.[31]

By creatively supposing that the "their" in the verse refers to the Egyptian homes, the passage must be claiming that Israelites miraculously enjoyed illumination even when they went into the homes of the Egyptians. Elsewhere this imaginative reading supposes that the Egyptians relied upon the Israelites for everything during those days. They even came to appreciate the Israelites at this time since Israelites could have robbed Egyptians blind any time they liked. The fact that they didn't—the Bible doesn't say they did, so they didn't—proves the character of the Israelite people.

Rabbis were able to find other ways in which the plagues had beneficial outcomes.

> The plagues that the Holy One brought upon the Egyptians were the means of establishing peace for them. How so? There had been a dispute between the Ethiopians and the Egyptians, the Egyptians claiming, "Our borders extend to here," and the Ethiopians claiming, "No, our borders extend to here." But when the frogs came, they made peace between them, for the frogs entered only the Egyptian territory and thus the fields that did not belong to the Ethiopians were clearly identified.[32]

We must realize that, as funny as this sounds to us, it was also amusing to rabbis. Rabbis felt comfortable playing with Scriptures in ways that would keep their congregations interested and chuckling. But they also had a serious intention: to search out and discover the goodness of God and God's providential care hidden in the folds of the garments of Torah. They also may want to remind readers that the worst of life's tragedies often have unexpected benefits.

---

31. *Exod. Rab.* 14:3.
32. *Exod. Rab.* 10:2.

7

The Plundering of Egypt

THIS CHAPTER WILL TAKE a different turn from those previous. Instead of skipping over the surface of the biblical narratives, this chapter will pick one narrative and delve deeply into related *haggadic* traditions for that passage alone. Here we will dig deeper by investigating every rabbinic interpretation of a single passage. This study provides an interesting window into the way rabbis defended their faith against anti-Jewish slander. It also exemplifies a key case in which Christian Bible interpreters learned from rabbinic scholars in their own debates with the gnostics; they plundered the plunderers of Egypt.

Few passages in the Hebrew Bible have caused more embarrassment for Jewish and Christian commentators than those that recount the plundering of the Egyptians (Gen 15:14; Exod 3:21–22; 11:2–3; 12:35–36). Soon after the completion of the plagues and the story of the first Passover, we read the following. "The Israelites did as Moses instructed and asked the Egyptians for articles of silver and gold and for clothing. The Lord had made the Egyptians favorably disposed toward the people, and they gave them what they asked for; so they plundered the Egyptians" (Exod 12:35–36).

The problem begins with the verb translated "ask." The same verb also means "borrow" and borrowing is the most reasonable understanding in this context. Since Moses had only asked for some time off work to offer sacrifices to God in the wilderness, the Egyptians expected the Hebrews to

The Plundering of Egypt

return to Egypt.[1] While many have attempted to explain this as something other than deception, Israel's enemies certainly saw it to be proof of Moses' moral duplicity.

They conclude that the Egyptians, by divine compulsion, loaned the Hebrews gold, silver, and clothing, which they expected to receive back when the Israelites returned from their worship in the wilderness. It is particularly critical that Exod 12:36 says that the Hebrews *plundered* the Egyptians. If these treasures were understood by the Egyptians as gifts, given free and clear, the children of Israel could not have plundered Egyptians as the text claims. The claim that the event, whatever else it may have been, was a plundering of Egypt, necessitates that we read the verb as "to borrow."

The detractors of Jewish or Christian faith used these very passages as proof either that the God of the Israelites was demonic (a central tenet of Gnosticism) or that the religion and character of the Jews—and Christians by extension—was inferior and despicable. Several rabbinic (see below) and patristic (e.g., Tertullian, *Against Marcion* 2:20) passages tell of actual Egyptian attempts to seek remuneration for their valuables stolen during the despoliation. Tertullian's argumentation against Marcion indicates that the gnostics (or at least the Marcionite gnostics) were using the despoliation of Egypt as a test case to prove the moral inferiority of the Hebrew God, a central tenet of their *gnosis*.[2] There are, therefore, two issues at stake with which the rabbis contended. First, does Exodus describe a case of fraud whereby the Jewish people absconded with borrowed Egyptian goods (the standard anti-Jewish rhetoric)?[3] Second, does this prove the moral inferiority of the Jewish God (the gnostic claim)?

We will seek answers to several questions as to the role this text played in its historical context. Was this interpretation intended to be

---

1. Contrary to the movie portrayals, Moses does not say to Pharaoh, "Let my people go" but some variation of "The Lord says, 'Let my people go that they may worship me in the wilderness.'" The text seems to indicate that Pharaoh expects their return in that he negotiates with Moses on who will get to leave. First he suggests that only the men go worship the Lord in the wilderness. The assumption of return is clearly in play. In Exod 8:8, Pharaoh clearly expects the children of Israel to return to Egypt when he partially relents after the plague of frogs saying, "I will let your people go offer sacrifices to the Lord." The text gives clear reason to think Pharaoh expected their return and at no point is it clear that Pharaoh expected them to leave for good.

2. Pétrement claims that the unifying characteristic of all gnostic sub-groups was the belief in a fundamental distinction between the good God of the gospel and the evil God of the Old Testament (*A Separate God*, 9).

3. Childs, *Exodus*, 175.

Jewish Biblical Legends

used apologetically—a public response to the gnostic challenge—and if so, would it have been effective? Because of the large number of texts to be examined, our present study is constructed as a broad survey of rabbinic exegetical options rather than as a detailed examination of the progression of a particular *midrashic* concept.

TEXTS THAT EMBRACE THE MORAL PROBLEM

The first set of texts we shall survey can be described as texts that embrace the moral problem. Four texts comprise this category: *Exod. Rab. (Bo)* 14:3; *Exod. Rab.* 21:5; *Est. Rab.* 7:13; and *Mek. (Pesiqta* 13).

The Ninth Plague and The Plundering

The context of *Exod Rab.* 14:3 treats the plague of darkness. The critical portion follows.

> Now during the three days of darkness, the Holy One, blessed be He, gave the people favor in the eyes of the Egyptians so that they made loans to them. For an Israelite would go into the homes of the Egyptians and would see in the homes vessels of silver and gold and clothing. If they [the Egyptians] would say, "We don't have anything to loan to you," the Israelite would say to them, "Look, here it is in such-and-such a place." At that time [later during the exodus], the Egyptians were saying, "If they wanted to deceive us, they would have taken them during the days of darkness, and we would not have known it. Look, they already saw the items previously. Since they didn't touch them without our permission, in the same way, they will not hold on to them (that is, fail to return the items we loan them)." So they loaned them their belongings. This happened to fulfill what Scripture says, "And afterwards, they will come out with great provisions." (Gen 15:14)

The narrative logic of this story is a bit tricky to unravel. The *midrash* is based on the idea that the Israelites, during the days of darkness, had light wherever they went, so that an Israelite could walk into an Egyptian home and see clearly, even though the Egyptians were unable to see. The textual key to the *midrash* is the unexpected meaning for the suffix "their" in the claim that all the Israelites had light in *their* dwellings (Exod 10:23). If the *their* refers to the homes of the Egyptians, as this view claims, the

The Plundering of Egypt

Israelites could see even outside of the land of Goshen and in the homes of the Egyptians. If the Egyptians were blind and the Israelites could see, they could easily make away with whatever they pleased, leaving the Egyptians completely vulnerable. The Israelites proved themselves to be fully trustworthy by not taking advantage of their situation, and thus they attained favor in the eyes of the Egyptians.

This midrash conflates the stories of the plague of darkness and the plundering so that it could be paraphrased *God gave the Israelites favor in the eyes of the Egyptians during the days of darkness with the result that, (during the exodus) they continued to loan them their belongings*. In this case, it functions as an introduction to what follows; the Israelites did not steal Egyptian goods even though they could have done so with impunity. The point of the story intends to explain the means by which God gave the Israelites favor; they won the trust of the Egyptians during the days of darkness, a time of particular Egyptian vulnerability.

A shorter version of this idea begins as a saying of R. Jose the Galilean explaining the biblical phrase, "And the Lord gave the people favor." "They [the Egyptians] trusted them [the Israelites] on account of the three days of darkness saying, 'If when we were in darkness and they in the light they were not suspect, shall they now be under suspicion?'"[4] Because of the respect won by the Israelites in the days of darkness, the Egyptians are certain that the Israelites could be trusted *not* to make away with the valuables. The narrative logic of the story demands that the Egyptians loaned their goods; you don't need to trust someone when you give something free and clear. If you loan something to someone, trust becomes an important factor. As such, this passage embraces and even accentuates the trickery involved. The Egyptians were *not* giving their treasures away free and clear; they believed their treasures would be returned.

Perhaps these passages could be understood as an attempt to justify the plundering (category 2). If the Egyptians were overly trusting because of their previous experience such that they foolishly gave up their treasures, the plunder might be seen as justified in some way (the Egyptians got what they deserved for their naiveté). Perhaps this *midrash* wants us to understand these Egyptians as having been so trusting that they didn't work out the details carefully enough. Because of their experiences with the Israelites during the ninth plague, they assumed that the Israelites were wanting loans and that they could be trusted. Thus, they gave their wealth

---

4. *Mek., Pesiqta* 13.

Jewish Biblical Legends

freely on loan. The Israelites did not realize the confusion on the part of the Egyptians and thus were not morally responsible. In other words, the Israelites thought they were being given gifts, but the Egyptians thought they were making loans.

If this is the case, this passage attempts to justify the action. However, one would expect this line of reasoning to be more explicit. It simply demands that one read too much into the text. As it is, one cannot help but wonder: What is the literary function of such a tradition in the rabbinic community? As it is, this passage seems an almost Odyssean kind of reveling in the deception, and thus it accentuates and embraces the plundering with all its moral dubiousness and duplicity, perhaps in terms of divine providence and vengeance. These passages are unique in that they bind together the biblical claim of favor received with the behavior of the Israelites during the plague of darkness. These *midrashim* seek to explain the question arising from the biblical narrative, "Exactly how did God arrange the giving of favor to our ancestors?" The *midrash* does not seek to justify the despoliation in the face of the anti-Jewish or gnostic challenges but instead accentuates the trickery involved.

An Anti-Semitic History of Israel

The following *midrash*, which also embraces the moral problem, provides insight into the way in which the history of Israel may have been retold from the anti-Jewish perspective. The *haggadic midrash* is an expansion on Esth 3:9, "If it please the King, let it be written that they be destroyed." Here, Haman, their arch-enemy, tells Israel's story from his jaundiced and wrathful perspective. Jews are depicted as a haughty, ungrateful, and malevolent people who seek the destruction of other races.

> Take for instance poor Pharaoh. What did they do [to him] when they went down to Egypt? He received them with a hospitable attitude. He had the people settle in the best part of the land, and provided for them during the years of famine and fed them with the best food in the land. He had palaces to build and they were building there. With all this, he was unable [to gain their loyalty]. Not only that, but they came to him in trickery and they said to him, "We will go three day's journey to sacrifice to Adonai our God, and afterwards, we will return. If you please, loan us vessels of silver and gold and clothing." And so they loaned them their silver and gold and the nicest clothes they had. And every one of

them [the Israelites] loaded up as many donkeys as he had. There were more than one could count. The end result was that they plundered the Egyptians, as the Bible says, "And they plundered the Egyptians" (Exod 12:36). And when Pharaoh heard that they were fleeing, he went after them to retrieve his money.[5]

The trickery of Moses comes off as knavish fraud in Haman's letter. Pharaoh plays the role of tragic protagonist whose trust and helpfulness is sorely abused. This *midrash* makes explicit the deception involved in the request to offer sacrifices to God in the desert by the addition "and afterwards, we will return." The quantity of valuable items taken is grossly exaggerated. The Egyptians give all the gold, silver, and nice clothing they possess. The Israelites have donkeys without number fully loaded with loot. When Pharaoh realizes that the Israelites have ungratefully taken advantage of his good graces and that the slaves had no intention of returning with his valuables, he makes chase after them, not so much to re-enslave them, but to retrieve his stolen property!

What is remarkable about this passage is the force with which it presents the anti-Semitic version of the exodus. It, of course, fails to mention that Pharaoh enslaved the Israelites and compelled them to do hard labor under the worst of conditions, or that he murdered their firstborn sons. According to the version presented here, Pharaoh received the people warmly, settled them in the best part of the land and provided food for them in the time of famine, as if the Pharaoh of the Joseph story and the Pharaoh of the exodus were the same person. The Israelites were only asked to help him build a few palaces—hardly much to ask in return. Yet in the face of all his kindness they deceived him, took the Egyptians' money, and made escape. While this version of the story is not true to the biblical text, it is in fact much closer to the biblical version of the exodus than the scurrilous versions of the exodus collected by Josephus in *Against Apion*. There, Moses led a group of Egyptian lepers who had been expelled from Egypt, among other things, for the contagion they were spreading (*Ag. Ap.* 1.230–50).

This begs the question: What is the literary purpose for the construction of this version of the exodus in this context? In *Ag. Ap.*, Josephus preserves the slander in order to refute it and to defend his people. But there is no direct response to the version preserved here, though there hardly needed to be. Placing these traditions in the letter inspired by Haman is refutation enough. Perhaps the reader is expected to revel in their victory,

---

5. *Est. Rab.* 7:13.

morally dubious as it was, by thinking, "We got the best of them and they still haven't gotten over it."

Perhaps the purpose of this story is to offset the egregious nature of the crimes committed by the Jews against their enemies toward the end of the book of Esther. The description of the request to slaughter the Jews as a *minor matter* earlier in the letter may also play a role here. In other words, if the Persians under Haman's influence could consider the destruction of the Jews as a minor request, and if they could so convincingly and so deceptively manipulate their sacred story so as to put the Jews in such a bad light, the Jews were justified in taking the actions that are described at the end of the book of Esther. These traditions may have intended to present Jewish history in the worst light possible, to accentuate their enemies' anti-Jewish hatred, a hatred which was so malevolent as to justify the extreme measures taken.[6] If this is correct, the above text doesn't so much embrace the moral problem of the biblical story as it embraces the anti-Jewish version of the moral problem. It intends to make known the way in which their sacred story had been unfairly and malevolently manipulated. As such, it also minimizes the moral problem (category 2), not that of Exod 12:35–36, but the moral problem stemming from the horrific ending of the book of Esther. In any case, it is likely that this text does not preserve the gnostic position so much as that of anti-Semites in general, seeing that there is little interest here in proving the moral inferiority of the Hebrew God. The focus here is on the haughtiness and bellicosity of the Hebrew people.

TEXTS THAT MINIMIZE THE MORAL PROBLEM

The second grouping deals with texts that minimize the moral problem of the plundering of Egypt. These texts can be subdivided by their various claims: a) the plunder was fair wage or back-payment for slavery; b) Pharaoh was a fool and the despoliation was his just desserts; c) the treasures were not loans but gifts given free-and-clear; d) the plundering was an act of justified vengeance; e) there is no sense in being overly apologetic with nothing to apologize for; f) the treasures of Egypt were ours to begins with; and g) it all worked out in the end.

---

6. This explanation was suggested to me in a personal conversation with the late Dr. David Weisberg of Hebrew Union College—Jewish Institute of Religion.

The Plundering of Egypt

Backwages for Slaves?

The following texts fall into the first category: *Tanh* 4:8, *Gen. Rab.* 61:7, *b. Sanh* 91a. *Genesis Rabbah* will serve as representative. All texts place the debate about the plundering of the Egyptians in an imaginary legal context, as a case brought against the Jews by Egyptians for remuneration of the plundered treasures of Egypt. In this case, Alexander of Macedon is the judge, the Egyptians are the plaintiffs, and the Jews are the defendants.

> The Egyptians said, "We are making our claim against them on the basis of their own Torah." 600,000 men went up out of our land loaded up with vessels of silver and gold, as it is said, "and they plundered the Egyptians." Let them give to us our silver and our gold." Gebiah the son of Kosem said to him, "O King, 600,000 men worked for them 210 years, some of them were silversmiths and goldsmiths, who should receive as their wage a dinar per day." The mathematicians sat down and figured it out and they had not come to 100 years before the land of Egypt was found to be in forfeit, and so they left in disgrace.

The clothing is not mentioned as part of the plundered treasure. As we shall see, there are other *midrashim* in which the clothes are the most valuable items taken; here they seem not worthy of mention. Several competing elements of interest come to the fore. Tertullian (in *Against Marcion* 2.20:1–3) claims that Egyptians had by his time actually sought reparations from the Jews for the despoliation of Egypt. We thus have reason to believe that these texts may reflect such events. At least, Tertullian knew this tradition and saw it as an historical witness to events in the recent past. The whole event was set back in the period of Alexander as if to say, "This matter has already been handled definitely and authoritatively." Yet this argument could hardly have been taken seriously at all as an actual legal case. The Israelites were slaves, and slaves are not paid wages, much less back-wages according to either Greek or Roman law. No attempt is made to show that the Israelites were unjustly enslaved and thus deserving of back-wages. Watson draws attention to a passage in Pomponius Sextus (a prolific Roman lawyer of the second century AD) who states that even in a time of peace, a person who has been captured by the Romans becomes a slave if he or she was a member of a community that had no official ties or treaties of hospitality with Rome.[7] No such claim is here made. If this case was pre-

---

7. Watson, *Roman Slave Law*, 20.

sented in a court of Roman law, Gebiah would have come off very badly. In the Sanhedrin version, Gebiah tells the Sages, when he asks for permission to provide defense for the Jews, that if he is defeated they should say that they have merely defeated an ignorant man. In an actual court of law, this is exactly what would have transpired. For this reason, we must again assume that this tradition was meant for in-house consumption only.

Pharaoh Was a Fool

Tanḥ (Buber) *Beshallah* 4:8 (par. *Pesiq. Rab Kah.* 11:3) seeks to explain the triple punishment of Pharaoh (plagues, loss of treasures, loss of slaves) as the result of his own foolish obstinacy. A parable is told in which a king asks a servant to buy him a fish. The servant returns with a rotten fish. The king gives the servant his choice between three punishments: eat the fish, pay for it, or be flogged with one hundred lashes. The servant, because of his foolishness and obstinacy, ends up undergoing all three. The passage continues,

> So it was with Pharaoh. His enslavement of Israel in Egypt was excessive. The Holy One said to him (in Exod 5:1), "Let my people go." He said (in Exod 5:2), "I do not know the Lord." He brought ten plagues upon him, but he did not let them go. The Holy One said to him, "By your life, you have to give them compensation." Thus it is stated (in Exod 12:36), "And the LORD gave the people favor in the eyes of the Egyptians to give them loans. Thus they despoiled the Egyptians."[8]

The implication is that if Pharaoh had cooperated, one of these punishments should have been enough. But due to his stubbornness, he brought all three upon his head. As the text reads, it is possible that the goal of the passage is not to directly answer the gnostic problems related to the plunder of the Egyptians, but to answer a gnostic charge that God was excessive in his punishments of Pharaoh generally. Its interest in the plundering of the Egyptians is tangential. It is surprising that the image of the divine courtroom as the setting for the adjudication of the grievance was not used by the Rabbis to greater effect. It seems the logical way to shore up an otherwise weak case. And even with this in play, one cannot help but imagine that the gnostic would respond saying, "How is God justified to compensate past wrongs by being deceitful and committing fraud?"

---

8. Translation of J. Townsend, *Midrash Tankhuma*, 2:79–80.

The Plundering of Egypt

Bon Voyage Gifts

The general tradition that the Egyptians gave their gifts voluntarily—something on the order of bon voyage gifts to their departing friends—has a long history that first appears in Josephus *Ant.* 2:314.[9] In the rabbinic literature, this tradition takes many forms. Both *Mek.* (*Pischa* 13) and *Mek. Rab Simeon* (*Bo* 12:35–36) illustrate one variety.

> Rabbi (Judah the Prince) says, "What does the Scripture say about when they were living in Egypt? 'A woman shall ask of her neighbor and of her who is visiting in her home' (Exod 3:22), showing that they were visiting together with them. What does the Scripture say about them when they ceased from bondage? 'And each man asked from his friend' (11:2), showing that they were their friends. And concerning the time they were released from servitude, what does the Scripture say concerning them? 'And they asked them to take' (12:36). What they asked them to take, they [the Israelites] wouldn't touch, and they [the Egyptians] were insisting that they take the goods against their wishes, showing that they feared them as people tend to fear their masters. Also they were saying, 'Soon the people will see them in the desert and will say, "Look how rich these Egyptian slaves are!"'"[10]

The point is clear: the Egyptians were on very friendly terms with the Israelites. Their friendship turned into respect and awe as the plagues progressed. The passage goes on to describe how one Hebrew escapee would have been able to pay for the expenses of the tabernacle and its furnishings. This exaggeration emphasizes the friendship and respect the Egyptians had for the Israelites expressed in abundant gifts.

This *midrash* claims that there really was no despoliation; what was given was given free and clear. The Israelites only took the spoils when they were pressed even against their will (see also *b. Ber.* 9b below). Apart from this, the Egyptians had ulterior motives for their generosity: they wanted others to see just how wealthy their slaves were. Those who did would be inclined to draw the conclusion that the wealth of Egypt was vast. So not only were these gifts of good will and respect, they were given out of vanity. What we have here is a hodgepodge of motivations: friendship, fear, and vanity. But in all cases, the Israelites didn't ask and weren't interested; the Egyptians insisted on

---

9. See my chapter on Josephus in *The Despoliation of Egypt*.

10. My translation follows the Hebrew text of Epstein and Melammed, *Mekhilta d'Rabbi Shim'on*, 31.

giving (for whatever motivations) and thus Egypt was not plundered. There are several goals for these interpretations: to exonerate Israel, to remove any question of reparations, and to increase the glory of their ancestors in answer to the anti-Jewish traditions that defamed them.

In the rabbinic case being presented here, the freedom with which the Egyptians behaved is brought to the fore. The Egyptians acted freely and with their full volition and with enthusiasm such that they gave more than was asked. *The Mekhilta of Rabbi Ishmael* represents here a collection of traditions that provide various motivations for the enthusiasm with which the Egyptians gave their treasures. Again, while several motivations are presented, the free volition with which the Egyptians gave is the point.

The emphasis on the volitional gift-giving of the Egyptians may be a specific means of answering gnostic charges. This is not absolutely clear since there is no other clearly anti-gnostic element to the passage. But if we assume the passage as an anti-gnostic purpose, it is difficult to assess whether this argument could have been successful. An antagonist could simply respond: If the Egyptians gave their gifts freely, what does the text mean when it says that the Israelites *plundered* Egypt? Those who are plundered have not given up their goods freely! If this problem was solved by saying that the word *plundering* is hyperbole, and not to be taken literally, an effective apology might be made. If the Gentile interlocutors knew several answers we have discussed above, they could have played them off each other: How can the rabbis claim, on one hand, that the Egyptians brought their case to Alexander of Macedon to retrieve their plundered gold and silver, and then claim that the Egyptians gave that property freely? They appear to cancel each other out. These arguments seem to primarily be in-house and no such challenge would be expected. Also, this kind of juxtaposition of traditions would have been virtually impossible seeing they arise in different sources at different times. The point here is only that theoretically a knowledgeable gnostic might have made such a point.

An Act of Justified Vengeance

Surprisingly, there is only one text that places this spin on the story; *Exod. Rab.* 18:8–10.

> Israel spread out into all Egypt at that time, as Scripture says, "And the Israelites did what Moses required and asked for loans of the Egyptians." But Moses was occupied with the bones of Joseph, and

The Plundering of Egypt

with the vessels of the tabernacle which Jacob our father had prepared, and thus David said, "The righteous will rejoice when he sees vengeance." (Ps 58:11)

Kasher notes that a *midrash* in *Gen. Rab.* 94.4 stands behind this passage; Jacob had prophetically foreseen that the Israelites would build a tabernacle in the wilderness. When he went down to Egypt he brought the necessary trees for its construction, trees that Abraham had planted at Beer Sheba (Gen 21:33).[11]

So while Moses busied himself making plans for the tabernacle and collecting the bones of Joseph, the people spread through the land asking for treasures of the Egyptians. Since the preparations made by Moses for the tabernacle can have nothing to do with righteous vengeance of Ps 58, this *midrash* clearly understands the plundering of Egypt as righteous vengeance. The text cited would have been inappropriate and ineffective for direct confrontation with the gnostics, but may have been quite effective with the rabbinic students. A gnostic may have answered essentially with a *two wrongs don't make a right* response.

It Was Ours Anyway!

The following two *midrashim* come from a section of *b. Pesah* 119a that Neusner has called "a meandering composite."[12] I will follow his translation.

> Said R. Judah, "All the silver and gold in the world did Joseph collect and bring to Egypt: 'And Joseph gathered up all the money that was found in the land of Egypt and in the land of Canaan' (Gen 47:14). I know only about what was in the land of Egypt and in the land of Canaan. How do I know about that in other lands? Scripture says, 'And all the countries came to Egypt to Joseph to buy grain' (Gen 41:57). And when the Israelites went up from Egypt, they brought it up with them: 'and they despoiled the Egyptians.'" (Exod 12:36)[13]

The purpose and strategy of this *midrash* is hardly opaque; it intends to justify the despoliation by claiming that the gold and silver taken from Egypt originally belonged to Israel by associating the plunder of Egypt with

---

11. Kasher, *Biblical Interpretation*, 8:79.
12. Neusner, *The Talmud of Babylonia*, 90.
13. Ibid., 87.

Jewish Biblical Legends

the money collected by Joseph in the period of the famine. Not only was money taken from the land of Egypt and Canaan, but, based on Gen 41:57, R. Judah speculates that Joseph gathered all the silver and gold in the world. This dual strategy also glorifies their ancestors by magnifying the value of what was taken (all the world's silver and gold!). The *midrash* seems to assume that when the Israelites made their exit from Egypt with plundered Egyptian treasures, they were in fact only taking back what originally belonged to Joseph. Here is something on the order of, "The Egyptians took the money of the world from Joseph first; so we only received back what was originally ours."

If a detractor could have been convinced that this indeed was the case, it would go a long way toward justifying God and reducing the moral problem.

It All Worked Out in the Wash

The final means to be described here is essentially the claim that the subsequent plundering of Israel's treasures by the Egyptian army negates any need for compensation or apology. Chapter 41 of *Abot R. Nat.* expounds on *Abot* 4:17, which reads, "R. Simeon said, 'There are three crowns: the crown of the Torah, the crown of the Priesthood, and the crown of royalty; but the crown of a good name excels them all.'" Paragraph nine reads:

> Three things returned to their original place: Israel, Egypt's wealth, and the heavenly writing. Israel returned to their original place, as it is stated, *Your fathers dwelt of old time beyond the River* (Josh 24:2) and it is also stated, *And carried the people away into Babylon* (Ezra 5:12). Egypt's wealth returned to its original place (to Egypt) as it is stated, *And they despoiled Egypt* (Exod 12:36) . . . and it is also stated, *And it came to pass in the fifth year of king Rehoboam, that Shishak king of Egypt came up against Jerusalem; and he took away the treasures of the house of the Lord.* (1 Kgs 14:25f)[14]

It is possible that this *midrash* understands that Shishak took away the *very* vessels of gold and silver taken from Egypt, since the wilderness Tabernacle, the Temple's precursor, was believed to have been furnished with the gold and silver (and often bronze) taken from Egypt.[15] This being the case, the argument advanced is that the very vessels plundered from Egypt,

---

14. Translation of Cashdan, *The Minor Tractates*, 1:207.
15. Kugel, *The Bible as it Was,* 325, note 13. See also *Exod. Rab.* 18:18 above.

The Plundering of Egypt

by the providence of God, have already been returned to Egypt. While this approach doesn't exactly solve the moral problem directly, it resolves it in terms of outcome; God saw to it that the treasures of Egypt were returned. Especially if the Egyptians were seeking repayment for their lost valuables, this line of argumentation could have been effective. It would not, however, completely answer the original charges made by the gnostics and other anti-Jews concerning the morality of the biblical narrative.

B. Pesahim 119a carries this argument in a different direction by claiming that this treasure had no final value (like a pond without fish) since, after it was taken by Shishak from Rehoboam, it was stolen from Shishak by a minor potentate from whom the treasure was again stolen. A succession of robberies prevented the treasures of Egypt from having any real value. The treasures of Egypt made a journey around the world until they ended up in Rome. While both these interpretations take an "it all worked out in the wash" approach, the second seeks to further minimize the problem by emphasizing the ultimate worthlessness of the treasures taken. Perhaps by claiming that the treasures ended up in Rome, the midrashist is implying that the Romans are the ones who should pay back the riches originally stolen from Egypt! It is hard to imagine this was taken seriously; they would have been laughing up their sleeves if they had any. Both *midrashim* appear to have general anti-Jewish sentiment in focus and not gnosticism in particular. These texts might alleviate pressures put on Jews for reparation. They do not seek to answer the gnostic challenge per se; God still appears to have orchestrated fraud.

Virtue Out of Vice

The third grouping of texts seek to make a virtue out of a vice. This category is not always clearly distinguishable from the previous one, as both try to justify the past. My criterion for this distinction shall be as follows. The texts in this category justify the past by means of an interpretation of the story that highlights the virtue and honor in what transpired. In this way, virtue overshadows vice and the moral tension is assuaged. The texts can be sub-divided into five groupings; 1) texts that emphasize the amazing ability of the Hebrew people to keep a secret, 2) texts that emphasize the ability of the Hebrew people to order their priorities rightly in relation to the items taken in the plunder, 3) a single text that highlights the positive outcome of the Egyptian plunder, 4) texts that claim that the plundering of Egypt was to bring about the destruction of Egyptian idols, and 5) the claim that the plundering was necessary as a fulfillment of the promise made to Abraham in Gen 15:14.

Keeping the Secret Secret

In this first category we find the following: *Mek.* (*Pesiqta* 5), *Lev. Rab.* 32:5, *Num. Rab.* 20:22, and *Cant. Rab.* IV 12:1. All transmit a very similar tradition, although in two cases the words are attributed to R. Huna in the name of Bar Kappara (*Lev. Rab.* and *Cant. Rab.*) and in one case the tradition is attributed to our rabbis (*Num. Rab.*). Also, *Num. Rab.* cites Exod 3:22 while the other two cite Exod 11:2. The saying of R. Huna from *Cant. Rab.* will suffice.

> R. Huna in the name of R. Kappara says, "Israel was redeemed from Egypt on account of their merit in four cases; they did not change their names, they did not change language, they did not engage in gossip, and none of them was unrestrained in terms of sexual promiscuity.[16] They did not change their names; since Reuben and Simeon went down (to Egypt) and Reuben and Simeon came up (from Egypt). They didn't call Reuben Rufus and they didn't call Simeon Julian or Joseph Listis, or Benjamin Alexander. They also didn't change their language, since elsewhere it is written, 'One who had escaped came and told Abram the Hebrew...' (Gen 14:13). And in this other text it is written, 'The God of the Israelites appeared to us...' (Exod 5:3). It is also written, 'For it is my mouth that is addressing you' (Gen 45:12) in the Holy Language. And they didn't gossip, as Scriptures says, 'Speak now in the ears of the people that everyone should inquire of his friend...' (Exod 11:2). One finds that this matter was revealed to them twelve months previous, yet there was not found among them one who made it known to his companion. And there was not found among them one person unrestrained in their sexuality, as it says, 'And a son of an Israelite woman went out... and the son of the Israelite woman blasphemed' (Lev 24:10), which points out the superiority of the Israelites, for there was not found among them (any immoral persons) but this one, and the Scriptures divulges her."

It is fascinating to consider that the very passage that was used by some as the centerpiece of the case for the moral inferiority of the Jews and

---

16. Literally: *unrestrained in terms of their sexual organs*.

The Plundering of Egypt

their God is found here to be proof of the opposite. In fact, it was the ability of the Israelites to keep a secret concerning their plan—to ask for loans and escape into the desert with borrowed goods—that won them favor with God. God saw fit to redeem them from their bondage because all of them resisted the urge to divulge the secret for twelve months, even though presumably there would have been financial incentive to do so.

Clearly, the Rabbis read the passages very carefully, seeking to creatively find the virtue in the putative vice. The twelve months arise from the notion that the period of the plagues lasted about a year. If God told Moses to announce to the people that they were going to plunder Egypt in Exod 3, before the plagues began, and the plundering eventuated in Exod 12, then the people kept this a secret for at least a whole year. If any one of them had been unable to control their tongue, the plan would have failed—the Egyptians would have been ready for them, and would not have loaned them anything. God's reason for telling them of the plan in advance was a test of their ability to keep a secret, a test which they passed with flying colors.

This interpretation goes against the grain of the biblical text; Moses commanded the Israelites to ask for Egyptian treasures only in Exod 11:2, which takes place just before the first Passover and the last plague. This would only be days before the exodus, not a year before. Moses, according to the biblical text, didn't apprise the people of the plan until the eve of the last plague. When we come to Exod 11, the people still haven't been commanded to ask for loans and Moses needed to be reminded by God to get on with the plan. We see that the rabbis are hard pressed to make their case here and play loose-and-free with the biblical story by implying that Moses divulged the plan before the Bible says that he did.

Interestingly, this interpretation also demands that the Egyptian plunder was loaned, not given. They were to ask for treasures on loan and then were to make their way to freedom. If the goods taken were to be given voluntarily, there would be no need for such secrecy. Again, we see a line of argument that would not play well with the gnostics or other anti-Semites. Their detractors could too easily point out that the storyline of the biblical narrative does not support the rabbis' view, and that the ability to keep secret a plan of great deception and despoliation is hardly a mark of moral superiority. This tactic would also have been unhelpful with anti-Semites generally; it clearly is intended for the synagogue insider.

Jewish Biblical Legends

The Clothes Are Worth Most!

Two texts fall into this category; *Gen. Rab.* 60:11, and *Exod. Rab.* 3:11. *Exodus Rabbah* will provide our representative sample.

> The biblical citation "And every woman shall ask from her neighbor and guests vessels of silver and gold and clothing" shows that the clothing was the more valuable to them, for at the time that a man goes out on the road, if he doesn't have proper clothing, he is put to shame. "And you will plunder (*nizzaltem*) the Egyptians"; Egypt in the future will be like a fishpond (*metzulah*) in which there are no fish.

The point of this passage is that since clothing is mentioned last, it is considered the most valuable. Of all the items taken in the plundering, the clothing was the most valuable because it was needed for their journey. We noted above some texts that do not find the clothing to be worth mentioning at all. Yet here, the Israelites cannot be faulted because the clothing they took was needed for the journey. This was their primary aim and that the clothes were the most important to them is proved in that they are listed last in the biblical text. The biblical description of the plundering shows the virtue and prudence of the Hebrew people; they were able to rightly order their priorities.

Typically, in a list, things mentioned first are the most important, but under certain circumstances this can be reversed. In this instance, the latter is the case: the clothes are most important because they were necessary for their trip across the desert. The gold and the silver were niceties that could have been done without. The general strategy seems here to be to assert that the Israelites did not plunder the Egyptians out of a desire to rob them of their precious metals. They were primarily interested in getting the clothing they needed to survive in the desert. The silver and gold were not very important to them, but were "icing on the cake" so to speak.

This text does more than deny that they plundered Egypt for the love of riches. It seems to imply that they were the more honorable because they listed clothing last, proving that they valued clothes the most. Such an argument would have done little more than make the gnostics roll their eyes with dismay. Again, it has little value except when preaching to the choir.

The final sentence plays on the linguistic connection between "plunder" (*nizzaltem*) and "fishpond" (*mezulah*—cf. the tradition in *b. Pes.* 119a). The point seems to be that all of Egypt's valuables in the future will

The Plundering of Egypt

be completely destroyed, making it a worthless place—a fishpond without fish. It appears to announce retribution upon Egypt for their cruelty to their Hebrew slaves; all their wealth will be stripped away.

Chasing the Spoil

In *Song Rab.* 1:26 we encounter the ethical opposite of the above. This passage is a saying of R. Azariah that seeks to explain the meaning of the biblical citation, "Draw me after you, let us run" (Song 1:4). It is understood in this context as, "Draw me, we will run after you." The passage is rendered as follows.

> R. Azariah says, "The community of Israel said to the Holy One, Blessed be He, Sovereign of the Universe, 'On account of the fact that you have given to me the spoil of my neighbors, we will run after you.' For as Scripture says, 'Each woman shall ask of her neighbor' (Exod 3:23). [For the sake of] the spoils of Egypt and the spoils of Sihon and Og and the spoils of the thirty one kings, we will run after you."

This is an "ends justifies the means" explanation. In the rabbinic interpretation, the words "after you" are construed with what follows, rather than what precedes. In its biblical context, the words are spoken between two lovers; "draw me after you, let's run away." In the rabbinic context, the plural "let's run away" refers to the community of Israel running after God, not two lovers running together; thus, "we [the community] will run after you."

In this interpretation, the plunder and the profit gained in divine service is that which motivates Israel to pursue God, to run after him rather than the other gods. Since, in the rabbinic worldview, this is the highest good and the merit by which the world is sustained, all else is justified; the end justifies the means. The world is sustained by Israel's pursuit of God, which comes as a result of God's giving them the plunder of their neighbors. The community of Israel did plunder Egypt for the love of riches but this very love spurred them on in their love of God who gave the riches, and thus it motivated the keeping of the commands. The plundering of Egypt is justified when one sees the greater perspective and the ultimate good that came from a relative evil.

We may again have a case in which this argument functioned as a subpoint in a complex argument. If, for instance, the Egyptians were motivated by the Holy Spirit such that they gave most freely, and even gave more than what the Israelites asked for, these gifts could have spurred the Israelites on to pursue their God and to observe his statutes. Taken in such a dosage, the Jewish detractors could possibly have been effectively answered. But on its own, this argument would have failed to meet the gnostic and/or anti-Semitic challenge and there is no clear evidence that these traditions functioned together in such a fashion.

Destroying the Idols

Only one text makes the following claim: "'And they despoiled the Egyptians' shows that their idols melted and ceased to exist [as idols] and returned to their initial state."[17] This passage seems to be reading the verb *natzal*, which normally is translated "despoil," to mean "destroy," which is a rarer but possible meaning. If this is indeed the way the *midrash* is reading the text, the Israelites didn't plunder Egypt to acquire Egyptian gold but to destroy that which was idolatrous in Egypt. The terms "vessels of gold and silver" in the Bible does not necessarily refer to idolatrous items, but here in this *midrash* they are taken to at least include idols or idolatrous paraphernalia. Again, we have here an attempt to justify the Israelites' actions by turning vice into virtue; the plundering of Egypt took place to destroy Egyptian idols, not to acquire wealth. However, we again are dealing here with an argument aimed at their own disciples since such a tack would have come off as tactless to the typical pagan or gnostic.

Promise to Abraham Fulfilled

The Hebrew reluctance to take the treasures of Egypt is also present in *b. Ber.* 9b, where it is emphasized that the Israelites did not want to borrow from the Egyptians and that they were satisfied with their freedom only. Here the Israelites took but never asked for Egyptian treasures. They simply did not care for riches but God insists that they ask for Egyptian treasures so that Abraham would not be able to complain that the promise made to him went unfulfilled (Gen 15:14). The plundering of the Egyptians was necessary as a fulfillment of God's promise to Abraham. Beginning with the Exod 3:21 (And I will give this people favor . . .) it continues in the divine voice.

---

17. *Mek.* (Pesiqta 13).

I said to Abraham, "And after this, they will come forth with great possessions" (Gen 15:14). In the future I will cause them to be in favor with the Egyptians, so that they will make loans to them and they come away fully loaded, in order that Abraham would have no excuse to say, "The saying, 'They will serve them and oppress them' was fulfilled in their case, but the statement 'and after this, they will come out with great possessions' was not fulfilled."[18]

This argument aims to point out that God was keeping the divine promise to Abraham concerning the despoliation of Egypt. Promise-keeping, in itself, is a moral virtue, in spite of the problems relating to how this promise was kept. On its own this tactic would not hold much sway for the gnostics as they could too easily point out that to keep a promise by defrauding someone else is still reprehensible. God's goodness is exactly the point that the gnostics were questioning, and this argument does not fully account for the problems being raised. Again, we are dealing with in-house arguments that are not designed for the rough-and-tumble challenges that might be made by skeptics and gnostics.

Forced to Say "Sorry"

Another text that seeks to minimize the moral problem is *Exod. Rab.* 21:5.

> So what is the meaning of, "And Pharaoh drew near" (Exod 14:10), but that he brought Israel to (the point of) repentance, which they did. R. Berekiah said, "Pharaoh's attack on Israel was more efficacious [for Israel] than one hundred fasts and prayers. Why? Because when they pursued after them and they (the Israelites) saw them, they were terribly frightened, and they looked for help from on high, and they made repentance, and prayed. As Scripture says, 'So the children of Israel cried out to God' (Exod 14:10). The Israelites said to Moses, 'What have you done to us? Now they are coming after us and are going to do to us all that we have done to them. For we killed their firstborn and we took their money and ran. Didn't you tell us, "And a woman should borrow from her neighbor" and so on?'" (Exod 3:23 or 11:2).[19]

This *midrash* continues telling that after their attempt to blame Moses for their difficulties ("Didn't you tell us?") Israel cried out to the Lord in

---

18. *Exod. Rab.* 3:11.
19. *Exod. Rab.* 21:5.

prayer and repentance, which was God's purpose for allowing the whole event. When the passage reaches its climax, Exod 14:10 is repeated with the point that Israel had repented fully. Thus, Exod 14:10 both introduces and concludes this *midrash*.

In the *midrash*, the words "we killed their firstborn and we took their money and ran" are not a confession or repentance mentioned by R. Berekiah in the previous sentence, but a response of fear, anger, and unbelief. As the passage is structured, as is not uncommon in rabbinic literature, the first point (R. Berekiah's claim) telescopes the point of the fuller narrative that follows. The main point of the passage is that God used the Egyptian advance to cause Israel to cry out in prayer even though their initial attitude had been fear, anger, and self-pity ("we killed their firstborn," etc.). As such, the text seems to seek to minimize the moral problem by suggesting that the despoliation of Egypt led up to Israel's repentance (under duress but repentance just the same) and this brings a good end to a questionable beginning. This passage is perplexing in that, not only do the Israelites admit that they plundered the Egyptians (which they did at God's command through Moses), but they also claim to have killed the Egyptian firstborn, something for which they were not directly responsible. In any case, the advancement of the Egyptian army is that which moved them from fear and self-pity to repentance.

The focus of the context, before and after, is clearly upon God's desire to hear Israel repent. God allowed Pharaoh to advance upon Israel because God desired that they cry out to him. In the biblical text, Israel cries to God due to fear (Exod 14:10), which is expressed in anger at Moses (vv. 11–12). The *midrash*, in its elaboration and dramatization of the narrative, transforms verse 10 into a pious cry of repentance and confession of sin. But why this particular charge against Moses? Why does the *midrash* have the Israelites claim, even in fear and anger, that Moses made them kill the firstborn of Egypt along with the plundering of Egypt? On one level, this is simply rhetorical hyperbole meant to account for Egypt's angry pursuit. It constitutes simply a mindless lashing-out against Moses due to excessive fear. Yet one cannot help wonder why these particular admissions were made when at least one of them (death of Egypt's firstborn) goes against the grain of the biblical narrative.

In the first case, there is no biblical warrant at all since it was the angel of death that did the killing. The Israelites were specifically *not* involved in the death of the Egyptian firstborn but were in their homes celebrating the

The Plundering of Egypt

first *Pesach*. This admission "we killed the Egyptian firstborn and stole their money" is interesting in that it yokes together that which is a possible biblical meaning (our ancestors left Egypt with borrowed items) to what cannot be accepted on the biblical level (they did not kill the Egyptian firstborn). In both cases, what is admitted here is done under duress caused by the approach of an enemy. The implication may be that, due to external pressures, we can be pressured into admitting guilt falsely. We should, in fact, cry out to God, for he longs to hear our voice.

CONCLUDING THOUGHTS AND OBSERVATIONS

It is rather obvious from the start that the *midrashim* above do not appear to have been suitable for use outside the walls of the *beth midrash*. However, even in the case of the *midrashim* that do seek to minimize the moral problem, the degree to which these *midrashic* endeavors seem, by and large, to be addressed to the community of faith and not to the anti-Semitic/gnostic challengers is noteworthy.

I have argued elsewhere that among the Christian interpreters, Irenaeus and Tertullian design their arguments to be used in a public context as is the case with Philo and Josephus.[20] The "fair wages" theory was known outside the rabbinic *beth midrash* since Philo and Tertullian not only made use of it but expanded upon it. But, as we have seen, even here one suspects that that tradition originally came into being with the spiritual needs of the rabbinic disciples in view. A skeptical listener could have asked, "How is it that slaves can expect wages in the first place?" It is this question Philo and Tertullian had to answer; they explain in legal terms how the Israelites had been unjustly enslaved and thus worthy of remuneration. Josephus speaks of the plundering of the Egyptians in terms of *bon voyage* gifts and rewrote the whole story from the start so there was absolutely no deception involved; that is, he eliminates the plea for time off to offer sacrifice in the wilderness. The Josephan Moses demands complete manumission from the start. Re-written in those terms, *bon voyage* gifts make sense.

But in the rabbinic literature, there is no version of the story that could be used as a full explanation and justification of events. The fact that the preponderance of the arguments put forth by the rabbis are directed toward the *beth midrash* leads one to suspect that the moral challenges related to

---

20. See my *The Despoliation of Egypt* for interpretations of Philo, Josephus, Irenaeus, and Tertullian.

Jewish Biblical Legends

the biblical texts had a real disconcerting effect on the typical rabbinical student. Meeting these challenges was their main concern. These charges were ones that compelled the rabbinic masters to put their creative genius into high gear so as to arrive at spiritually satisfying solutions. Their concern was not to win converts or respond publicly to their detractors so much as to answer questions that arose among their disciples. To be even more cautious, it must be pointed out that these passages never make any specific reference to the gnostics. It may well be that rabbis are answering in-house concerns about general anti-Jewish attitudes with these interpretations. This may also account for the fact that there has not been developed any cohesive answer to the moral problems raised by the biblical text.

However, by providing clusters of interpretive possibilities, it is perhaps expected by the rabbinic community that those who are in direct contact with Jewish detractors would choose from the buffet of options and weave together several options into a new whole. I have shown elsewhere that Philo applies a similar maneuver in *Moses* 1:140–42, where he combines a legally nuanced fair-wage defense with a despoliation of defeated enemy argument.[21] One could argue the following: God fulfilled his promise to Abraham—that he would bring him out of Egypt with great possessions—by using the foolishness and hardheartedness of Pharaoh, who set up both himself and his people for judgment. Through their own greed, the Egyptians took what had originally belonged to Joseph for themselves and unjustly enslaved and oppressed the Hebrew people. God orchestrated events by giving the children of Israel great favor in the eyes of the Egyptians so that the Egyptians gave their treasures willingly and in superabundance. This constituted a fair and decent wage for all the Israelites' years of unjust enslavement. While it did involve trickery, it eventuated in a justifiable vengeance and the return of goods to their original owners.

Biblical Justification

How did the author(s) of Exodus understand the moral justification of the despoliation of Egypt? A central feature of the exodus narrative is the clarification of Yahweh's nature and character, in contradistinction to the gods of Egypt. The question of the character and nature of God becomes particularly manifest in Pharaoh's proud question, "Who is Yahweh?" (Exod 5:2).

21. See my *The Despoliation of Egypt*. Chapter 6 deals with Philo's literal interpretation (beginning on page 91).

The Plundering of Egypt

The story from that point develops so as to answer that question, and to make the Lord known, not only to the Hebrews (6:3, 7; 10:2) but to Pharaoh and the Egyptians (7:5; 8:10, 22; 9:14, 29; 11:7; 14:4, 18) and eventually to all the peoples of the earth (15:14–15; 18:8–12). In Gen 15:13–14 Egypt is to be punished for its enslavement and mistreatment of the Hebrews. But Exodus itself does not strongly emphasize the plagues as punishment for Pharaoh's sins. Words for sin are strangely missing from Exod 1–15 (only 9:27 and 10:16ff, used by Pharaoh himself, not in judgment against him).[22]

God's purpose for the plagues is most clearly identified in 9:14–16 in words to be spoken to Pharaoh himself.

> 14 For this time I will send all My plagues upon your person, and your courtiers, and your people, *in order that* you may know that there is none like Me in all the world. 15 I could have stretched forth my hand and stricken you and your people with pestilence, and you would have been effaced from the earth. 16 Nevertheless I have spared you for this purpose: *in order to* show you My power, and *in order that* My fame may resound throughout the world. (NJPS)

The three purpose clauses heighten the rhetorical force of the passage in the narrative flow. The point of all the suffering and pestilence brought by God upon Egypt is identified in three positive statements: "that you may know that there is none like me in all the earth," "to show you my power," and "so that my fame may resound throughout the world." God is in a showdown with Pharaoh to determine who is most powerful in the world. By displaying God's power, God will prove that there is no similar deity in the whole world.

Gowan points out that the use of the word "know" is associated with the words "wonders" and "signs." *Wonders* are mighty and awe-inspiring acts or miracles. *Signs* are events that are intended to convey information of some kind about God.[23] In Exod 10:1ff the nexus of "signs" and "knowing" results from the hardening of Pharaoh's heart. Pharaoh's heart and the hearts of his servants are hardened to provide opportunity for God to provide signs in Egypt so that the knowledge of God may become unavoidable to their land. Pharaoh is the learner in 9:14 and Israel in 10:2. The purpose of the hardening of Pharaoh's heart and the resulting plagues ceases to be judgment and increasingly becomes salvation through the knowledge and glory of God.[24]

---

22. The situation is slightly more complex than explained here. See Gowan, *Theology of Exodus*, 133.

23. see *TDOT* 1:167–88.

24. Gowan, *Theology of Exodus*, 134.

Jewish Biblical Legends

The destruction of the Egyptian army at the sea is explicitly tied to this purpose in Exod 14:4, 17. In chapters 5–15 the words for oppression and suffering do not occur at all, yet the verb "know," with either the Egyptians or Israel as the subject, is the thread that holds the whole account together. Gowan says,

> When Moses and Aaron first encounter the pharaoh with their request that the Hebrews be permitted to go into the wilderness to sacrifice, the king's scornful answer is, "Who is Yahweh, that I should heed his voice and let Israel go? *I do not know Yahweh*, and moreover I will not let Israel go" (5:2). The rest of the story, through 14:18, tells how God remedied that deficiency.[25]

The signs are thus intended to be revelation to both Israel and Egypt. This knowledge is more than intellectual apprehension of a fact, but includes adoration and orientation toward the one who makes the claim.[26] Thus Israel understood the hardening of Pharaoh's heart and the resulting plagues of its exodus as a show of power and sovereignty to provide an unavoidable opportunity for Egypt to know Yahweh as the true God worthy of worship.

The despoliation, in this interpretive context, takes on new shades of meaning that move toward justification. The purpose of all the tragedies experienced by Egypt was not to humiliate and punish the Egyptians. God's purpose was to make God's name and identity known, not only to Israel but in Egypt and the rest of the world. This can only be accomplished with acts that make God's absolute sovereignty unavoidable. From the vantage point of the biblical writer, this is their salvation. Complete and overwhelming victory was necessary to humble Pharaoh and his proud nation to confess Yahweh as God. The plundering of Egypt is the final evidence of the utter defeat of the Egyptians. As Childs has it, "The Israelites do not slink out of the country, but go as a victorious army who has plundered their oppressors."[27] As the victorious army left with Egyptian goods, the Egyptians could do nothing but conclude that Yahweh was God, and their deities were not.[28]

---

25. Ibid.
26. Ibid., 137.
27. Childs, *The Book of Exodus*, 201.
28. This motif could be called a "severe mercy" (to borrow a phrase used by C. S. Lewis).

8

At the Sea and Beyond

BICKERING AT THE RED SEA

"And the Lord said to Moses, 'Why are you crying out to me?'" (Exod 14:15).

As the children of Israel prepare to pass through the Red Sea, the rabbis tell of a disagreement that broke out between the tribes of Israel as to which of them would be able to pass through first. In one version, the tribe of Benjamin springs forward and rushes to pass through first. This is why the tribe of Benjamin was honored by having the temple later situated that tiny stretch of land. While the wrangling continued, Moses was standing and praying at some distance away.

> So the Holy One said to him, "My beloved are on the verge of drowning in the sea, and you spin out lengthy prayers before me." Moses spoke up to God, "But Master of the universe, what else can I do?" God replied, "Speak unto the children of Israel, that they go forward. And lift up thy rod," etc. (Exod 14:16).[1]

This passage is full of humor and enjoyment. Rabbis are playing with Scripture again. While Scripture is a profound holiness to them, it is also

---

1. *Exod. Rab.* 21:8. In chapters 8 and 9, I have presented not translations but spot-checked paraphrases based on various English translations.

their friend and we laugh with friends. What is so funny to them? They find it humorous that God asks Moses, "Why do you cry out to me?" (Exod 14:15a). It seems like Moses is making lengthy prayers and God needs to tell him to attend to tasks at hand. It is also humorous that God had to tell Moses to tell the people of Israel to head out into the sea. You would think the people would have headed out immediately with no coaxing and that Moses would not have had to be coaxed to get them moving.

Why would God have had to tell people to do what is so obvious? God had to spurn them forward because they were preoccupied arguing over who gets to go first. Some were even throwing stones at others who were trying to get down to the water. And all the while, Moses was having a lengthy prayer meeting off to the side. So God brings order to the chaos and enlightenment to the reader. While the biblical text depicts Moses as praying when he should be acting, the rabbis expand the narrative to make the point—there is a time for prayer and there is a time for action. This was not the former.

JUDGMENT AND MERCY AT THE RED SEA

"Then the Lord said to Moses, 'Stretch out your hand over the sea'" (Exod 14:26).

When God was about to send the waters of the Red Sea down on the armies of the Egyptians, the rabbis imagine that an angelic prince of Egypt went before the Lord to plead their case. "You created the world by the measure of mercy. Why then do you wish to down my children?" The Lord calls a heavenly court to adjudicate and sends Gabriel down to gather evidence. Gabriel exposes a dead Hebrew infant killed by the Egyptians saying, "Master of the universe, thus did the Egyptians enslave your children." The Lord then acted with justice and drowned the Egyptians in the sea.

> That instant the ministering angels longed to sing before the Holy One but He rebuked them, saying, "The works of my hands are drowning in the sea, and you would sing in my presence!"[2]

This legend looks at the drowning at the sea from two angles. On one hand, the Egyptians had brought great grief to the children of Israel through their harsh enslavement. The rabbis want to see the destruction at the sea as justifiable punishment; it accords with the laws of just

---

2. *b. Sanh.* 39b.

retribution: an Egyptian for every Hebrew child. However, it is still a tragedy and not something to be happy about. All angelic rejoicing is put to a quick end. It is worth pointing out that the book of Exodus itself does not emphasize the plagues as divine punishment on Egypt but as a severe mercy intended to deliver even the Egyptians from their own spiritual blindness (see Exod 9:14).[3]

Attitudes toward the Egyptians vacillate between understanding (the above) and vindictive fury, as is seen in the following tradition. This tradition imagines the scene at the Red Sea after the Egyptian soldiers' bodies have washed ashore.

> "Israel saw the Egyptians dead" (Exod 14:30). What did the children of Israel do to them? Each man in Israel took his dog, went down, and, placing his foot upon an Egyptian's neck, said to his dog, "Eat of this hand, which used me as a slave. Eat of these bowels, which had no mercy on me."[4]

We've encountered many humorous texts heretofore, but there is certainly no laughing here. This is *schadenfruede* pure and simple; it is unsettling from the perspective of our modern moral sensitivities. Readers from the ancient world have no such qualms about expressing hatred and revenge. Of course, if our immediate ancestors had been cruelly enslaved for hundreds of years, we might have similar feelings. Texts like this would have been understood as celebrations of justice; the vindication of the oppressed and the demotion of the arrogant tyrants.

This tradition is one that perceives the plunder that might have occurred at the Red Sea. So great was this plunder that the Israelites didn't want to leave the region.

> "And Moses made Israel move on from the Red Sea" (Exod 15:22). He had to force them to move on against their will because they were not ready to leave the shore. Why not? When Israel left Egypt, Pharaoh, together with all those hosts, set out to pursue them. What else did he do? As he set out in pursuit of Israel with his chariots and horsemen, he had all the horses beautified with precious stones and pearls. When they reached the sea and the Holy One drowned them, all these precious stones and pearls floated on the surface and were thrown upon shore, so that every day Israelites would come down and gather them.

---

3. For more on this, see the section of chapter 7 called "Biblical Justification."
4. *Midr. Psalms* 22:1.

> That is why they did not wish to move from there. Moses, seeing this, said, "Do you think that the sea will continue to bring up precious stones and pearls for you every day?" So, against their will, Moses had them move on.[5]

On a biblical level, this passage flows from Exod 15:22; the NJPS translation has it, "Then Moses caused Israel to set out . . ." Why so reluctant to leave? They were gathering precious stones from the shore. The passage seeks to exalt even further the glorious manner in which the exodus brought benefit to their ancestors and provided the provisions needed to construct the tabernacle.

VINE OUT OF EGYPT

"Then Moses and the Israelites sang this song,'I will sing unto the Lord, for he has triumphed gloriously'" (Exod 15:1).

Rabbis spent a lot of time pondering their special status as a slave-people, specially chosen by God to be bearers of Torah. When they read in the Scriptures of a lily among thorns (Song 2:2), they were reading of themselves; *they* were a lily among thorns. One interpretation of this is found in *Exodus Rabbah*.

> "You picked a vine out of Egypt" (Ps 80:9). R. Tanhuma bar Abba asked, "Why is Israel compared to a vine? Think of what owners of a vine, seeking to improve it, do. They pluck it from its place and replant it where it flourishes. So too, when the Holy One wished to make Israel known throughout the world, what did He do? He took them out of Egypt and brought them into the wilderness, and there they began to thrive. There they received the Torah and their name went throughout the world."[6]

While such an interpretation may strike the reader as self-aggrandizement, passages such as this play an important role in the development of a community ethos necessary for survival. The rest of the world, much of it Christian, was convinced that Jews had no continuing value because of their rejection of Christ. In a typically hostile world, the rabbis were adept at reminding themselves and their communities of God's special love for

---

5. Tanhuma, *Be-shallah*, 16.
6. *Exod. Rab.* 44:1.

At the Sea and Beyond

them in spite of appearances. The remarkable survival and prosperity of the Jewish people, in spite of all adversity, is in part due to the fortitude engendered by traditions such as this one.

THE BREAD OF ANGELS

"The manna was like coriander seed and looked like resin" (Num 11:7).

Rabbis told many stories about the manna, some of which were outlandish. According to one, manna tasted differently to different people: like bread to the young, honey to the old, and oil to the infants. In another, righteous persons were said to gather manna as baked bread, ordinary Israelites as unbaked dough, and the wicked as grain yet to be ground into flour. Each interpretation was based on hints in the text.

> "And the taste of it was the taste of a cake (*leshad*) baked with oil" (Num. 11:8). R. Abbahu said: [Read not *leshad*, "cake," but *shad*, "breast"]. Hence, just as an infant, whenever he touches the breast, finds many flavors in it, so it was with manna. Whenever Israel ate it, they found many flavors in it. Some read *leshad* as *le-shed*, "of a demon." Even as the demon changes himself into many shapes, so manna changed into many flavors.[7]

Apparently, it was believed that a mother's breast milk tasted differently and had various flavors. The Hebrew text didn't have definite vowel-pointing at this time; this was added by later scribes. As a result, the text can be imagined with different vowels as we see above. One cannot help but wonder if rabbis thought about how people could possibly eat and enjoy the same food for the whole forty years of wilderness wandering. Wouldn't anyone become completely disgusted with manna after time? Not if it changed flavors like breast milk!

---

7. *b. Yoma* 75a; Braude, *Book of Legends*, 76.

9

Moses, Torah, and Sinai

THE LAW AT SINAI

"And God spoke all these words . . ." (Exod 20:1).

Rabbis grappled with narrative questions that would never trouble contemporary readers—Jewish or Christian. For instance, in the following, rabbis wondered why the law was not given to Moses immediately upon the exit from Egypt? If the Torah is such a precious and necessary gift, why make the children of Israel wait until they arrived at Sinai? Their answer was they needed time to recover from the rigors of Egyptian slavery.

> R. Isaac said, "The Israelites were worthy of receiving the Torah immediately upon leaving Egypt. But the Holy One said, 'Because of their enslavement making clay into bricks, my children's healthful appearance has not yet returned and therefore they cannot receive the Torah yet.' God's delay in giving the Torah is like this story of a king's son who had just got up from his sickbed. His tutor said, 'Let your boy go back to school.' The king replied, 'My son still does not look healthy and yet you say that I should let him go back to school? Let my son be indulged for two or three

Moses, Torah, and Sinai

months with good food and drink, so that he may regain his ruddy appearance. Then he can go back to school.' Likewise, the Holy One said, 'My children's healthful appearance has not yet returned. They have just been released from hard labor with clay and bricks. Shall I give them the Torah now? Let my children take it easy for two or three months. They will have manna, water and quail to eat. Then I will give them the Torah.'"[1]

This whole question would probably not trouble a modern reader. If someone did think of it, it would seem that God was simply waiting for the people to make their way down to the holy mountain where God earlier promised they would meet after the exodus (Exod 3:12). But this reason hardly suffices for the rabbis. Why not promise to give the law sooner? If the Torah is as critical and life-giving a gift as all that, like medicine it should be administered as soon as possible. So why the wait? Because God, as a loving parent, wanted his children to have time to fully recover from the rigors of slavery so they would be rested up and able to enjoy the law in its fullness and have the energy needed for their study of it.

A FIERY LAW

"The Lord came from Sinai . . ." (Deut 33:2).

Rabbis pondered the question, "Why were we chosen of God to receive the gift of Torah?" By giving Israel the Torah, God definitively proved the great import of their being chosen; they were to be bearers of and witnesses to God's instructional pathway called "Torah." The question more specifically was, "Why did God choose to give Torah to Israel as opposed to all the other nations of the world?" Because, they supposed, God tried to give Torah to other nations but they rejected it.

The biblical text used to warrant this claim was Deut 33:2, which the rabbis translated, "The Lord came unto Sinai having risen at Seir unto the people there, then having shined forth at Mount Paran, He came unto the holy myriads with a fiery law[2] in his right hand for them." The verse was understood as describing the Lord moving from Seir to Mt. Paran and finally approaching the holy myriads (Israel) at Mt. Sinai. Seir was located in

---

1. *Eccl. Rab.* 3:11.

2. NJPS translates the word *dat* as lightning. But the word commonly means "decree," which rabbis see as the Torah (here "law") to be given to Moses.

Jewish Biblical Legends

Edom and Edomites were thought to be descendants of Esau. Paran in the Arabah region of southern Israel was understood to refer to Ishmael and thus the Arabs. In rabbinic reading, this text describes the Lord, with his holy law in hand, approaching other nations to see if they would accept the Torah before he approached Israel with it.

> When He who is omnipresent revealed Himself to give the Torah to Israel, He revealed Himself not only to Israel but to all the other nations as well. At first God went to the descendants of Esau. He asked them, "Will you accept the Torah?" They asked in insolence, "What is written in it?" He replied, "Thou shalt not murder." They said, "Master of the universe, this goes against our nature. Our father, of whom it was said 'these hands are the hands of Esau' (Gen 27:22), taught us to rely only on the sword, because his father told him, 'By your sword you will live'" (Gen 27:40).[3]

Esau came to be associated with Rome in rabbinic imagination due in part to the systematic brutality of the Roman empire, which was prefigure in the sword by which Esau was said to have lived. Rome, like Esau, was by nature a murderer who lives by the sword. The *haggadah* goes on to imagine the Lord approaching the children of Ammon and Moab and making the same offer. They likewise asked, "What does the law demand of us?" God said, "You shall not commit adultery." They also refused the law claiming that adultery goes to the core of their existence. The rabbis supported this with a biblical verse in which their ancestor Lot impregnates his two daughters (Gen 19:36).

God then moves on to the children of Ishmael with similar results. They ask about the law's requirements and are told, "Thou shalt not steal." They reject the law noting that their whole substance and nature depends upon thievery. They point out that the Scriptures say of their ancestor Ishmael that the hand of everyone was against him (Gen 16:12). What could this mean but that everyone resented Ishmael due to his thieving ways? All the nations were offered the Torah and rejected it once they learned its contents. Yet when God offered the Torah to Israel, they responded quite differently: "Everything that the Lord has said, we will obey" (Exod 24:7). For this reason, they were chosen to receive Torah.

This text may seem xenophobic and self-congratulatory to modern ears. Yet, in a world that celebrated violence, in a world filled with prostitution and sex slavery, in a world in which thievery typically went unpunished,

---

3. *Sif. Deut.* §343.

Moses, Torah, and Sinai

especially when carried out by the powerful, it is hardly surprising that Jews felt their laws set them apart from other nations and provided a signpost of their inherent superiority. It was not their superiority in power or influence that set them apart but their enthusiasm for and acceptance of God's Torah. The law was and is a gift of God; theirs due to the insight of their ancestors to accept it when offered.

THE MAGNIFICENCE OF THE MOUNTAIN

"The sound of the trumpet grew louder and louder" (Exod 19:19).

The whole Sinai event was interpreted by the rabbis as of exceeding magnificence on many levels. In one *haggadah*, when the word of the law issued forth from the mouth of the Holy One the whole world was filled with the fragrance of spices.[4] In another, the word of the Lord was a unique sort of word that altered itself in accordance to the capacity of the hearer. For instance, to the elderly, the word was heard in accordance with their elderly capacity. To the young, the word mysteriously altered itself to be heard in their capacity. The point of this tradition is to explain why no person died when they heard the words spoken by God on the mountain. One would think that no human could survive the experience in light of Deut 5:26. But in God's mercy, he adjusted the word out of concern for the listeners.

Support is found in Job: "God thundered marvelously with his voice" (Job 37:5). This wasn't any spoken word, it was "marvelous" in that it adjusted itself according to what the listener could handle. One rabbi compares it to the manna, which was also believed to take different flavors in accordance to the eater's desires and needs.[5] Rabbis love playing with these ideas; if God is so much more magnificent than humans, how much more wonderful are his words and deeds than anything human.

In another tradition, the word of the Lord spoken on the mountain automatically transmuted itself into seventy different languages. It was compared to striking an anvil with a hammer and sending sparks into many different directions. Another rabbi compares it to striking a rock with a hammer and sending chips flying in all directions.[6] The main point is that when God says what is really important (and nothing is more important than the law

---

4. *b. Shab.* 88b.
5. *Exod. Rab.* 5:9.
6. *b. Shab.* 88b.

Jewish Biblical Legends

given on the mountain!), he can make himself understood in many languages at once. God's word has worldwide significance and people of all nations have access to it. God has made this possible right from the beginning.

THE GOLDEN CALF

"Come, let us make gods..." (Exod 32:1).

The golden calf episode in Exod 32 functioned for the rabbis as something of an original sin story. All human sins, in rabbinic perspective, were versions of idolatry and here we encounter the fundamental idolatry story. But rabbis were keen to exonerate Aaron and the rest for their participation in the crafting of the golden calf. Complaints concerning Moses' delay on the mountain were brought by 40,000 of the mixed multitude, which included two Egyptian magicians. When Hur rebuked them for their impatience, he was murdered and the people then turned to Aaron and threatened to do the same to him if he didn't build them a golden calf.

Aaron tried to delay them with subterfuges. He requested earrings from their wives ears to build the calf, thinking the women would not give up their jewelry only recently plundered from Egypt. The wives did refuse, but not only because they wanted to keep their golden earrings, but also because they didn't want to have anything to do with idolatry. Aaron then insisted on building the altar himself, hoping to delay until Moses came down from the mountain. He declared, "Tomorrow shall be a festival to the Lord" (Exod 32:5), hoping to delay by throwing a party.[7]

Rabbis had much to say about Moses' conversation with God on the top of Mt. Sinai concerning the golden calf (Exod 32:7ff). In one particularly fascinating story, rabbis imagine Moses trying to ameliorate the severity of the crime so that God's wrath would wane. Moses asks God why God is so angry against his people whom he brought up out of Egypt (Exod 32:11). Why did Moses use the word "Egypt" in this context? It doesn't seem to be necessary to the narrative flow at this point. He mentioned Egypt here because he wanted to remind God that it is only normal for a people who have lived for so long in Egypt—a land where every animal imaginable is worshipped—to worship a calf.

A parable is told to explain the aptness of Moses' argument. In the parable, a sage built a perfume shop on a red-light district. When his son

---

7. *Tanhuma, Ki Tissa*, §19, *b. Shab.* 89a.

Moses, Torah, and Sinai

ended up being caught with the hookers, the father is outraged to the point of killing his own son. But the father's wise friend reminds him that he bears some responsibility for his son's actions.

> "You yourself ruined the boy, and now you are yelling at him? You left behind all other occupations and taught him to be a perfumer. You ignored all other streets and opened a shop for him on a street known for its hookers." Likewise, Moses said, "Master of the universe, you ignored the entire world and deliberately enslaved your children in Egypt where the inhabitants worship calves. Your children learned from the Egyptians, and now have even made a calf for themselves." It is for this reason that Moses said, "... your people that you have brought out of the land of Egypt." He means to tell the Lord of the kind of place out of which his people had only of late come.[8]

This story illustrates something powerfully at work in rabbinic literature; rabbis believed it was their duty and privilege to argue with their God. Rabbinic spirituality was and is a curious mixture of contrite piety and contentious bellicosity. Of course, this is a feature on parade in certain biblical texts as well. Abraham's argued with God over the destruction of Sodom (Gen 18:22–32) and here Moses argues with the Lord over the destruction of the people of Israel. What is striking here is how the rabbis refine Moses' argument by making it even more strident; God himself bears some of the responsibility for the construction of the calf. This is not a feature of the argument employed by the biblical Moses.

Moses is imagined here to argue that God should have expected the golden calf, and there was no good reason to be angry about it. After bringing Israel to Egypt for 400 years, God should not be surprised that the Israelites pick up on some Egyptian ways and customs. Egyptians worship animals as a matter of custom. Why should God be angry at his people who have lived among Egyptians for so long to have picked up on Egyptian ways?

It is often said, by those who despise people of religious faith, that faith destroys human reasoning capacity. Revelation forces all conversation to a halt and all religious beliefs must be "approved" or come under ecclesiastical sanction. Religion, it is said, destroys freedom of thought. Yet both Christianity and Judaism, in spite of what its detractors may say, claim a robust place for the mind and reason. God created humans as thinking animals and expects us to use our minds as a meaningful way we worship

---

8. *Exod. Rab.* 43:7.

Jewish Biblical Legends

God. Adam's first job was to name animals, a task that would have taxed his brain in the extreme. Jesus famously taught us to love the Lord with our minds (Matt 22:37). Here, God seems to invite a robust challenge and rabbis see their enhancement of Moses' argument in defense of his people as perfectly sensible and rational.

Rabbinic scholars know well the story of "the oven of Akhnai," where Rabbi Eliezer was arguing a point of *halakah* and brought every imaginable argument to the table but the assembled rabbis rejected his proposal. Finally, a voice from heaven (a *bat qol* in Hebrew or "daughter of a voice") chimed out that the *halakah* resides with Eliezer. The other rabbis cried foul and decided to ignore the heavenly voice and rule with the majority and against the heavenly voice! What was God's response? The *bat qol* spoke again in laughter saying, "My children have defeated me! My children have defeated me!"[9] In other words, God welcomed the intellectual challenge and was willing to accept defeat with good cheer. God respected the rabbinic majority opinion even though he sided with Eliezer in the minority! God clearly respected their thoughts and the reasoning process that stands behind it. This is no religion of mental restriction and intellectual servitude.

SILVER AND GOLD

"Tell the people that the men and women alike are to ask their neighbors for articles of silver and gold" (Exod 11:2).

This *midrash* is similar to the above in which the rabbis argue that God should not have been overly surprised and angry about the creation of the golden calf. In this *haggadah*, Moses protests on the basis of the plundering of Egypt, which we have discussed thoroughly in chapter 7. Here, the rabbis note that the silver and gold that the Holy One rained down upon Israel was in itself temptation to make of it a golden calf. A lion does not roar over a heap of straw, but he goes crazy over a pile of freshly killed meat. A lion could hardly be blamed for eating meat laid out before it. Similarly, Israel having ended a 400 year sojourn in an idolatrous nation like Egypt, and being presented with all the implements of idolatry (gold, silver, and vessels), can hardly be blamed for building a calf.

A parable is told to illustrate this point. A man had a heifer that was lean but with a huge appetite. When very tasty food was brought to it, in its

9. Benin, "Jews, Christians," 14.

joy it inadvertently kicked the master who had just fed it. The man realizes that he is partly to blame because he should have expected a kick from such an eager eater. Again, God could have and should have expected a great act of idolatry under these circumstances. It is natural for a hungry calf to kick as it is fed; if you are standing too close and are hurt, you have only yourself to blame! Rabbis even find a verse that can be read (with a little creative tweaking) to this end: "I multiplied silver and gold for her. [I should have known] they would use it for Baal" (Hos 2:8).[10]

Both the two above traditions flow from a common-sense awareness that people are influenced by their environment and while the outcome may be negative it is none-the-less understandable. Environmental influence should be brought into the matrix of factors considered when assigning guilt. These traditions seem a bit out-of-sync with the section on Cain above (chapter 2) where Cain tries to justify himself by saying that God is ultimately responsible for his sin since God should have created him without an evil impulse. In that case, the sages determined that he only had himself to blame for his actions. There may be something of a distinction to be made; Cain tried to blame God for his own evil impulse that he failed to control. The Israelites, the rabbis claim, having lived in Egypt for 400 years were naturally going to be influenced by the Egyptian ways and God bore some responsibility for their sojourn there. While the two claims are somewhat similar, the second seems the more reasonable and less contentious.

LONG-SUFFERING WITH THE WICKED

"Come, let us make gods . . ." (Exod 32:1).

Some rabbis approached the same golden calf episode from a different frame of reference but come out in much the same place as the above two traditions. Moses is standing before God on Mt. Sinai and notices that God is writing down the attribute of "long-suffering" or "patience." Moses supposes that God is referring to God's own patience with the righteous. God corrects him; God speaks also of his own long-suffering with the wicked. Moses thoughtlessly pronounces a curse on the wicked, but God warns him that soon enough Moses will come to appreciate God's patience even with the wicked as well as the righteous.

---

10. *b. Ber.* 32a.

Jewish Biblical Legends

When Moses comes down from the mountain, he learns of the great sin being committed there at the very place made holy by the giving of the law. God reminded Moses later that Moses had only just expressed appreciation for God's patience with the righteous, but now he needed God to be long-suffering with the wicked Israelites. For this reason, it is said, the Scriptures teach us that the Lord is slow to anger (Num 14:18).[11]

This *midrash* works quite differently from the two previous but to similar ends. Above, the midrashist critiques God's anger at Israel for their sins and believes that God should shoulder some of the blame for placing them in such seductive surroundings. Who could help but stumble? Here, God's long-suffering ways—proclaimed to Moses in Exod 34:6—are the key to understanding God's response to the golden calf episode. As angry as God seems to come off in Exod 32 (God says they acted perversely in verse 7), he is actually always long-suffering, even with the wicked. It is this patience that saves the day and on which Moses calls (Exod 32:11–14). It is because God is patient with the wicked that God relents from his intent to punish and allows Israel to stand as the people of the covenant. This *midrash*, perhaps more in line with the biblical text itself, emphasizes the love and mercy of God and expands upon it. Here it is not Moses chastening God for being too angry with the wicked, but Moses who is schooled by God for his petulant curse on the wicked and his failure to appreciate God's patience with the wicked. Even Moses must learn that strains of wickedness run through the saints.

---

11. *b. Sanh.* 111a–b.

10

The Ethics of the Fathers

THE LAST CHAPTER WILL survey several rabbinic sayings that are not specifically associated with Scripture. Particularly we will ponder readings from an important document we have already mentioned: *Pirke Avot* or sometimes just *Avot*. The title means "Chapters of the Fathers" and is sometimes translated more meaningfully "Ethics of the Fathers" since the topics are often ethical in nature. It lies in the fourth division of Mishnah called, "The Order of Damages" and is a mysterious repository of sayings of wisdom. It is mysterious in large part because its location is perplexing. Mishnah is the earliest collection of *halakah* to be written down and could hardly be more forensically dense. *Pirke Avot*, almost breezy in comparison, seems something like a sports car parked in a garage full of earth-moving equipment.

Mishnah, originally oral law, spells out how Israel is to live out the written laws of the Torah in daily life. According to one tradition, when God gave Moses the written law on Mt. Sinai, he also whispered in Moses' ear an oral commentary that was intended to be retained only in memory. During the days of Jesus and Paul, these "traditions of the elders" were still being orally transmitted. Designated students were "repeaters" charged to memorize the oral law completely. Eventually, around 200 CE, these oral laws were edited into a volume called Mishnah. *Pirke Avot* bears witness to the process by which this oral tradition was handed down from one generation to the next.

Jewish Biblical Legends

PRUDENCE IN JUDGMENT

In the first lesson of *Avot*, the transmission of the oral Torah is described as follows.

> Moses received Torah at Sinai and handed it on to Joshua, Joshua to elders, and elders to prophets. And prophets handed it on to the men of the great assembly. They said three things. (1) "Be prudent in judgment. (2) "Raise up many disciples. (3) "Make a fence for the Torah."[1]

The "great assembly" was a gathering of 120 sages and scribes who played a critical administrative role spanning the gap between biblical prophets and the beginnings of the rabbinic movement in the first century CE. As this text says, they passed on the Torah (meaning they transmitted both written Torah and oral Torah), but they also helped define the perimeters of the biblical canon and made other administrative and juridical decisions. Three things these elders commended to those who follow in their train.

First, be prudent in judgment. Not only were rabbis scholars; they also functioned as legal advocates. They did more than spin-out legal theories in academic ease; they provided real legal counsel to people in various predicaments. The advice being given here could hardly be more practical; remember that these laws affect average folk in the daily life. The word *halakah* actually means "the walk of life." People have to be able to live with this law and it shouldn't be too burdensome. Be prudent in judgment.

Second, raise up many disciples. The job of the sage requires a "paying it forward" factor. Just as your teacher (or father) poured his heart and knowledge into you, you must pour the same into your disciples. Don't take on an affected humility that says, "I could never assume that others should look to me as an example." Your life should be boldly imprinted on the souls of your disciples and you should make sure they know not only how you interpret the law but how your teacher and his teacher and his teacher interpreted. It isn't enough to know the law and to expound on it brilliantly. You must train others to do what you do and to do it better than you do it. Raise up many disciples.

Make a fence for the Torah. This is a central idea to Rabbinic Judaism involving the distinction between the written Torah and the oral Torah. The

---

1. *Avot* 1:1. Translation of Neusner, *Mishnah,* 672. The rather unorthodox usage of quotation marks correctly transcribes the source.

The Ethics of the Fathers

written Torah is essentially the five books of Moses, which Christians call the "Pentateuch." The oral Torah includes the legal traditions that spell out the details as to how that written Torah—particularly the 613 specific laws of the Pentateuch—is applied to daily living. For instance, the Mosaic law forbids labor on the Sabbath in numerous places. Exactly what does this mean? Can I light a match to start a fire on the Sabbath? Exactly when does Sabbath start? Can I pick up something the size of a grape off the floor on the Sabbath? How about something the size of an orange? What happens if I forget and do some work on the Sabbath? All these questions needed answering and the Mishnah, like an opaque thicket, provides a whole host of sometimes conflicting legal opinions. Talmud, a commentary on the Mishnah, constructs a pathway through the forest of the Mishnah.

So the "fence for the Torah" refers to the oral traditions of Mishnah, which seek to define how Israel is to be faithful to the written law. The oral Torah increases the probability of living in obedience to the written law. For example, if the speed limit (the written law) is 70 mph, the oral law may specify more clearly circumstances whereby one should not drive over 50 mph and when one could drive 68. Thus, knowing the oral law, we are more likely to be compliant with the written law. Rabbis hoped to create, through these oral traditions, a holy Israel worthy of King Messiah and thus be able to receive the kingdom of God.

On a very parenthetical note, the comment frequently encountered in *Avot* encouraging rabbis to "raise up many disciples" helps us to appreciate the context in which Jesus called his disciples. The value of knowing something about this culture of raising up disciples was brought to my attention recently when I heard an atheist calling into question the genuineness of Christian faith and the hypocrisy of modern Christianity by implication. He averred that few Christians who claim to be modern disciples of Jesus actually do what Jesus demands; few leave their families and wealth to hit the road of itinerant ministry. For instance, Jesus said to a rich man, "One thing you lack. Go, sell everything you have and give to the poor, and you will have treasure in heaven. Then come, follow me" (Mark 10:21). In the Sermon on the Mount we read,

> Do not store up for yourselves treasures on earth, where moths and vermin destroy, and where thieves break in and steal. 20 But store up for yourselves treasures in heaven, where moths and vermin do not destroy, and where thieves do not break in and

> steal. 21 For where your treasure is, there your heart will be also."
> (Matt 6:19–20)

The point is that Jesus is calling disciples to leave all and enter into his tutelage. In Luke 14:26 Jesus similarly calls followers to discipleship requiring that they "hate" their own biological families. This language, odd in our day, was a way of emphasizing the strong priority of discipleship over family obligations. Jesus clearly called disciples to leave their families and enroll in his college of ambulatory education.

According to said atheist, the fact that modern Christians don't leave their families and hit the road for Jesus proves the hypocrisy of our faith. But this is a failure to appreciate that Jesus' calling to discipleship was perfectly well situated in his own culture but unsuited and almost impossible in ours. For modern believers to go on some itinerant journey of mendicant self-imposed poverty would be weird and counter-productive. In Jesus' day, it was perfectly understandable. Francis of Assisi was used by God to actually imitate the lifestyle of Jesus. But it is thoughtless to say that modern Christians are hypocrites for calling themselves disciples of Christ without taking on the life of an itinerant. We must reasonably appropriate the calling of discipleship to our own culture as Christ's calling to discipleship was well-suited in his.

DEEDS OF LOVING KINDNESS

In the ocean of *haggadic* wisdom-sayings, one precious droplet is of such beauty it has been incorporated into the rituals of synagogue worship. Jews who attend synagogue even periodically are likely to be familiar with this saying since it is sung regularly in worship. It comes second in *Pirke Avot* just after the one above.

> Simeon the Righteous was one of the last survivors of the great assembly. He would say: "On three things does the world stand: (1) "On the Torah, (2) "and on the Temple service, (3) "and on deeds of loving kindness."[2]

To say that the world "stands" upon something, as one might expect, conveys crucial importance to the thing identified. These actions, it was believed, sustain and invigorate the power by which God holds all things

---

2. *Avot* 1:2; Neusner, *Mishnah*, 672. The odd usage of quotation marks is exactly the way it was used in the source for some reason unbeknownst to me.

The Ethics of the Fathers

together, almost the way Aaron and Hur held up Moses' praying hands sustaining victory over the Amalekites (Exod 17:8–16).

The first empowering agent on which the world stands is simply "Torah." As one might imagine, this word is rich with meanings that are contextually based and rather fluid. As we have seen already, the word meant something more like "instruction" than "law." The law for the rabbis isn't simply a set of rules by which to justify one's self before God. They believed they were already people of the covenant so no self-justification was necessary. The "Torah" was more an expression of thanks than a set of constricting rules. Torah was perceived as the "instruction" by which God shaped, consecrated, and blessed daily life. We have noted above that the word *halakah* is based on the verb "to walk" as in "walk through life." "Torah," contrary to all expectation, is not so much "law" as "life."

So rabbis were not interested in rules for the sake of rules, but living for the sake of righteousness by which they sustained the whole world. The word "Torah" in this context refers to the study of both oral and written Torah and living out of its precepts. It was the study of and living of this Torah that sustains the whole world and motivated God's gracious perseverance of it. The study of Torah was considered to outweigh other commandments such as visiting the sick, honoring one's parents, or bringing peace between people (*B. Shab.* 127a). A very famous rabbi named Meir—a student of Rabbi Akiba—said that when one studies Torah for its own sake, the creation of the world was worthwhile for that person alone, and God is made to sing for joy (*Avot* 6:1). A single day of Torah study is worth 1,000 sacrifices (*b. Shab.* 30a).[3] Study of Torah eventually replaces the temple completely.

The second element on which the world stands is, in the Neusner translation above, "Temple service." In Hebrew, the word *avodah* means simply "service" or "worship." It originally referred to the whole system of divine service centered in the Jerusalem temple, but after the destruction of the temple by the Romans in 70 CE, the word came to refer to the worship of God generally. The meaning of the word broadens to refer to *any* true worship and service of God. To serve God is to sustain the world. The world depends for its very existence upon those who truly worship and serve God in sincerity.

For the rabbis, acts of simple duty and worship took on profound meaning; to save a person's life is seen as saving the entire world (*m. Sanh.* 4:5). Each person's life has a profound impact upon the world, and if we

---

3. See "Torah Study" in *Wikipedia*.

save one person's life, it is as if we preserve the world that was meant to be. By saving a life we, by our act of self-sacrifice, prevent the world from sliding into perversity. The same thinking is felt here: to serve and worship God is to profoundly impact one's environment and change things for the better. The world stands on divine service.

The last foundation consists of "deeds of loving kindness." The words in Hebrew are *gemilut hasadim* and refer to deeds of kindness for others done with absolutely no interest in retribution and repayment. If someone hopes for or seeks to be paid back in kind, those deeds fail to qualify. These are the deeds of simple charity such as clothing the naked, housing the homeless, feeding the hungry, and seeking justice for the disenfranchised. These deeds humanize not only the person being helped but the person helping. One is reminded of Jesus' teaching that when we give to the needy, we are not to let our left hand know what our right hand is doing (Matt 6:2). Here, Jesus is expressing a very rabbinic social value; self-sacrifice is only meaningful in God's eyes if it is done for goodness sake (and for God's sake) alone.

BENEFIT OF A DOUBT

> Joshua b. Perahiah and Nittai the Arbelite received [the Torah] from them. Joshua b. Perahiah says, (1) "Set up a master for yourself. (2) "And get yourself a fellow disciple. (3) "And give everybody the benefit of the doubt."[4]

The modern world champions individuality and autonomy; we can hardly imagine ourselves taking on a *master*! Rabbinic culture emphasized community, communal solidarity, and communal wisdom. The requirement to retain huge bodies of knowledge demanded sustained attention and effort. Yet this culture and its values were assimilated into sub-consciousness through daily repetition the way an Olympic swimmer, after years of diligent practice, speeds instinctively through the water to finish the race. We can hardly bear hearing the same thing twice; they reveled in going back to the same sources again and again. In one of the teachings of *Avot*, we read the words of a rabbi with a very funny name.

> Ben Bag Bag says [in Aramaic], "Turn it over and over because everything is in it. "And reflect upon it and grow old and worn

---

4. *Avot* 1:6; Neusner, *Mishnah*, 673.

The Ethics of the Fathers

out in it and do not leave it, [in Hebrew] for you have no better lot than that."[5]

The point of this passage is that one can turn the same biblical text over again and again and find new jewels of meaning and new avenues of interpretation with every turn. Having a good teacher could hardly have been more crucial; an inspiring teacher instructs the disciple how to mine for gems in sacred writ, even after fifty readings.

Rabbis also believed that study of sacred texts could not be done alone; you must find fellow-disciples. There were to be no lone-wolf rabbinical students. You absolutely must study in groups and bounce ideas off each other in a ritual of competitive mutual-inspiration. Almost the way a running partner who is slightly more advanced can elicit greater effort from their running mates, a good study partner is critical in the study of Torah. Study simply must not be done alone; Torah study was too important to be pursued as an individual.

The advice "give everyone the benefit of a doubt" is intended to provide something of a balance to the other two sayings. While the first two motivated Torah study, rabbis realized that people can become just a little kooky after too much time cooped up in the *beth midrash*. They can become critical of others through their hard work. When one person aspires to great things, that person can become puffed up by their knowledge and look down upon other students who are perhaps less motivated or less intelligent. Those advanced students are advised to be very slow to be critical of others and to work just as hard on their own patience as they are working hard to improve their knowledge of the Torah.

THE SHY LEARNER AND IMPATIENT TEACHER

If there is any sagacious word of wisdom covered in this book that is likely to be known, and even quoted, by your Jewish—and sometimes even non-Jewish—friends in the course of daily life, this is it. It is attributed to Rabban Gamaliel, son of Judah the Patriarch. It has become a rather stock proverb in Jewish educational circles and conveys the very core of the Jewish psyche and culture. Jewish culture is bookish and intellectually rigorous because of

---

5. *Avot* 5:22; Neusner, *Mishnah*, 689. Again, Neusner's use of quotation marks is inscrutable.

what is here conveyed. The selection includes five observations, only two of which are commonly quoted: numbers 3 and 4.

> He would say, (1) "A coarse person will never fear sin, (2) nor will an average Joe ever be pious, (3) nor will a shy person learn, (4) nor will an intolerant person teach, (5) nor will anyone too busy in business get wise."[6]

I will comment here only the third and fourth sayings here since, as we have noted, these are the two that have become a commonplace in modern Jewish parlance. The sayings are typically addressed to a student who, with great trepidation, lifts their hand and says, "This might be a dumb question, but I was just wondering . . ." The educator will respond saying, "There are no dumb questions. Remember that a shy person can't learn and an impatient person can't teach."

The point of the saying is two-directional. First, it is intended to encourage students to gin up courage in themselves to ask questions. Shy people who are too embarrassed to ask their question cannot learn from the answers they would have received had they asked. Typically, when we sit in our seats and worry about whether our question will make us look foolish, the reality of the situation is that other students are asking similar questions but are also feeling too shy to ask. Education becomes transformational when it involves more self-discovery than lecture. But for this to occur, students must be coached to master their fears and let the questions fly. Boldness enhances the learning process and fear de-rails it.

The other half of the dictum exhorts the person at the front of the room. If master rabbi is feeling testy and a bit snide, he (or "she" in a modern classroom) can belittle students when they stumble around trying to figure out what to ask. If a teacher becomes impatient with students who are full of questions or intolerant of the slower students in class, it is easy for that teacher to upbraid the student using the authority of the office to intimidate into compliance. This kind of response hinders the whole educational process at least for those students who feel threatened. When someone feels frightened of looking stupid, they mentally shut down and education comes to a screeching halt. Good educators are patient, tolerant,

---

6. *Avot* 2:5; Neusner, *Mishnah*, 676. Where I have above "average Joe" the Hebrew has *am ha 'aretz*, which literally means, "people of the land" but came to mean something like the Greek "*hoi polloi*" (which translates roughly as "the common folk"). In Talmud, *am ha 'aretz* comes to mean uneducated folk who are uninterested in rabbinic teachings.

The Ethics of the Fathers

and able to coach students up to potential by encouraging them to have the boldness to ask their hardest questions with no fear of reprisal.

WHO IS FOR ME?

Hillel is accredited with wisdom of such probing simplicity, his questions echo in the mind like a mighty shout reverberating forth and back again.

> He would say, (1) "If I am not for myself, who is for me? (2) "And when I am for myself, what am I? (3) "And if not now, when?"[7]

The first question should not be read in the context of Paul's "If God is for us, who can be against us" (Rom 8:31). Hillel's interest here is not on mighty streams of theology like Paul but on the daily trickle of life. There are many things that we simply must do for ourselves. No one will brush our teeth for us and no one will study Torah for us. There is a certain self-interested practicality that should at all times be called upon. In one sense, we study Torah because by it the world stands. In another, we study for our own sake and benefit. We must realize our own stock is invested in this bank and that when the bank prospers we are paid the dividends. No one else will do for you what you must do for yourself.

Yet, question number 2 brings us in an almost opposing direction: "When I am for myself, what am I?" If you are for yourself, watch out! Like Narcissus of myth, we can come under the thrall of our own image in the reflection pool and languish there. Selfishness is the evil doppelgänger of self-interest; we can hardly but must tell the two apart. Hillel warns us here of the dangers of this pathway, yet it is a road down which we must travel to achieve anything worthwhile.

Finally, he asks, "If not now, when?" With all the dangers and potentials of life, it is possible to become paralyzed by fear and procrastination. Today is the day for life to begin anew. Every sunrise is thick with the mist of Easter morning. Tomorrow may never come and yesterday will never come back. Almost as the Taoist says that a journey of a thousand miles begins with a single step, Hillel encourages the procrastinator with the question, "Why not now? What is wrong with today? Enough with the excuses already; let's start that journey!" More than likely the journey to which he refers is the study of Torah but the questions are appropriate for any major endeavors in life, including the composition of this book. That journey has here come to an end.

---

7. *Avot* 1:14; Neusner, *Mishnah*, 674.

Glossary

Avot of Rabbi Nathan (abbreviated *Avot R. Nat.*)—a compilation of *haggadic* sayings from the Geonic period (700–900 CE) often printed with the minor tractates of the Talmud. It contains many proverbs and sayings that are not retained in the earlier collections.

Amoraim—the rabbinic "spokesmen" who were teachers and compilers of Jewish Law from the critical period of 200–500 CE (the *Amoraic* period). The *Tannaim*—the earlier period of rabbinic history—initially collected and encoded Jewish oral law into the Mishnah, which the Amoraim expanded on and clarified in what became the Talmuds.

Berishit—the Hebrew name for the biblical book of *Genesis*. In Hebrew it means, "In the beginning," following a common custom of naming books from the first few words of the book.

Beth midrash ("house of interpretation" or "house of learning")—the study centers where disciples are trained in rabbinic biblical knowledge and interpretation. Sometimes, but not always, these study centers are associated with a synagogue.

Babylonian Talmud (often shortened lovingly to *Bavli*)—the massive rabbinic legal corpus from the Babylonian rabbis of the Amoraic period (200–500 CE). It expounded upon, clarified, and explicated the confusing array of legal opinions in the Mishnah applying them to the needs of Babylonian Jews. *Bavli* contains both the text of the Mishnah with commentary (called the Gemara) alongside, representing 300 years of analysis from the centers of Babylonian rabbinic learning. Strikingly, *Bavli* has a much higher status in the rabbinic world than the other Talmud from the land of Israel (the Jerusalem Talmud). When someone refers to "the

Glossary

Talmud," they are designating the Babylonian Talmud. It is, when cited, abbreviated with a simple "*b.*" as in *b. Sanh.*

Berachot (abbreviated *Ber.*)—the tractate in Mishnah and the Talmuds that regulate the saying of the traditional prayers.

Darshan—one who interprets and expounds upon Scripture.

Ecclesiastes Rabbah (abbreviated *Eccl. Rab.*)—a collection of *haggadic* interpretations on the book of Ecclesiastes. It is included in the compilation *Midrash Rabbah*.

Exodus Rabbah (abbreviated *Exod. Rab.*)—a collection of *haggadic* interpretations on the book of Exodus. It is included in the compilation *Midrash Rabbah*.

Genesis Rabbah (abbreviated *Gen. Rab.*)—a collection of *haggadic* observations on the book of Genesis. It is included in the compilation *Midrash Rabbah*.

Haggadah or *haggadic literature*—the non-legal literature of the rabbis. Typically, if associated with Scripture, these stories interpret by telling parables or relating what other rabbis have said about the text. Many *haggadoth* (the plural of *haggadah*) relate stories about famous rabbis or rabbinic wisdom-sayings. If *The Haggadah* is spoken of in common parlance, it refers to the *Passover Haggadah*, which is the liturgy to be used at home during Passover (or *Pesaḥ*).

Halakah—the legal literary output of the rabbis. *Halakah* (plural *halakoth*) is based on the Hebrew verb "to walk" and refers to the legal traditions that governed the way the biblical laws of Moses (all 613 of them) were applied to daily life. The primary collection of *halakoth* is the *Mishnah*, which contains oral traditions said to have been whispered by God in Moses' ear at Mt. Sinai as an oral commentary on the biblical law.

Jerusalem Talmud (called *Yerushalmi*)—the collection of rabbinic legal opinions from the Palestinian rabbis of the Amoraic period (fourth and fifth centuries CE). It is actually the work of the Galilean Rabbis (from Tiberias and Caesaerea) and for this reason is often called the Palestinian Talmud rather than the Jerusalem Talmud. It clarified and explicated the *halakah* of the Mishnah and applied these legal matters to contemporary legal questions in the Galilee. It contains both the text of the Mishnah and commentary (called the Gemara) alongside. It predates the Babylonian Talmud by about 200 years but does not have the authority of the

Glossary

Babylonian Talmud. When someone speaks of the Talmud, they typically refer to the Babylonian Talmud unless context makes clear otherwise.

Mekhilta of Rabbi Ishmael (abbreviated *Mek.*)—a collection of *halakhic* midrashim on the book of Exodus representing the opinions of the rabbinic school of Rabbi Ishmael. There is also a collection titled *Mekhilta of R. Shimon bar Yochai* which contains *halakic midrashim* from the competing school of rabbi *Akiba*.

Mitzvah (plural *mitzvoth*)—commandments of God which stand as fundamental to all Jewish life. There were 613 *mitzvoth* in the written Torah (the Pentateuch), which were accepted by the Jews on Mt. Sinai and seven more rabbinical *mitzvoth* for a total of 620 commandments.

Midrash—rabbinic biblical interpretation that seeks to interpret Scripture often by telling imaginative stories (*haggadoth*) typically based on hints in the biblical text. The purpose of *midrash* is to solve problems raised by difficult texts using principles of interpretation and philology (*middoth*) and bring out hidden meanings, which are edifying to the community.

Midrash Rabbah—a collection of *haggadic* midrashim on Genesis, Exodus, Leviticus, Numbers, Deuteronomy, Song of Songs, Ruth, Esther, Lamentations, and Ecclesiastes.

Mishnah ("repetition")—the first major collection of rabbinic teachings or oral law that stands at the core of the Talmud. It remained an oral text (thus called the "repetition" since it needed to be repeated and remembered) until Rabbi Judah haNassi (the Prince) redacted it into a written text by 220 CE. It contains six major divisions and is mainly written in "Mishnaic Hebrew." It reflects the legal opinions of rabbis of the first and second centuries who are often called the *Tannaim*. Each of the tractates of the Mishnah also became a tractate in the Talmuds since the Talmuds are essentially commentaries on Mishnah and follow its six divisions. When a Mishnah text is cited, it is often abbreviated with an "*m.*"—as in "*m. Hag.*"

Numbers Rabbah (abbreviated *Num. Rab.*)—a collection of *haggadic* interpretations dealing with the book of Numbers. It is included in the compilation *Midrash Rabbah*.

Palestinian Talmud—see Jerusalem Talmud.

Pesachim—The third tractate in the "Order of Festivals" in both Mishnah and the Talmuds. It regulates the celebration of Passover and the title means "Passovers."

Glossary

Pirke Avot—the only non-legal tractate in the Mishnah that retains sayings of the rabbis of the Mishnaic period (the *Tannaim*).

Rabbi—a teacher of rabbinic law and Torah. The word (meaning "my master") reflects the way a student would refer to his teacher; the word *rab* essentially means "great one." In the Pharisaic period up to 70 CE, the term was only informally used if at all. Official ordination to the rabbinate began in the Tannaitic period and the title is first mentioned in the Mishnah. The first known rabbis were Rabban Gamaliel the elder, Simeon his son, and Johannan ben Zakkai, who were presidents of the Sanhedrin. "Rabban" is a variation of "rabbi;" it means "our master" and refers typically to the chief rabbi.

Sanhedrin (abbreviated *Sanh.*)—a tractate in Mishnah and the Talmuds that deal with criminal law. Sanhedrin also refers more broadly to the legislative body of rabbis who ruled on legal questions and developed the outlines of Jewish legal life.

Sifre Numbers and Deuteronomy (abbreviated *Sif.*)—a rabbinic verse-by-verse commentary on Numbers and Deuteronomy that finds generalizations and governing principles in the biblical text. It probably dates to the third century CE.

Sotah ("wayward wife")—a tractate in Mishnah and the Talmuds that specifies the manner in which one carries out the biblical ordeal of bitter water (Num 5:11–31), which is used when a wife is expected of but not proven to have committed adultery.

Tanhuma—a name given to two midrashim on Torah. They were named after Tanhuma bar Abba, a Palestinian rabbi of the amoraic period who was one of the leading preachers of his time. These texts were not collected by him but influenced by his homiletical style.

Tannaim—rabbis of the critical first two centuries when the Mishnah was still in oral form (thus the *mishnaic* period).

Yoma ("the day")—the tractate in the Mishnah and the Talmud, which lays out the regulations for the Jewish holiday *Yom Kippur*.

Bibliography

Abelson, Joshua. *The Immanence of God in Rabbinic Literature.* London: Macmillan, 1912.
Achtemeier, Paul et al. *Introducing the New Testament: Its Literature and Theology.* Grand Rapids: Eerdmans, 2001.
Alexander, P. "The Fall into Knowledge: The Garden of Eden/Paradise in Gnostic Literature." In *A Walk in the Garden,* edited by Paul Morris and Deborah Sawyer, 92-105. Sheffield, UK: JSOT, 1992.
———. "Midrash." In *A Dictionary of Biblical Interpretation,* edited by R. J Coggins and J. Houlden, 450-60. Philadelphia: Trinity, 1990.
———. "Retelling the Old Testament." In *It is Written: Scripture Citing Scripture,* edited by D. A. Carson and H. G. M. Williamson, 99-121. Cambridge: Cambridge University Press, 1988.
Allen, Joel S. *The Despoliation of Egypt in Pre-Rabbinic, Rabbinic and Patristic Traditions.* Supplements to *Vigiliae Christianae.* Leiden: Brill, 2008.
Allon, G. "Jews, Judaism and the Classical World." In *Studies in Jewish History in the Times of the Second Temple and Talmud,* 18-47. Jerusalem: Magnes, 1977.
Attridge, H. W. "Historiography." In *Jewish Writings of the Second Temple Period,* edited by M. E. Stone, 157-83. Philadelphia: Fortress, 1984.
Attridge, H. W., J. J. Collins, and T. Tobin. *Of Scribes and Scrolls.* Lanham, MD: University Press of America, 1991.
Bacher, Wilhelm. *Die Agada der Babylonischen Amoraër.* Strassburg: Trübner, 1878.
———. *Die Agada der palästinensischen Amoraër.* 3 vols. Strassburg, 1882-99. Reprint. Hildesheim: Georg Olms, 1965.
———. *Die Agada der Tannaiten.* 2 vols. Strassburg: Tübner, 1884-90.
Barclay, J. "Manipulating Moses: Exodus 2.10-15 in Egyptian Judaism and the New Testament." In *Text as Pretext: Essays in Honour of Robert Davidson,* edited by Robert P. Carroll. Sheffield, UK: Sheffield Academic, 1992.
Bartlett, J. R. *Jews in the Hellenistic World.* Cambridge: Cambridge University Press, 1989.
———. *Pharaoh's Counselors.* Chico, CA: Scholars, 1983.
Benin, S. "Jews, Christians and the Authority to Interpret." In *With Reverence for the Word: Medieval Scriptural Exegesis in Judaism, Christianity and Islam,* edited by J. McAuliffe et al., 13-32. Oxford: Oxford University Press, 2010.
Bickerman, E. *The Jews in the Greek Age.* Cambridge: Harvard University Press, 1998.
———. "The Septuagint as a Translation." In *Studies in Jewish and Christian History,* 1:167-200. Leiden: Brill, 1976.

Bibliography

Birch, Bruce, Walter Brueggemann, Terence Fretheim, and David Petersen. *A Theological Introduction to the Old Testament.* Nashville: Abingdon, 1999.
Blowers, Paul. "Origen, the Rabbis, and the Bible." In *Origen of Alexandria,* edited by C. Kannengiesser and W. L. Petersen, 63–96. South Bend, IN: University of Notre Dame Press, 1988.
———. "Origen, The Rabbis, and the Bible: Toward a Picture of Judaism and Christianity in Third-Century Caesarea." In *Recent Studies in Early Christianity,* edited by Everett Ferguson, 2–22. New York: Garland, 1999.
Bohak, G. "The Impact of Jewish Monotheism on the Greco-Roman World." *Jewish Studies Quarterly* 7.1 (2000) 1–21.
Bowker, J. *The Targums and Rabbinic Literature.* Cambridge: Cambridge University Press, 1969.
Bowman, John. "The Exegesis of the Pentateuch among the Samaritans and among the Rabbis." In *Oudtestamentische Studiën,* edited by P. A. H. De Boer, 8:220–62. Leiden: Brill, 1950.
Boyarin, D. "Inner Biblical Ambiguity, Intertexuality, and the Dialectic of Midrash." *Prooftexts* 10 (1990) 29–48.
———. "On the Status of the Tannaitic Midrashim." *Journal of the American Oriental Society* 112 (1992) 455–65.
Braude, William G., translator. *Book of Legends/Sefer Ha-Aggadah: Legends from the Talmud and Midrash.* Edited by H. N. Bialik and Y. H. Ravintzsky. New York: Schocken, 1992.
Carroll, James. *Constantine's Sword: The Church and the Jews.* New York: Mariner, 2002.
Cashdan, Eli. *The Minor Tractates of the Talmud.* London: Soncino, 1965.
Childs, Brevard. *The Book of Exodus: A Critical, Theological Commentary.* Philadelphia: Westminster, 1974.
Coats, G. W. "Despoiling the Egyptians." *Vetus Testamentum* 18 (1968) 450–57.
Coggins, R. J. *Samaritans and Jews.* Atlanta: John Knox, 1975.
Collins, J. J. *Between Athens and Jerusalem: Jewish Identity in the Hellenistic Diaspora.* 2nd ed. Grand Rapids: Eerdmans, 2000.
Conzelmann, Hans. *Gentiles, Jews, Christians: Polemics and Apologetics in the Greco-Roman Era.* Translated by M. Eugene Boring. Minneapolis: Fortress, 1992.
Dershowitz, Alan. *The Genesis of Justice: 10 Stories of Biblical Injustice that Led to the 10 Commandments and Modern Morality and Law.* New York: Grand Central, 2001.
Drijvers, H. "Jews and Christians at Edessa." *Journal of Jewish Studies* 36 (1985) 88–102.
Enns, Peter. *Inspiration and Incarnation: Evangelicals and the Problem of the Old Testament.* Grand Rapids: Baker Academic, 2005.
Epstein, J. N., and E. Z. Melammed. *Mekhilta d'Rabbi Shim'on b. Jochai.* 1955. Reprint. Jerusalem: Mekize Nirdamim, 1979.
Evans, C. A. *Early Jewish and Christian Exegesis.* Atlanta: Scholars, 1987.
Feldman, L. H. "Anti-Semitism in the Ancient World." In *History and Hate: The Dimensions of Anti-Semitism,* edited by D. Berger, 15–42. Philadelphia, 1986.
———. "Reflections on the Jews in Graeco-Roman Literature." *Journal for the Study of the Pseudepigrapha* 16 (1997) 39–52.
Fink, W. *Der Einfluß der jüdischen Religion auf die griechisch-römische Religion.* PhD diss., University of Bonn, 1932.
Fischel, Henry A. *Rabbinic Literature and Greco-Roman Philosophy.* Leiden: Brill, 1973.
Fishbane, M. *Biblical Interpretation in Ancient Israel.* Oxford: Clarendon, 1985.

Bibliography

———. *The Exegetical Imagination: On Jewish Thought and Theology.* Cambridge: Harvard University Press, 1998.

———. *Garments of Torah; Essays in Biblical Hermeneutic.* Bloomington, IN: Indiana University Press, 1989.

———. "The Well of Living Water: A Biblical Motif and Its Ancient Transformations." In *Sha´arei Talmon: Studies in the Bible, Qumran, and the Ancient Near East Presented to Shemaryahu Talmon,* edited by M. Fishbane and E. Tov. Winona Lake, IN: Eisenbrauns, 1992.

Folliet, Georges. "La Spoliatio Aegyptiorum (Exode 3:21–23; 11:2–3; 12:35–36) Les Interprétations de cette Image chez les Pères et Autres Écrivains Ecclésiastiques." *Traditio* 57 (2002) 1–48.

Fraade, S. D. *Enosh and His Generation: Pre-Israelite Hero and History in Post-Biblical Interpretation.* Chico, CA: Scholars, 1984.

———. *From Tradition to Commentary.* Albany, NY: SUNY, 1991.

Freedman, Harry, and Maurice Simon, translators. *Midrash Rabbah.* New York: Soncino, 1992.

Fretheim, Terence E. *Exodus.* Louisville: Westminster John Knox, 1991.

———. "The Plagues as Ecological Signs of Historical Disaster." *Journal of Biblical Literature* 110 (1991) 385–96.

Frizzell, L. "'Spoils from Egypt,' between Jews and Gnostics." In *Hellenization Revisited,* edited by Wendy Helleman, 383–94. Chico, CA: University Press of America, 1994.

Gager, John. *Moses in Greco-Roman Paganism.* Nashville: Abingdon, 1972.

Ginzberg, L. *Legends of the Jews.* 2 vols. Philadelphia: Jewish Publication Society, 2003.[1]

Goldenberg, D. "The Halakhah in Josephus and in Tannaic Literature." *Jewish Quarterly Review* 67 (1976) 30–43.

Goldin, Judah. *Studies in Midrash and Related Literature.* Edited by Barry L. Eichler and Jeffrey Tigay. Philadelphia: Jewish Publication Society, 1988.

Gowan, Donald. *Theology of Exodus.* Louisville: Westminster John Knox, 1994.

Greenberg, Moshe. *Understanding Exodus.* New York: Behrman House, 1969.

Griffith, Paul. "Seeking Egyptian Gold: A Fundamental Metaphor for the Christian Intellectual Life in a Religiously Diverse Age." *The Cresset* 63.7 (2000) 5–16.

Harris, Jay M. *How Do We Know This? Midrash and the Fragmentation of Modern Judaism.* New York: SUNY, 1995.

Halperin, D. "Origen, Ezekiel's Merkabah, and the Ascension of Moses" *Church History* 50 (1981) 261–75.

Hata, G. "The Story of Moses Interpreted within the Context of Anti-Semitism." In *Josephus, Judaism and Christianity,* edited by Louis H. Feldman and Gohei Hata, 180–197. Detroit: Wayne State University Press, 1987.

---

1. In all footnotes for Ginzberg above, I provided citation based on the original English translation of this work (1909). This was translated by the famous Henrietta Szold (Zionist and founder of the Hadassah Women's Organization) and was divided into six volumes. Therefore, 2:142 in the text above would refer to volume 2, page 142. The sixth volume consists only of footnotes. The older edition can be downloaded for free today from Amazon! The newer edition listed in the bibliography here is the same translation improved several ways; only two volumes with footnotes located conveniently at the bottom of each page. If you are using the newer edition, it is quite simple to find texts I've cited by following the biblical order.

Bibliography

Hick, John. *Evil and the God of Love*. 2nd ed. San Francisco: Harper, 1977.
Heinemann, J. *Aggadah and Its Development*. (Hebrew) Jerusalem: Keter, 1974.
Hengel, M. *Judaism and Hellenism*. Philadelphia: Fortress, 1974.
Horbury, W. *Christians and Jews in Contact and Controversy*. Edinburgh: T. & T. Clark, 1998.
Hunter, G. *The Celtic Way of Evangelism: How Christianity can Reach the West . . . Again*. Nashville: Abingdon, 2000.
Kamesar, Adam. "The Church Fathers and Rabbinic Midrash." In *Encyclopedia of Midrash: Biblical Interpretation in Formative Judaism*, edited by Jacob Neusner and Alan J. Avery Peck, 20–40. Leiden: Brill, 2004.
———. "The Evaluation of the Narrative Aggada in Greek and Latin Patristic Literature." *Journal of Theological Studies* 45 (1994) 37–71.
———. *Jerome, Greek Scholarship, and the Hebrew Bible: A Study of the Quaestiones Hebraicae in Genesim*. Oxford: Clarendon, 1993.
———. "The Literary Genres of the Pentateuch as Seen from the Greek Perspective: The Testimony of Philo of Alexandria." *Studia Philonica Annual: Studies in Hellenistic Judaism* 9 (1997) 143–89.
———."The Narrative Aggada as Seen from the Graeco-Latin Perspective." *Journal of Jewish Studies* 45 (1994) 52–70.
———. "Philo, *Grammatikē*, and the Narrative Aggada." In *Pursuing the Text: Studies in Honor of Ben Zion Wacholder on the Occasion of his Seventieth Birthday*, edited by J. C. Reeves and J. Kampen, 216–42. Sheffield, UK: Sheffield Academic, 1994.
———. "Philo and the Literary Quality of the Bible: A Theoretical Aspect of the Problem." *Journal of Jewish Studies* 46 (1995) 55–68.
———. "Philo, the Presence of 'Paideutic' Myth in the Pentateuch, and the 'Principles' or *Kephalaia* of Mosaic Discourse." *Studia Philonica Annual: Studies in Hellenistic Judaism* 10 (1998) 34–65.
Kasher, D. M. *Encyclopedia of Biblical Interpretation: A Millennial Anthology*. 9 vols. New York: American Biblical Encyclopedia Society, 1970.
Kimmelman, Reuven. "Rabbi Yohanan and Origen on the Song of Songs: A Third-Century Jewish-Christian Disputation." *Harvard Theological Review* 73 (1980) 567–95.
Kinzig, W. "Closeness and Distance: Towards a New Description of Jewish-Christian Relations." *Jewish Studies Quarterly* 10 (2003) 274–90.
———."'Non-Separation': Closeness and Co-operation between Jews and Christians in the Fourth Century" *Vigiliae Christianae* 45 (1991) 27–53.
Klein, M. "Converse Translation: A Targumic Technique." *Biblica* 57 (1976) 515–37.
Koskenniemi, Errki. "Greeks, Egyptians and Jews." *Journal for the Study of the Pseudepigrapha* 13 (2002) 17–31.
Krauss, S. "The Jews in the Works of the Church Fathers." *Jewish Quarterly Review* 5 (1983) 139–49.
Kugel, James. *The Bible as It Was*. Cambridge: Belknap, 1997.
———. *In Potiphar's House: The Interpretive Life of Biblical Texts*. San Francisco: HarperCollins, 1990.
Kugel, James, and Rowan Greer. *Early Biblical Interpretation*. Philadelphia: Westminster, 1986.
De Lange, N. R. M. *Origen and the Jews: Studies in Jewish-Christian Relations in Third-Century Palestine* Cambridge: Cambridge University Press, 1976.

Bibliography

Lauterbach, Jacob Z. *Mekilta de-Rabbi Ishmael*. Philadelphia: Jewish Publication Society, 1933.
Layton, B. *The Gnostic Scriptures*. Garden City, NY: Doubleday, 1987.
Leiman, S. D. *The Canonization of Hebrew Scripture: The Talmudic and Midrashic Evidence*. Hamden, CT: Archon, 1976.
Levenson, J. D. *Death and Resurrection of the Beloved Son*. New Haven, CT: Yale University Press, 1993.
Levine, L. *Caesarea under Roman Rule*. Studies in Judaism in Late Antiquity 7. Leiden: Brill, 1975.
Lewis, C. S. *Mere Christianity*. New York: Macmillan, 1952.
Lieberman, Saul. *Greek in Jewish Palestine*. New York: Jewish Theological Seminary, 1942.
———. *Hellenism in Jewish Palestine*. New York: Jewish Theological Seminary of America, 1942.
Liebeschuetz, W. "The Influence of Judaism among Non-Jews in the Imperial Period." *Journal of Jewish Studies* 52.2 (2001) 235–52.
Loewe, Raphael. "The 'Plain' Meaning of Scripture in Early Jewish Exegesis." In *Papers of the Institute of Jewish Studies, London*, edited by J. G. Weiss, 1:140–84. Jerusalem: Magnes, 1964.
Löhr, W. A. "Gnostic Determinism Reconsidered." *Vigiliae Christianae* 46 (1992) 381–90.
Marmorstein, Arthur. "The Imitation of God in the Haggadah." In *Studies in Jewish Theology*, edited by J. Rabbinowitz and M. S. Lew, 106–21. London: Oxford University Press, 1950.
McGuckin, John A. "Origen on the Glory of God." *Studia Patristica* 21 (1989) 316–24.
———. "Origen on the Jews." In *Recent Studies in Early Christianity*, edited by Everett Ferguson, 23–37. New York: Garland, 1999.
Morgenstern, J. "The Despoiling of the Egyptians." *Journal of Biblical Literature* 68 (1949) 1–27.
Mulder, M. J. *Mikra: Text, Translation, Reading, and Interpretation of the Hebrew Bible in Ancient Judaism and Early Christianity*. 1988. Reprint. Peabody, MA: Hendrickson, 2004.
Neusner, J. *Aphrahat and Judaism*. Leiden: Brill, 1971.
———. "Augustine and Judaism." *Journal of Jewish Studies* 53 (2002) 49–65.
———. *Introduction to Rabbinic Literature*. New York: Doubleday, 1994.
———. *The Rabbinic Traditions about the Pharisees Before 70*. Vol. 3. Leiden: Brill, 1971.
———. *The Talmud of Babylonia: And American Translation Volume IV.E: Pesahim Chapters 9 and 10*. Atlanta: Scholars, 1993.
Neusner, J., and William Scott Green. *Writing with Scripture: The Authority and Uses of the Hebrew Bible in Formative Judaism*. Minneapolis: Augsburg, 1989.
Nickelsburg, G. W. E. "The Bible Rewritten and Expanded." In *Jewish Writings of the Second-Temple Period*, edited by Martin Stone, 89–152. Philadelphia: Fortress, 1984.
Peck, M. Scott. *People of the Lie: Hope and Healing for Human Evil*. New York: Touchstone, 1983.
Pétrement, Simone. *A Separate God*. Translated by Carol Harrison. New York: Harper, 1984.
Petuchowski, J. J. "Halakhah in the Church Fathers." In *Essays in Honor of Solomon B. Freehof*, edited by W. Jacob et al., 257–74. Pittsburg: Rodef Shalom Congregation, 1964.

Bibliography

Radday, Y. T. "The Spoils of Egypt," *Annual of the Swedish Theological Institute* 12 (1983) 127-47.
Renolds, L., and N. Wilson. *Scribes and Scholars*. 3rd ed. Oxford: Clarendon, 1991.
Rivkin, Ellis. *A Hidden Revolution: The Pharisees' Search for the Kingdom Within*. Nashville: Abingdon, 1978.
Robinson, James M. *The Nag Hammadi Library*. New York: Harper and Row, 1978.
Rokeah, D. *Jews, Pagans and Christians in Conflict*. Studia Post-Biblica 33. Leiden: Brill, 1982.
Safrai, S. *The Literature of the Sages*. Philadelphia: Fortress, 1987.
Sarason, Richard. "Interpreting Rabbinic Biblical Interpretation: The Problem of Midrash, Again." In *Hesed Ve-Emet: Studies in Honor of Ernest S. Frerichs*, edited by Jodi Magness and Seymore Gitin, 133-54. Atlanta: Scholars, 1998.
———. "Toward a New Agendum for the Study of Rabbinic Midrashic Literature." In *Studies in Aggadah, Targum, and Jewish Liturgy in Memory of Joseph Heinemann*, edited by Jadob Petuchowski and Ezra Fleischer, 55-73. Jerusalem: Magnes, 1981.
Schechter, Solomon. *Aspects of Rabbinic Theology*. New York: Macmillan, 1909.
Schürer, E. *The History of the Jewish People in the Age of Jesus Christ*. 4 vols. Revised and edited by G. Vermes, F. Millar, M. Goodman, and M. Black. Edinburgh: T. & T. Clark, 1986.
Segal, A. *Two Powers in Heaven: Early Rabbinic Reports about Christianity*. Leiden: Brill, 1977.
Silverman, William B. *Rabbinic Stories for Christian Ministers and Teachers*. Nashville, Abingdon, 1958.
Smallwood, E. Mary. *The Jews under Roman Rule from Pompey to Diocletian*. Leiden: Brill, 1976.
Sparks, Kenton. *God's Word in Human Words: An Evangelical Appropriation of Critical Biblical Scholarship*. Grand Rapids: Baker Academic, 2008.
Stark, Rodney. *The Rise of Christianity: How the Obscure, Marginal Jesus Movement Became the Dominant Religious Force in the Western World in a Few Centuries*. San Francisco: Harper, 1997.
Stern, David. "Introduction." In *The Book of Legends: Sefer Ha-Aggadah: Legends from the Talmud and Midrash*, 17-22. New York: Schocken, 1992.
Stern, Menahem. *Greek and Latin Authors on Jews and Judaism*. Jerusalem: The Israel Academy of Sciences and Humanities, 1976.
Stone, M. E. *Jewish Writings of the Second Temple Period*. Philadelphia: Fortress, 1984.
———. *Scriptures, Sects and Visions*. Philadelphia: Fortress, 1980.
Strack, H. L., and G. Stemberger. *Introduction to the Talmud and Midrash*. Minneapolis: Fortress, 1992.
Stroumsa, G. G. *Another Seed: Studies in Gnostic Mythology*. Leiden: Brill, 1984.
Tcherikover, Victor. *Hellenistic Civilization and the Jews*. Translated by S. Applebaum. New York: Atheneum, 1985.
Townsend, John T. *Midrash Tankhuma: Translated into English with Introduction, Indices, and Brief Notes. S. Buber Recension*. 2 vols. Hoboken, NJ: KTAV, 1997.
Urbach, E. "The Homiletical Interpretations of the Sages and the Expositions of Origen on Canticles and the Jewish-Christian Disputation." *Studia Hierosolymitana* 22 (1971) 247-75.
———. "Homilies of the Rabbis on the Prophets of the Nations and the Balaam Stories." *Tarbiz* 25 (1956) 272-89.

Bibliography

―――. *The Sages: Their Concepts and Beliefs*. Translated by Israel Abrahams. Jerusalem: Magnes, 1975.

Vermes, G. "Bible and Midrash: Early Old Testament Exegesis." In *The Cambridge History of the Bible*, edited by Peter Ackroyd et al., 1:199–231. Cambridge: Cambridge University Press, 1970.

―――. *Scripture and Tradition in Judaism*. Leiden: Brill, 1975.

Visotzky, Burton L. *Fathers of the World: Essays in Rabbinic and Patristic Literatures*. WUNT 80. Tübingen: Mohr Siebeck, 1995.

Wacholder, B. Z. "Biblical Chronology in the Hellenistic World Chronicles." *Harvard Theological Review* 61 (1968) 451–81.

Watson, Alan. *Roman Slave Law*. Baltimore: Johns Hopkins University Press, 1987.

Wilken, R. *Judaism and the Early Christian Mind*. New Haven, CT: Yale University Press, 1971.

Wise, Michael, Martin Abegg, and Edward Cook. *The Dead Sea Scrolls: A New Translation*. San Francisco: Harper, 1996.

Scripture Index

OLD TESTAMENT/HEBREW SCRIPTURES

Genesis

Ref	Pages	Ref	Pages
1:1	14–17	8:20–22	56
1:1–2	17	10:9	57
1:2	17–20	10:23	115
1:26	22–24, 25, 29	11:3	58
1:27	27, 40	11:4	58
2:4	20–22	11:7	58
2:16–17	45	11:9	58
2:17	41	11:27	58
2:21	37	12	61
2:22	35	12:1	67, 68
2:23	40	12:2	68
3:2–3	44	12:1–3	67
3:3	41	12:5	69
3:5	42, 43	12:10	72
3:6	41, 44, 44n6	12:11	73
4:1	47	12:10–20	67
4:2	49	14:12	126
4:3–4	47	14:13	61, 126
4:5	47	15:1	74
4:8	48, 49	15:5	78
4:9	47, 49, 50,	15:6	63, 74
4:10	50	15:8	74
4:12	52	15:9	74
4:13	53	15:14	108, 112, 114, 130, 131
4:16	52	15:13–14	74, 135
5:29	53	16	73n16
6:6	22	16:12	144
7:1	54	17	91
		18	69, 71

173

Jewish Biblical Legends

18:22–32	147	3:13	102
19:36	144	3:14	102, 103
21:33	69, 123	3:21	130
22:2	76	3:21–22	112
22:3–4	76, 77	3:22	121, 126
22:11–12	78	3:23	129, 131
22:13	79	4:26	91
22:16	78	5:1	103, 120
24:64	5	5:2	103, 104, 120, 134, 136
27:22	144	5:3	126
27:40	145	6:3	135
33:10	80	6:7	135
35:22	86	7:3	106
37:25	82	7:5	135
39:3	84	7:9	105
39:7	85	7:12	105
39:8	84	8:2	109
41:8	86	8:8	113n1
41:57	123, 124	8:10	135
45:12	126	8:11	109
47:14	123	8:22	135
49:1	86	9:14	107, 135, 136, 139
49:33	88	9:24	110
50:13	88	9:29	135
50:15	88	10:1	136
		10:2	135, 136
Exodus		10:19	110
		10:23	111, 114
1–15	135	11:2	113, 121, 126, 127, 131, 148
5–15	136	11:2–3	112
1:8	90	11:7	135
1:10	92	12	127
1:13	92	12:36	113, 117, 120, 121, 123, 124
1:22	93	12:35–36	112, 118
2	97	14:4	135, 136
2:1	93, 94	14:10	131, 132
2:10	95	14:11–12	132
2:11	96	14:15	137, 138, 139
2:12	97, 98, 109	14:16	137
2:15	98	14:17	136
2:16	98	14:18	135, 136
2:17	99	14:26	138
2:19	99	14:30	139
3	127	15:1	140
3:1	99, 100	15:14–15	135
3:3	101	15:22	139, 140
3:6	102		
3:12	143		

Scripture Index

17:8–16	155
18:8–12	135
19:19	145
20:1	142
24:7	144
32	146, 150
32:1	146, 149
32:5	146, 147
32:7	146, 147, 150
32:11	146, 147, 101
32:11–14	150
34:6	150

Leviticus

24:10	97, 126
24:11	97

Numbers

11:7	141
11:8	141
14:18	150
35:30	53

Deuteronomy

5:26	145
32:4	24
32:6	25
33:2	143

Joshua

5	91
24:2	124

I Kings

14:25	124

Ezra

5:12	124

Esther

3:9	116

Job

36:22	107
37:5	145

Psalms

58:11	123
80:9	140
90:4	44n7
105:25	91
113:9	94, 95
148:4	19n33
115:3–8	65
115:5–7	64
121:1	78
125:2	75
135:15–18	65
137	75

Song of Songs

1:4	129
2:2	140

Isaiah

19:11	104
19:11–13	103
40:18–20	65
44:9–20	65
44:20	65
45:7	19n8
63:9	101

Jeremiah

10:1–16	65

Ezekiel

1:4	75

Hosea

2:8	149

Amos

4:13	19n8

Jewish Biblical Legends

Habakkuk
2:19	66

Wisdom of Solomon
14:8–11	65
14:12–21	65
14:17–20	65

Sirach
3:21–22	18
25:24	45

NEW TESTAMENT

Matthew
5:5	37
5:48	35
6:2	156
6:19–20	154
6:34	103
18:19–20	76
22:34	34
22:37	148
23	31
23:3	32
23:5–7	32
23:8–12	32
23:16–22	33
23:23–24	32
23:23–25	33

Mark
10:21	153

Luke
10:25–28	34
14:26	154
16:10	101

Acts
5:34–40	38n58
22:3	38n58
26:4	37n58

Romans
3:3	63
3:19	51
4:17	20
8:31	160

I Corinthians
13	46

Philippians
2:3–8	37

I Timothy
2:13–14	45

Hebrews
11:3	20

I Peter
3:7	39
3:15–16	39

www.ingramcontent.com/pod-product-compliance
Lightning Source LLC
Chambersburg PA
CBHW020850160426
43192CB00007B/858